STACEY CLARE is a ̶̶̶̶̶̶, writer, activist, Buddhist and co-founding member of the East London Strippers Collective (ELSC). She grew up in northern England and began working as a stripper while on a gap year from her Fine Art degree at Glasgow School of Art.

Stacey has danced in clubs throughout the UK, as well as travelling to dance in Paris and Australia. While working as a stripper, Stacey encountered a variety of conditions within the industry. Early in her career she became interested in sex workers' rights, finding that when clubs were run respectfully stripping could be empowering; but she also found her welfare and autonomy were rarely acknowledged by club bosses, or regulating authorities.

In 2014, Stacey helped co-found the ELSC in a concerted effort to unite dancers around common grievances about their own industry, including the poor representation of strippers in public and media. She also helped establish the sex workers' trade union branch United Sex Workers, which has fought several successful labour-abuse cases for strippers in the UK. She lives between London and Scotland, sharing her time between art/theatre projects, activism and writing.

THE
ETHICAL STRIPPER

*Sex, Work and Labour Rights
in the Night-time Economy*

Stacey Clare

unbound

First published in 2022

Unbound
Level 1, Devonshire House, One Mayfair Place, London W1J 8AJ
www.unbound.com

Text design by Ellipsis, Glasgow

A CIP record for this book is available from the British Library

ISBN 978-1-78965-133-1 (paperback)
ISBN 978-1-78965-134-8 (ebook)

Printed and bound in Great Britain by Clays Ltd, Elcograf S.p.A.

1 3 5 7 9 8 6 4 2

This book is dedicated to Samantha Sun, Lauren Elise, and everyone who has contributed to the East London Strippers Collective.

SUPER PATRONS

Philll Kay

Cathy Keen

Alistair King

Kim Loliya

Seani Love

Will Macleod

G Martin

Lotta Mattila

Fiona Meth

Alastair Monk

Jenni Murphy

Petrea Nes-Iadicola

Lauren O'Connor

Christine Orient

Andrew Parsons

Keith Ramsey

Jessica Risqué

Malcolm Roderick

Anna Sampson

Michelle Sarah

Andrew Stys

Samantha Sun

Kit Swing

Attila Szakacs

The Great Smell of Brute

Morgan Trowland

Vijay Varman

Giulia Viaggi

Caroline Walker

Ray Ward

Dale Warren

Louise Wells

Rebecca Whelan

Alex Winter

CONTENTS

INTRODUCTION

Many of my colleagues and customers over the years will testify that this book is long overdue. In fact, after listening to me lamenting on the injustices of a business model that forces women to tolerate appalling abuses and acts of discrimination on a regular basis, more than a few of them have suggested it to me. Usually while I'm at work, sitting on a bar stool in stripper garb and high heels, pontificating on my lack of employment rights on a slow day shift in an East London strip joint. 'Blimey, Stacey. You should write a book,' they say. 'I'm going to,' I say. What happened instead was a decade of surviving in London, one of the most expensive cities in the Western capitalist world, while at the same time trying to be an effective activist, before I could get anywhere close to having the resources I needed to start writing. During this time, I watched my industry slowly and steadily disintegrate as economic, cultural and political conditions repeatedly undermined the women working in it.

This is a book about labour rights. As much as I'm writing with my own community in mind, this book also aims to reach a wider audience who are unaware of the complex realities of sex work. As we move into a stridently feminist post #metoo era, conversations about the sex industry are more frequent and wide-reaching than ever. The mission of the sex workers' rights movement is harm-reduction – a concept I'll explore throughout this book – and our challenge is building a critical mass of allies and supporters who are able to deliver the essential information so crucial to our efforts. Considering the centuries of criminalisation, censorship, shaming, violence, marginalisation, silencing and state-sanctioned brutality of sex workers, this is no mean feat. Public discourse has been dominated by morality and prejudice for so long that the work of disseminating information isn't just a matter of simply sharing data. The real task lies in breaking down the historical barriers that have prevented key expertise and language, developed by generations of committed sex working activists, from being shared with well-meaning, potential allies – a problem that I hope this book, at least in part, may help remedy.

At times, it seems to me that activism in general is a lot like needlework – patient, slow, diligent and persistent, progress is barely perceptible and reveals itself over time. As an advocate, I'm required to patiently unpick the tightly woven social fabric of stigma, which is slow and tedious work indeed. Like our great-great-great-grandmothers of first wave feminism, who objected to sitting in quiet composure over their needlework, behaving like 'good little women', our instinct is to set fire to the hegemonic tapestries woven from centuries of underpaid and undervalued women's work.

There isn't time for patience, though. For transgender sex workers, for BIPOC sex workers, for undocumented, street-based sex workers, for the most vulnerable members of the sex industry who have no access to state protections or legal resources, differences between legal regimes and policies can mean life, survival or death. It can mean targeted police oppression, loss of income, poverty and destitution, children separated from caregivers, migrant incarceration and deporta-tion. There isn't time to do the required amount of emotional labour, for sex workers to carefully and tenderly hold space while the rest of society processes their internalised discomfort and unease, one conversation at a time, stitch by stitch. To quote Juno Mac and Molly Smith, sex workers and authors of the hugely authoritative book, *Revolting Prostitutes*,

> It is not the task of sex workers to apologise for what prostitu-tion is. Sex workers should not have to defend the sex industry to argue that we deserve the ability to earn a living without punishment. People should not have to demonstrate that their work has intrinsic value to society to deserve safety at work.[1]

A stripper writing an autobiography isn't groundbreaking these days, and those wishing to read about the emotional rollercoaster of working in a strip club in vivid detail are spoiled for choice. Lap dancing was big business at the turn of the twenty-first century, and public fascination for those who disrobe for money hasn't shown any signs of abating since then (although the actual marketplace has changed considerably). It stands to reason that plenty of strippers have cashed in on their own experiences by publishing their memoirs. There have been so many stripper autobiographies in the last twenty years that they are virtually a sub-genre in their own right, and glancing through some of the titles is practically a form of entertainment: *Girl, Undressed,* Ruth Fowler, 2009; *The Beaver Show,* Jacqueline Frances, 2015; *Strip City: A Stripper's Farewell Journey Across America,* Lily Burana, 2003; *Spent,* Antonia Crane, 2017; *Two Decades Naked,* Leigh Hopkinson, 2016; *Candy Girl: A Year in the Life of an Unlikely Stripper,* Diablo Cody, 2005; *Bare: The Naked Truth About Stripping,* Elizabeth Eaves, 2004; *The Stripper Next Door,* Emma Lea Corbett, 2018; *Stripping Down: A Memoir,* Sheila Hageman, 2012; *Anything But a Wasted Life,* Sita Kaylin, 2018; *Dirty Money: Memoirs of a Stripper,* Erin Louis, 2015.

Dr Brooke Magnanti is probably the most widely recognised author of the genre, whose *Intimate Confessions of a London Call Girl,* 2005, became an international bestseller. Her pen name 'Belle de Jour' has become synonymous with the contemporary erotic biography. Thanks to the success of the series, which was eventually turned into a prime-time BBC TV show, Belle de Jour is verging on a household name. Magnanti's achievement has given rise to a cornucopia of copycat writers replicating the format of sex industry kiss-and-tell exposés over and over again.

Public appetites for sex workers' stories are understandable: for the consuming public it's all just a bit of fun, a titillating distraction from ordinary life, right? Maybe. But for sex workers there is a far more serious edge to it. The problem arises when fiction is confused with reality, when narratives presented in popular culture are assimilated as fact. If films, TV shows and tabloid articles inform wider beliefs about sex work, a void opens up between fantasy and reality into which empirical data and evidence-based research are lost, making information increasingly difficult to share. Mainstream narratives shape public opinion in ways that can't be underestimated, and when the desire to consume is greater than the thirst for knowledge then we have a cultural imbalance that is hard to rectify.

The urge to consume and the urge to tell all complete each other, like the Ouroboros, the symbolic snake eating its own tail. I could easily contribute to the cycle. I could have written a book revealing more personal details about my childhood neglect and dysfunctional upbringing, financial struggles, disastrous relationships and occasional substance use. It's tempting to lift the lid on all the painful realities, and the joys, the friendships, the glamour, the highlights and intensity, the *emotional rollercoaster*. But as a writer I wanted to use this book to make a contribution towards harm-reduction and sex workers' rights by disseminating information, knowledge and insight, rather than dishing the dirt. My story, like my body, is my own business.

Another greatly over-represented sub-genre in publishing is the academic study of the sex industry. Since third wave feminism in the 1970s sought to eradicate the sex industry, vast numbers of academic books and papers have been written by non-sex workers that take a pedagogic approach and have proven no less popular than sex workers' autobiographies. However, academic researchers have tended to take up opposing sides of an argument *for* and *against* the sex industry, ingraining divisions between 'sex-positive', pro-sex work feminists, who seek to empower sex workers by removing the burden of criminalisation on one side, and on the other, sex industry abolitionist, 'carceral' feminists, also known as Sex Worker Exclusionary Radical Feminists (SWERFs), who aim to end the sex trade by imposing and increasing state penalties and restrictions. The 'sex wars' are now rumbling along into their fifth decade. And while the two camps battle it out, with prominent mainstream feminists locked in conflict, creating another repetitive cycle, sex workers' voices are repeatedly ignored. Mercifully, more recent titles have been written by sex workers themselves, propounding a more circumspect view concentrated on safety and harm-reduction rather than a 'sex-positive' interpretation of sex work.

This book contains the apparatus of scholarly references, but it's not an academic publication. And while there are personal anecdotes throughout, it's not an autobiography either. I have chosen to write from two perspectives woven together, two voices speaking alongside each other to reflect my two personas: Stacey the stripper, the worker, the slut, and Clare, the researcher and the ideologist. Since I first began stripping as a plucky art student, I've been seeking to reconcile my personal experience with the variety of opinions, voices, beliefs and feminist narratives around me. I found one of the best ways to do this has been to divide myself for the sake of brevity, creating at least two different identities to allow for different and occasionally opposing ideologies to co-exist while I process and integrate them.

The term 'sex-positive' has started to become an unhelpful phrase within sex worker activist circles. Increasingly, sex-positivity has been entering the mainstream consciousness as an enlightened and empowered attitude to sexuality; the sex-positive ethos is that sex is nothing to be ashamed of, and sex-positive people are healthier and happier for exploring their sexual proclivities, safely and consensually. Sex work doesn't necessarily sit comfortably in this framework: if sex is only positive as long as it's safe and consensual, then in practice, many sex workers, whose work may be unsafe or whose consent may be undermined by circumstance, are left behind. Sex workers who enjoy high levels of privilege and consent may often identify with sex positivity to leverage further benefits and freedoms – which is how we arrive at the term 'happy hooker'. The sex-positive movement may celebrate sex work as an enlightening and meaningful activity, but this can be confusing if the lived experience of other sex workers is less than positive. There isn't much room for sex-positivity for survival sex workers, for instance.

Readers of this book may be more familiar with the term 'harm-reduction' in the context of public health and addiction, but perhaps not so much in relation to the sex industry. There are many clear comparisons to be made between decriminalisation of drugs and decriminalisation of sex work, since they both fall within a public health remit. The 'war on drugs' has been entirely counterproductive and has shown how criminalisation of substances has exacerbated the social conditions that increase vulnerability and addiction. Evidence from around thirty countries that have adopted some form of decriminalisation shows very clearly that there are improved social outcomes from shifting public policy away from criminalisation.[2] This is what harm-reduction looks like: evidence-based strategies that have positive results. Since the evidence shows that criminalisation does not lead to safety and harm-reduction (and that criminalised marketplaces are in fact the most violent and coercive marketplaces that exist) this book is therefore written from a position that supports the full decriminalisation of sex work.

Throughout the book, I use the terms 'stripper', 'lap dancer' and 'sex worker' interchangeably, since (to many of us) they mean the same thing. It's important to acknowledge that the term 'sex worker' applies to anyone who provides sexual services: strippers, lap dancers, full-service sex workers, escorts, prostitutes, porn performers, webcammers, pro-dommes, hostesses, glamour models, tantric practitioners, somatic sex therapists – essentially anyone trading on their erotic capital and performing sexual labour is a sex worker. As a group, we are all marginalised, and the reason I use the term is to build solidarity and challenge the stigma that unites everyone in the sex industry, no matter their job.

When I identify myself as a sex worker, I draw heavily on my experience as a stripper, having danced in strip clubs since 2006. I've also looked closely at licensing legislation in the UK, and since this is my greatest area of knowledge and research, I have been acting as an advocate for sex industry workers who work in licensed premises, i.e. sexual entertainment venues (SEVs). While the distinctions between stripping and full-service sex work (and their various crossovers) will be explored throughout, by focusing in on UK strip clubs as a sub-section of the wider sex industry, I hope to contribute in part towards a broader discussion of sex work policy.

The legislative distinctions between stripping and full-service sex work are widely misunderstood: stripping is legalised in the UK (for now) via the SEV licensing regime, while prostitution is criminalised in a number of ways. Criminalisation means full-service sex work must happen in secrecy, behind closed doors, while strip clubs can legally operate in publicly licensed premises. Practically speaking, this means that strippers can still organise and campaign for their rights within the workplace, while full-service sex workers cannot access labour rights since they do not have a workplace – any spaces where full-service sex work takes place in any kind of organised way are criminalised. By explaining these differences, it is not my intention to be divisive; rather I hope to demystify a lot of the confusing rules and policy decisions that keep some kinds of sex work more marginalised than others.

One of the objections from fellow sex workers to the chosen title of this book is that claiming to be an *ethical* stripper sets up a dichotomy, with the suggestion that some strippers are more ethical than others. This has never been the intended meaning behind the title of this book, which is written in the spirit of solidarity with other sex workers who are all too familiar with finding themselves on the wrong side of a mainstream moral binary. Such a binary reiterates the age-old trope that women who sell sex or sexual services are *bad women*. The very last thing I want to do is to create further divides by suggesting that some sex workers are 'good' in that they behave properly and follow the rules, while others are trangressive or 'immoral'. For this reason I have chosen the term 'ethical', where the ethical proposition *is* harm-reduction. It is not my intention to judge anyone's personal choices, but to focus on how suffering can be reduced at a systemic level, through collaboration and mutual support. In my experience, this is something to which sex workers are already fully signed up, successfully organising to a degree that is nothing short of inspiring.

Throughout the writing of this book, I have been navigating a considerable fear as an author that my words do not serve everyone in my community. I have agonised for months, not just over vocabulary and syntax, but also about representation and advocacy. What right do I have to speak on behalf of other sex workers? As a white, British-born, English-speaking, educated, cis female with access to power, justice and resources, I enjoy certain forms of privilege and comfort, as well as a public-facing role as a writer and media spokesperson. But my relative privilege hasn't made me impervious to adversity as a sex worker. The violence, toxicity, coercion, bullying, victimisation and trauma experienced by people in the sex industry are real; I'm also a survivor. There are countless vulnerable people in the sex industry who cannot access resources or self-advocate for so many reasons, and the challenge for anyone involved in activism is knowing how to share their platform and privilege with under-represented and at-risk groups. The fear for every sex worker who puts their head above the parapet and enters the world of activism and advocacy is that they may get it wrong, as they often do. I hope that I have not failed my colleagues who operate further out in the margins.

Perhaps to the disappointment of some, this book falls into traditional patterns of heteronormative language. Sadly, I don't think I can safely and carefully represent more marginalised LGBTQI+ and BIPOC groups, who are under-represented in this publication. For this, I apologise. To my own disappointment, this is a reflection of their under-representation within the strip club industry in its present form. There is still much work to be done before strip clubs can offer less misogynistic and more egalitarian spaces where all genders and identities can enjoy equal freedom and visibility. Incredibly, in July 2019, during the writing of this book, the first queer strip club in the UK, Harpies, opened the doors of their London venue, marking a hugely positive shift in that direction.

While I have referenced the work of many incredible authors and activists, this book is still polemical. I am a sex worker, and this is my version of events as I see them. The pitfalls of writing about my own experience as well as advocating on behalf of those who don't necessarily share it are innumerable. This book may be difficult and uncomfortable to read for others in the same field of work, if my story doesn't chime with theirs. There are untold sex workers whose experiences do not match my own, since the full range of issues of class, gender, age, immigration, ethnicity, ability/disability and economic disparity to be found in the global sex industry go a long way beyond what I have encountered. I cannot claim to represent all members of the sex industry; mine is one voice among many, and my greatest privilege of all is having a podium (no pun intended) to speak for myself.

There is occasional mention throughout this book of 'rumours' and 'hearsay' among strippers and sex workers, although I never divulge anything more than a vague reference to 'internal dialogue'. I cannot say where these rumours come from, since quoting their sources would jeopardise strippers' and sex workers' private networks. These forums are often carefully screened and curated, and have become essential resources for sex workers to share knowledge and information for staying safe. Therefore, one of the caveats of this book is that I am asking readers to respect our need for privacy and trust some of the information in this book that comes from sources that are protected for anonymity.

Another caveat is that, unfortunately, I have not used any of my word count to talk about male strippers. The phenomenon of 'Magic Mike' has placed male stripping in the public conversation and, to some extent, has helped move the dialogue forwards, not least by reminding mainstream audiences that there are also men who work in the sex industry. Pointing out the existence of male sex workers is essential, since it serves to disrupt some of the most ingrained core beliefs about victimhood and abuse being gendered. For the purposes of writing this book, however, when I talk about strip clubs, I am talking about a female workforce. While male strippers also fall into the category of precarious workers, the business model is very different when it comes to Butlers in the Buff, or male strip-o-grams.

Male strippers work for a fixed wage, either a performer's fee or a split of the profit, depending on whether they work for a club, an agency, or take private bookings. As far as I know there are no strip clubs where male strippers are paying house fees, fines and commissions, and hustling to sell private dances. They are not starting from a deficit, having paid out a house fee to a venue which then takes a cut of everything they earn on top; they are not at a permanent disadvantage, fearful for their jobs. The working environments between genders are not comparable, so I have therefore chosen to leave them out. Of course, I would welcome a book written by a man that divulges the employment conditions, cultural biases and forms of exploitation encountered by male strippers; I hear it's not a walk in the park either.

Since I began my stripping career, SEV numbers in the UK have dwindled from 350 clubs a decade ago to 150 at present.

Declining numbers of strip clubs may not sound like the most pressing issue at hand, but they are part of a wider picture. I started writing this book in 2019, ten years after the passing of the Policing and Crime Act 2009, the current law that regulates SEVs. The law sets out to control strip clubs and protect women by 'cleaning up' a fringe economy that has long been poorly managed. I began dancing on the club circuit in 2006, just a few years before the Policing and Crime Act 2009 was passed, and so have been able to observe conditions before, during and after. Present day conditions in the industry, ten years on, make a mockery of the idea that women have been protected. The law had a devastating effect on the industry and pushed those who work in it into ever worsening working conditions. This book aims to explain those conditions from the point of view of a social architecture of public policy and enforcement that has failed to achieve its mission.

Right now, sex workers are in crisis. Since the first draft of this book was completed, Covid-19 has devastated people's lives the world over. Precarious people have been made exponentially more precarious, and it's those who are closer to the bottom of the social ladder and most financially insecure who have been hit hardest. In the Afterword, I give a more detailed update of how sex workers have been impacted, and how club closures, loss of income and ever-increasing levels of insecurity have led thousands of women to turn to different forms of sex work to survive.

Covid-19 has revealed how badly strippers have been let down by their social architecture. One of the most egregious outcomes of the pandemic has been the extent to which club owners have benefited from the UK government furlough scheme. As part of a national economic crisis package, employers have been able to rely on bailout payments to pay their staff up to 80 per cent of their salaries while businesses have been under lockdown. In the case of strip clubs this has meant all employed staff – bar tenders, door security, managers – have been furloughed throughout the pandemic. Dancers, despite their integral role within the business, have been excluded from the furlough scheme, leaving them dependent on other forms of support, which for millions of self-employed, precarious workers, has been unreliable at best, and – for undocumented workers – non-existent.

Had public debate a decade ago not been couched in hysteria and ridicule, had dancers been properly included in the public and Parliamentary discourse, had club bosses been compelled to establish a business model that wasn't run on the misclassification and financial exploitation of its workforce – had sex workers been able to access their labour rights and establish their employment protections – then perhaps we would be seeing very different outcomes today.

The good news is that times are changing. If I've learned anything from over fifteen years of stripping, it's that sex workers are a resilient bunch. Throughout the writing of this book several momentous events took place, shifting the balance of power in favour of workers and changing the cultural landscape of the sex industry. Strippers have been engaging in trade union activism, making representations at local council meetings, demanding basic employment rights at work, and even, in some cases, campaigning to preserve licences when clubs have been under threat of closure in order to protect their own jobs. Landmark court cases have been fought and won by strippers, establishing once and for all that they do in fact have power in their workplaces and that the conditions they are working under are often unlawful. As a result of community-building and self-organisation, increasing numbers of strippers and sex workers have been turning away from the exploitative business owners running the clubs and setting up their own initiatives: pop-up alternative events run by indie collectives which challenge the stigma surrounding sex work have been appearing more frequently as acts of resistance and statements of political protest. The future of the sex industry is worker-led; big changes are on the way, and they are happening fast.

I

ETHICAL STRIPPING

> Everything great in life and business is born out of good
> communication.
>
> —Cindy Gallop[1]

A major inspiration for writing this book is the work of Dossie
Easton and Janet W. Hardy, writers of *The Ethical Slut*, first
published in 1997. In their *Practical Guide to Polyamory, Open
Relationships and Other Adventures*, Easton and Hardy offer an
understanding of the complexities of non-traditional relationship models and provide a language for communicating outside of traditional heteronormative monogamy. They are
quick to identify their choice of title and define its intended
meaning:

> As proud sluts, we believe that sex and sexual love are funda-
> mental forces for good, activities with the potential to

strengthen intimate bonds, enhance lives, open spiritual awareness, even change the world . . . Sluts share their sexuality the way philanthropists share their money: because they have a lot of it to share, because it makes them happy to share it, because sharing makes the world a better place.[2]

Here, Easton and Hardy identify their sexuality as a form of value, and their sluttish nature as their desire to give that value away. Some strippers and sex workers do identify as people who have enough sexuality to share around, but the idea quickly becomes murky and laden with moral baggage in the context of an economic marketplace. Being an ethical slut sounds nice in theory, but what about if you're charging for it instead of sharing it freely? What's ethical about stripping if it comes at a price? How can selling sex be ethical?

WHAT DOES 'ETHICAL STRIPPER' MEAN?

Ethics and morals are often used interchangeably, though they don't mean the same thing. Morality, as used here, comes from the idea that we have an internal 'moral compass' guiding us through life and pointing us towards 'good' and away from 'evil'; it refers to our individual sense of right and wrong. Morals are often seen as the foundation of our beliefs; they're not up for discussion, because to consider changing your morals is much the same as breaking them. To say 'It's just wrong!' is the same as saying 'It's just morally wrong.' Moral codes tend to be imparted implicitly, passed down via families, cultures or communities and – since the variety of alternative value systems, principles and purposes to live by is impossibly complex – there is some convenience in simply adhering to those we are born into. But there are also innumerable downsides to living by an inherited morality that is outdated or oppressive, without ever stopping to question or reject it.

Ethics, on the other hand, are centred on an external source of codes, rules or boundaries. These are decided by a group – such as a community, religion or business – and used to regulate individuals by a system of accountability. For example, a company can have its own code of ethics; a bank or charity may follow an agreed set of procedures that maintain their particular ethical viewpoint. Legislation is society's endeavour to regulate the behaviour of individuals by way of ethical codes of practice. Where morals may end up acting as an implicit or unconscious set of commands over one's value system, ethics are often explicit, written down or enshrined, and ideally edited and refined over time.

Discussions about the sex industry are often beset by confusion between the two. The subject of sex is energetically and emotionally charged enough to be a conversation that most people avoid. The idea of selling or paying for sexual services is, in turn, loaded so deep with social conditioning that it undermines attempts to have comprehensive, detailed and considered conversations about it. Some may follow their moral compass on the matter, trusting how they *feel fundamentally* about it; others may leave it up to the regulators to decide right from wrong, and trust there are enough checks and balances to protect people.

But neither approach accounts for the way sex work laws have developed, or the wider social impact they have. The creation and implementation of an ethical code that supports the rights and freedoms of those immediately affected by it becomes an incredibly intricate and convoluted process when there are so many competing and opposing viewpoints. The danger is, and has always been, that the voices of the most vulnerable groups in the process are drowned out by the dominant narratives held by more powerful stakeholders. Discourse is essential to the work of a society; laws, rules and ethical standards only emerge through dialogue and critical analysis. Therefore, the quality of the policies and laws developed to govern the sex industry depends entirely on the quality of the conversation being had about it.

Easton and Hardy wrote their book at a time when there was a growing awareness of the power of ethical consumption – the idea that an individual could make a positive impact on the world via their consumer choices. Publication of *The Ethical Slut* in 1997 coincided with the release of the first product to be certified with the Fairtrade stamp (chocolate made using cocoa beans from Belize). The stamp represents a policy of harm-reduction, an assurance that human suffering and environmental damage have been minimised in the product's supply chain. In this sense, the word 'ethical' connotes harm-reduction. *The Ethical Slut* clearly reflects the desire to do less harm and create more positive outcomes in the area of sexuality and non-monogamy, by inviting people to develop good communication and agreed codes of conduct around sex. By using the word 'ethical' rather than 'moral', Easton and Hardy sidestep traditional notions of right and wrong in sexuality and monogamy, and instead centre the discussion on creating value and avoiding harm. By framing sluts as sexual philanthropists, they don't examine the issue of selling sex and sexual labour, but by echoing the zeitgeist of ethical purchase, they have nonetheless chosen terms that fit very easily into a discussion on the explicit marketplace of sex.

Making a comparison between selling chocolate and selling sex may be in poor taste to some (although plenty of advertising executives seem to have made the same connection), but for many sex workers, the parallels between the two different labour markets stand up. Society has no problem with the idea of behaving ethically in the field of business, so if we can have an ethical chocolate industry, then why not an ethical sex industry? This is where *The Ethical Stripper* picks up the thread. Rather than getting bogged down in the morality of personal sexual behaviour, the aim is to take a wider view of the sex industry and begin asking how the *ethics of harm-reduction* can take shape.

SELLING SEX BY LAW

According to the World Health Organization:

> Modelling studies indicate that decriminalising sex work could
> lead to a 46 per cent reduction in new HIV infections in sex
> workers over 10 years; eliminating sexual violence against sex
> workers could lead to a 20 per cent reduction in new HIV
> infections.[3]

HIV is just one of the many pathologies that intersect with the
sex industry, and statistics like this are substantial enough to raise
serious questions about our current ethical regimes. In New
Zealand, where sex work has been fully decriminalised since
2004, the strategy has improved sex workers' safety. A study by
the University of Otago School of Medicine revealed that after
the legal reform 60 per cent of sex workers in New Zealand felt
more able to refuse a client, and 95 per cent felt they had more
rights and were able to seek justice or support.[4] New Zealand
has developed a clear strategy for harm-reduction, with demonstrable results. So the question we should be asking isn't 'how
can the sex industry be ethical?' but 'what is the most ethically
reliable approach for reducing harm in the sex industry?'

The legal regimes in which sex work occurs can mean the
difference between life and death. Criminal records or incur-
able illnesses become life sentences for affected individuals,

while prosecution, incarceration and public health costs place an enormous burden on state governments. The need to ameliorate the harmful consequences of an industry that creates so many victims is unquestionable, yet public opinion remains divided over the source of its harms. Opinion among sex workers themselves, though, is united the world over: full decriminalisation empowers sex workers to reclaim their own narratives, create their own working and regulatory environments, and fight exploitation by re-establishing their rights within a framework that recognises them as workers. The ethical framework of the sex industry must therefore be developed by sex workers themselves.

Sex industry regulations vary throughout the world as different communities and legal regimes have evolved; in some countries it is a criminal offence to be a stripper or sex worker, whereas in others it is an accepted part of the cultural and economic landscape. Even in countries where it is legal and legitimate, rules can differ between states or local authorities. Understanding where strip clubs fit into the sex industry requires a wider understanding of the industry itself and the legal regimes that exist from country to country. One of the best resources available for this is the Sex Work Law Map produced by the Institute of Development Studies.[5] The map functions as a wiki database showing the legal regimes applied to sex work in most countries in the world – it's the first calling point for anyone wanting to expand their knowledge of sex workers' rights. What the map doesn't include, however, is how strip clubs fit into the legislature, which countries regulate or criminalise stripping, and how, in some countries where full-service sex work is criminalised, strip clubs operate legally.

There are essentially four different legal regimes that govern sex work: criminalisation, legalisation, the Nordic model (otherwise known as partial-decriminalisation or the end-demand model) and full decriminalisation. It is easy to confuse legalisation with decriminalisation, but the distinctions are important. There are very few places in the world where sex work has been fully decriminalised; New Zealand was the first nation to adopt the approach, while the state of New South Wales, Australia, adopted the regime even earlier in 1995. During the writing of this book, in late 2019, the state parliament of Northern Territories, Australia, passed a bill to decriminalise sex work. In these regions, there are no legal restrictions on sex workers who work alone, except where no precautions have been taken against STDs. Independent sex workers don't need to pay for a special licence or register with local authorities; they are free to operate without interference from the police or the state. There are legal restrictions, however, when it comes to operating a business which offers sexual services: brothels can only operate with state approved licences, meaning that sex workers who want to work together or in the safety of a workplace (rather than alone, working from home or travelling to meet clients in private) still find themselves in a framework of legislation, albeit a relatively relaxed one. By decriminalising sex work, New Zealand has created a political pathway for sex workers to access their rights as citizens and workers. In 2014 a sex worker sued a brothel keeper for sexual harassment because she was able to access legal assistance without being prosecuted herself.[6] This cannot happen when sex work is criminalised.

In places where sex work has been *legalised*, such as Germany, Switzerland, or Nevada, USA, sexual services are strictly authorised and regulated by the state. Under legalisation there is a good deal of gate-keeping going on; sex workers are frequently required to register with local authorities, provide proof of identity, carry permits and attend regular health checks. In order to work legally, sex workers must make themselves identifiable and traceable by the state, which also produces an illegal marketplace outside of state rule. This in turn creates a social hierarchy between sex workers who have the relative privilege to operate within view of the state and those without. Undocumented migrants and people with *irregular immigration status* are automatically cast out of the legal system, instantly vulnerable to exploitation, criminalisation and/or deportation.[7] Commercial sex businesses require permits and governments collect tax on the revenue generated by the sex industry. Local authorities can also create zoned areas, which are effectively state sanctioned red-light districts, as well as controlling business operation hours with the use of licensing.

The state can control who has the right to sell sex, where and when it can be sold and, to some extent, how much it costs — if licence fees must be paid as a running cost then there are market forces at play influencing the nature and value of the transaction. It could be argued that under the legalisation model, the state actually fulfils the role of pimp, dictating who can work where, and taking their cut of the money.

The Nordic model, known also by a number of other names (Swedish model, neo-abolitionism, partial-decriminalisation, the 'sex buyers law' or the 'end-demand law') is an approach that was first adopted across most Scandinavian countries including Norway, Sweden, Finland and Iceland. These Scandinavian governments are otherwise known for their progressive social policies, with some of the highest levels of gender equality worldwide. The law has subsequently been ratified by other nations aiming to lead the way on women's rights, including Canada, France, Republic of Ireland and Israel. The Nordic model is known as the *kinder* version of criminalisation; it sets out to eradicate the sex industry by shifting criminal responsibility away from sex workers and onto the buyer. It is based on the principle that paying for sex is an act of gender violence, and by criminalising clients, it ends demand for sexual services by raising the stakes for people who pay for sex. It is a policy that has become extremely popular among prominent feminists and social reformers.

Sex workers have been protesting *against* the Nordic model

since it was first adopted in Sweden in 1999. From a sex worker's point of view, the law doesn't help – criminalisation has the same detrimental impact on sex workers, regardless of which side the burden falls. Criminalisation drives away trustworthy and reliable clients who have too much to lose, leaving behind those willing to break the law to pay for sexual services, and who know how to use stigma, fear and criminalisation for abusive and coercive purposes. The Nordic model still pushes sex workers to make snap decisions in stressful circumstances; screening clients becomes more difficult if they are unwilling to provide ID or comply with safety and accountability procedures.

Some countries that have adopted the Nordic model, like Iceland and Israel, also shut down their strip clubs, while others, like Canada, France and Ireland, did not. Strip clubs have always been places where clients and sex workers can solicit for business in clandestine surroundings, although as explained, the stakes are much higher for clients. Either way, the Nordic model helps create a culture of stigma, identifying all men who pay for sexual services as abusers, and assuming a paternalistic role towards sex workers by classing them as victims. This has a counterintuitive impact; rather than protecting sex workers, the policy robs them of their agency and ability to spot and weed out abusers.

In the UK, full-service sex work isn't illegal in and of itself; exchanging sex for money isn't technically against the law, but the act of doing so is criminalised in various ways. Present day legislation aims to curb prostitution by targeting how sex work is organised. Street solicitation is strictly prohibited, as are any visible forms of advertising. The Sexual Offences Act 2003 defines any premises used by more than one sex worker to see clients as a brothel, and therefore illegal. It's OK for one sex worker to see clients in their home, but as soon as there is another sex worker present, or some other type of worker who assists in the business of selling sex (even, for instance, a cleaner), they have broken the law. Sex workers are therefore required to make a choice between compromising their personal protection by working in isolation, or – if they work together for safety – risking up to seven years in prison and a lifelong criminal record.

Perpetrators of violence who are aware of this legal vulnerability can exploit, harass or violate sex workers, safe in the knowledge that women who work together cannot report crimes for fear of prosecution themselves.[8] In this sense, full-service sex workers are caught in a punitive bind that maintains their vulnerability and precarious status. Alongside brothel-keeping, advertising or public soliciting, assisting a sex worker with operations such as driving them to a client, or answering their phone to help organise bookings in return for a percentage of their income, known as controlling prostitution for gain, are all criminal offences. Under Section 53 (Schedule 1) of the Sexual Offences Act 2003, a person commits an offence if:

1. They intentionally control any of the activities of another person relating to that person's prostitution in any part of the world, and

2. They do so for or in the expectation of gain for themselves or a third party.

So, for example, answering the phone and organising bookings for a sex worker in return for a fee is illegal. All of the above conditions create a situation in which full-service sex work is organised with the utmost secrecy, out of view of any legal authorities.

In contrast, strip clubs in the UK operate under the legalisation model. Despite arguably being an organised sex business, stripping is a legal, licensable activity, where the state controls who operates the venues and where, via the implementation of current licensing laws. Strip clubs or lap-dancing clubs are known legally as 'sexual entertainment venues' or SEVs. The current law that regulates SEV licensing in the UK is the Policing and Crime Act 2009, a licensing regime that sets out to regulate strip clubs with the use of strict and, to some extent, complicated licensing conditions, which will be explored later. For the sake of context here, any licence can have conditions attached. A licence to sell alcohol, for example, may come with the condition that alcohol cannot be sold to someone already inebriated. Licence holders who are found to be in breach of the conditions of that licence may have it revoked either temporarily or permanently. In the UK, each county council has its own licensing authority overseeing licensable activities, including SEVs, through the use of licence application processes, hearings and reviews.

CLUB CULTURE: THE IDEAL ECONOMIC CONDITIONS FOR STRIPPING

Phrases like 'the oldest profession in the world' imply a universal truth that the sex industry exists everywhere and always has. But strip clubs really only operate successfully in locations where a certain set of socio-economic conditions line up, and they are only financially viable within certain global economies. The first and most obvious prerequisite for a strip club to be profitable is the level of disposable income in any locale. A strip club is selling a service rather than an actual product, besides alcohol (and in a very few cases, branded merchandise). A striptease or lap dance is an experience; when it's over, it only exists as a memory. Strip clubs are expensive places – it is really only a tiny percentage of the global population who can afford to literally throw cash onto a stage, or pay a considerable amount of money by the hour in a VIP room with someone they've only just met without being totally sure of what will happen once they are inside the room. Strip clubs as we understand them in pop culture, with the mirrors and chrome, champagne and sparkles, really only exist in the largest economies in the world where there is enough excess wealth to justify spending it on transient pleasures.

Another factor that allows strip clubs to become prosperous businesses is liberalism, defined as the willingness within society to accept and tolerate differing opinions and behaviours. The sex industry represents such a disruption to the traditional value systems sanctioned by the Christian church and Western colonisation the world over, upon which global economies have been founded, that it is usually only an accepted occupation where active attempts to liberalise society have happened. Parallels can be drawn with the decriminalisation of homosexuality or abortion, which both recognise our human right to bodily autonomy by returning those rights to the consenting individual. The degree to which religion has left a deep imprint on the culture and traditions of a place will shape the sex industry there, and this tends to be reflected in the Sex Work Law Map.

Although legislation varies widely from country to country, strip clubs are well established in the public imagination since they are so visible. Visions of flashing neon signs advertising 'Live Nude Girls' are synonymous with the sex industry, particularly in those liberalised affluent economies mentioned above. Strip clubs exist in something of a hinterland, not quite a brothel since penetrative sex is not traditionally for sale there, but the suggestion of it is. Stripping connotes a lack of physical contact; the age-old phrase 'you can look but you can't touch' preserves the cultural notion that a strip club does not supply full sexual gratification. But due to the variety of legal regimes globally, the experience on offer can vary from club to club. Criminalisation means a strip club is unlikely to be a premises for clients to attain actual climax, but it may provide a covert gateway to finding it. A strip club in the US where sex work is strictly criminalised will be a different experience from a strip club in, say, Germany, which might offer full-contact services (known as extras) in the private rooms. Even in countries where sex work is criminalised, strip clubs may offer contact dancing where customers may touch a dancer's breasts and thighs. Any one club can become a micro-economy where there are essentially a range of experiences available dictated by the legal and traditional ethics ingrained within it.

Because of the strict laws in the UK that criminalise full-service sex work, there have been concerted efforts within the strip club industry to build robust boundaries between stripping and other types of sexual services. Club owners have long been distancing themselves from the term 'sex work', separating themselves in an attempt to be seen as 'legitimate' businesses. The word 'legitimate' comes up over and over again in the public dialogue about strip clubs, carrying with it all the implied connotations, the stigma, the respectability politics and power struggles that demarcate *good* types of sex workers from *bad* ones.

Many people who work in the sex industry will argue that

there is a disjunct between the actual industry and the public discourse about it. Strippers and club owners are not the only interest groups with public or private agendas; there are also council officials, police district supervisors, local residents, feminist and human rights campaigners, and customers. Even the media play a role since the public often hear about local or national legal developments from the tabloid press, who are often quick to jump on stories about strip clubs regardless of accuracy. The following story illustrates the way in which a multiplicity of voices, opinions and narratives creates the cultural context in which we understand sex work; and how the *quality* of this discourse conditions our assumptions and beliefs.

THE CASE OF STACEY TIERNEY

On 19 December 2016, a British stripper, Stacey Tierney, was found dead in a strip club, Dreams, in Melbourne, Australia, after she had been working there for several months.[9] Her death was first reported in the press with scant information, but with no shortage of images of her in a bikini by a pool in the Australian sunshine, or at a festival with decorative gemstones accentuating her arrestingly pretty eyes. Early news reports declared her death, and named the venue in which her death had occurred, but with sparse information about the circumstances. Drugs and alcohol were mentioned, implying death by overdose before a full toxicology report was completed. It was two years until an inquest revealed the full details of her death, during which time no one was charged, the club remained trading as usual, and the narrative of a vulnerable female on her own in a foreign country who had suffered a tragic but somehow unavoidable misfortune was established.

Tierney's death was in fact suspicious, as became clear from the findings of the inquest. The news sent shock waves through the community, with many strippers, sex workers and allies using their social media accounts to demand answers from Victoria state police, who remained tight-lipped throughout the entire investigation. A year after her death a change.org campaign was launched by a local woman with some notoriety – Chase Paradise, an Australian stripper, comedian and performer who uses her platform to challenge stigma and advocate for sex workers. The petition titled 'What Happened to Dreams Dancer Stacey Tierney?'[10] ran for months, and helped draw attention to the worrying inconsistencies surrounding Tierney's death.

Details of the night as reported in the press are hazy, and piecing together the sequence of events from the segments released into the public still leaves questions unanswered. Tierney began her shift on Saturday 18 December at 8.30 p.m. and finished in the early hours of Sunday morning. She was seen on CCTV throughout the club looking sober and coherent. At 3.41 a.m. she entered the manager's office – the only part of the club not covered by CCTV – and didn't come out again alive. Her body was found on Monday morning, thirty hours after she went into the club. A stripper partying after hours at their workplace is no more unusual than a bar tender staying back for a drink when work is over. Nor is an after-party that goes on well into the following day, and night even, in a private office of a nightclub such an unusual occurrence in the party district of a major city, known for its nightlife. The use of illegal drugs at a private party would be at the discretion of a venue owner, and is ultimately their responsibility: for many people working and operating in the night-time industries these risks may seem relatively low. What happened to Tierney, though, was more than just an example of when things went wrong, but also a shocking indictment of a justice system that utterly failed in its duty of care.

Press reports around the time of Tierney's inquest stated that the party began with a group of six, eventually dwindling to leave Tierney with two men, Joseph Berhe and Tomas Mesfin. The men were nowhere to be seen when the club owner returned at 11.43 a.m. on Monday morning, by which time she had been dead for around six hours. The coroner's report estimated she had probably died around 5.30 a.m. Emergency services were called but by the time they arrived efforts had been made to clean up the room. Tierney's toxicology report came back with alcohol, heroin, cocaine and MDMA in her system. She died of an overdose, but the coroner recorded an open verdict. Berhe and Mesfin were questioned by police but not arrested until months later. They both gave inconsistent reports, claiming to be asleep through-out the session although phone records disproved this. A text from one of them was sent at 12.30 a.m. that read, 'this chick's passed out and I can't leave her. She's scaring me.' Another was sent at 5.43 a.m. on Monday, around about the estimated time of death, saying, 'I don't know what to do anymore.' Rather than calling an ambulance, the men fled.

Despite the worrying circumstances surrounding Tierney's death, no one has been charged or prosecuted. In November 2018 a UK inquest was held during which Coroner Ms Alison Mutch asked of Detective Superintendent Estelle Mathieson, from Greater Manchester Police, 'What is clear is that as she became unwell nobody sought any help for her . . . And the Australian police and Australian prosecuting authorities take the view that does not amount to a criminal offence?'[11] Detective Superintendent Mathieson replied, 'They can't prove a criminal offence. There's clearly been an attempt to clean up the scene, [which] made it difficult to gather evidence. Once she disappears from CCTV she's not seen alive again and the accounts we have been given are inconsistent.'

There are a staggering number of unanswered questions. Who permitted the club office to be used as an after-party hang out? If anything was changed at the scene before first responders arrived, isn't removing or tampering with evidence tantamount to obstructing the course of justice? Was the club searched for further evidence of drug abuse, or of drinks being spiked? Were glasses sent for forensic testing; if not why not? When police arrived on the scene, could any prejudiced beliefs about sex workers have meant they initially assumed her death was an overdose, leading them to overlook any traces of foul play? Why did the club not have its licence suspended while police investigations were under way? If police and prosecution services acknowledged inconsistences in the evidence, why has no one been prosecuted? Was it ever considered that Tierney's death should lead to any police restrictions on the club and the way it operates – and if not why not?

Perhaps the most disturbing detail of the case, among the pile of disturbing details, is how quickly the club returned to business as usual. Leigh Hopkinson, stripper and author of *Two Decades Naked*, an autobiography of life in the industry, wrote in an essay for Australian literary journal *Overland*, titled 'After Hours':

> What shocks me the most is the club's reopening the day after Stacey's death for 'Sexy Poker Tuesdays' . . . I guess death isn't part of the fantasy.[12]

No public statement of acknowledgement or condolence was ever made by Dreams. In the weeks and months after Tierney's death any public comments calling for accountability made by fellow strippers were quickly deleted from Dreams' social media accounts. At the time of writing, it appeared to be business as usual.

Australia is a popular destination for strippers. Sex work has been legalised in the state of Victoria, and fully decriminalised in New South Wales and Northern Territories, meaning that conditions for sex workers are conceivably the safest in the world. The death of Stacey Tierney, however, highlights so much of the systemic violence that still continues to surround the sex industry. Watching how police investigators and prosecution services appeared to fail in their duty to exact justice when there were considerable lines of enquiry, is indicative of an institutional bias that assumes the death of a sex worker is nothing other than a tragic but unavoidable accident. It's tempting to speculate that the lack of criminal prosecution may be explained by the fact that Tierney was a British citizen who died overseas. UK police face multiple challenges when it comes to investigating a crime in another country, not least when it happens on the other side of the planet; yet there are fewer obstacles when working alongside an English-speaking Commonwealth country with virtually the same criminal justice system. The apparently lackadaisical response from both Australian and UK police towards Tierney's death gives no indication that attitudes towards sex workers are any different between the two countries, despite the divergence in legal approaches.

When Tierney died, articles emerged immediately, particularly in the British press, containing all the predictable garishness that comes with the news of a sex worker's demise. As Hopkinson wrote:

The tabloids revert to tired tropes: Stacey's 'heartbroken family' had been unaware she was supporting herself by stripping . . . In *Daily Mail Australia*, Antoinette Aparo, the sister of Salvatore, the club's owner, insinuated Stacey's own culpability: 'I know strip clubs and I know the type of girls who work there.'[13]

Tierney was perfect tabloid fodder – a young, white, blonde-haired, beautiful female who met her untimely end in the sex industry. The story practically wrote itself, all it needed was a selection of highly gratuitous images taken from her social media pages, showing her posing like a Victoria's Secret model and showing off her amazing figure in a variety of swimwear. The actual details of the story didn't matter so much. Van Badham, an Australian feminist writer, theatre maker, critic and social commentator, wrote in the *Guardian*:

Stacey Tierney's story has got to me. For years I lived only a couple of hundred metres away from where her death occurred – and knowing it as a busy area, knowing how many people are always around even late on a Sunday night, the abandonment of her there is of a bleakness that is enraging. It is difficult to imagine a more profound disrespect of a human being than that shown to Tierney in death . . . until you see some media coverage of it. One British tabloid described her dancing job as a 'lucrative but seedy sideline' – accompanied by photos of her in a bikini.[14]

Online articles are riddled with mistakes, from dates to time-lines – but when the purpose is to simply objectify the victim, then consistency isn't the priority. To some extent, Tierney's death was reported with less venal avarice than similar stories about sex workers in the past. But questions still arise about the appropriateness of framing Stacey Tierney as a tragic victim of the sex industry. The facts of her death aside, people die of drug overdoses every day, regardless of their history of recreational drug use or addiction problems. If Tierney had died in the office of a regular nightclub, it is unlikely to have attracted the international attention it got. The one fact about Tierney's death that made the story press-worthy was her job as a stripper. Her death fitted with the entrenched value system, confirming a core societal belief about sex workers as victims.

At least some attempts were made to humanise Tierney in the press. Details emerged that she had studied dance and became a fitness instructor before moving to Australia. She had travelled on a work holiday visa with her boyfriend in 2014 before moving, a year later, to take advantage of the favourable economic opportunities there. Most of her family assumed she was working in a bar – some friends and loved ones knew what she was doing but were not necessarily accepting of it.

Looking through photos of Tierney, she had a healthy body type and glowing skin – images of her at the beach give the impression of someone enjoying life in the Australian climate. She didn't look socially isolated – photos of her in social situations imply that she was connected to a network of friends. It's hard to imagine her speedballing hard drugs at the weekend; the alarming cocktail of chemicals found in her system leans more towards the possibility of her drink being spiked, than of her dabbling with heroin, cocaine and MDMA at the same time. Of course, social media accounts rarely give a true picture of someone's life – no amount of profiling or stories about how happy and stable she was can shake the common assumption that, beneath the smiles and glitter, she was in fact deeply unhappy, vulnerable and at risk. Any attempt to humanise Tierney will always be competing with the typical personification of sex workers as poor tragic souls – an image so deeply ingrained in the popular imagination that it's almost impossible to write a narrative that doesn't end with Tierney's victimhood being bound up with her job.

The anniversary of Stacey Tierney's death falls only two days after 17 December, observed as International Day to End Violence Against Sex Workers. These coincidentally proximate dates underline an important point: violence is systemic as well as physical. The unexplained aspects of Tierney's death weren't fully investigated by the criminal justice system, and the press objectified her in order to sell newspapers and generate online traffic. The fact that her death happened in a part of the world known for its progressive attitude and legal approach to the sex industry illuminates the systemic violence that still befalls sex workers. She doesn't just leave behind a devastated family and a community of strippers in shock; her death also focuses attention on the growing need for sex worker safety. Could her death have been avoided had she been working in an environment and sector that valued her life; had she worked in an industry that respected her time and agency, which observed her employment rights; had she been able to rely on a legal system that upheld her right to safety; had she been surrounded by a support network of friends and family who all knew exactly where she was working and with whom, because she never felt like she had anything to hide; had she lived in a society where she could talk freely and openly about her work without fear of being shamed or pathologised?

A sex worker's death is not an isolated event divorced of context, and how a society reacts reveals the true nature of their prevailing moral tendencies about sex work. Do strippers die because their drinks are spiked? Because of addiction? Because of neglect? Or *because* they are strippers? For many the answer is the latter, and so Tierney's death becomes intrinsically linked to her sex working status, making the other questions circumstantial – i.e. strippers *are* neglected addicts whose drinks may get spiked, or worse. If the prevailing view is that working in the sex industry is wrong, then loss of life is ultimate proof of this, regardless of legal policy. Tierney's death apparently wasn't deemed worthy of rigorous and methodical investigation because it took place in the context of a moralistic belief system about sex workers – that their victimhood is inevitable.

Chapter 7 of this book, The Victimhood Industry, explores the web of charities, campaigners, journalists, politicians, academics and social critics with fixed views about sex work. Any stories of maltreatment, exploitation or abuse only serve to provide further grist for the mill of their efforts to abolish it, particularly when a stripper ends up on a mortuary slab. Keeping the prevailing views about sex work as an aberration firmly in place relies on a morality-based discourse, which merely sets up a right/wrong dichotomy – for anyone who falls on the wrong side, their demise will be inevitable. The moralistic patterning of right versus wrong uses sex workers' victimhood as evidence to prove the just-so story of why we shouldn't have a sex industry, but it does nothing to address the psycho-social environment in which violence still takes place.

What is needed is a shift towards an ethical paradigm, in which the death of a sex worker is seen as evidence that there is still much work to be done. Harm-reduction and safety for sex workers does not fit into the moralistic principle, if moralism does not allow for sex work to happen in the first place. An ethical approach aims to empower sex workers by providing a different psycho-social environment: one that takes a pragmatic world view, which no longer places sex work in a right/wrong binary. An ethical paradigm sees *sex work* as the inevitability and therefore seeks to restructure social norms to reduce violence and support workers' access to resources. There is no shortage of ideas on how to go about this, but the dividing lines seem to be continually drawn between morals and ethics.

Perhaps, then, the final say should go to those who are central to the dialogue. Sex workers and sex worker-led organisations the world over are united in the demand for decriminalisation. Harm-reduction cannot be built on a binary principle – making sex work safer can't happen if the end goal is to eradicate sex work by making it wrong. If Tierney's death shows us anything, it's that a mere change in the law is not enough. Regulating the sex industry is only worthwhile if there is a social restructuring going on alongside. The moralistic framework around sex workers like Tierney mean they are not protected, defended or humanised. Their work is legally permitted, but morally forbidden. If the goal is harm-reduction and safety for sex workers, then this is what needs to change.

I started stripping the same year that I became a Buddhist, the year I turned twenty-two. I was living in a shared flat with a fellow student from the Glasgow School of Art, who introduced me to Nichiren Buddhism, a Japanese religion with a philosophy that immediately caught my attention. He used to chant the words Nam Myoho Renge Kyo *every day in his room, and I started to join in. I starting going to Buddhist meetings once a week, hosted by a Japanese chef, which was a women's only meeting. I wasn't used to being separated by gender, and it was weird to me at first. At that age I was more comfortable in the company of men. I'd started to utilise my sexuality as a shield, a tool, or a resource, and I still had a lot to learn about my own boundaries. Practising Buddhism meant I quickly began to see things about myself, helping me become more aware of my life choices, and what was driving me – which was a valuable practice for the lifestyle I was about to embark upon.*

The words Nam Myoho Renge Kyo *come from an ancient Japanese dialect spoken by a thirteenth-century Buddhist monk, Nichiren Daishonin. Nichiren was motivated by a desire to heal human suffering; he studied for twenty years, reading every Buddhist text he could find until he discovered the* Lotus Sutra. *The phrase* Nam Myoho Renge Kyo, *which comes from the* Lotus Sutra, *roughly translates to mean 'I dedicate myself to the mystic law of the universe'. Legend has it that the original Buddha, the guy who sat under the Bodhi tree, the guy most people imagine as a giant golden head, was an Indian prince who left his palace one day for the first time and encountered the sufferings of his citizens outside the palace gates. He eventually gave up his wealth and dedicated his life to ascetic practices, which led to his enlightenment. According to historical legend, he gave lectures seated beneath the Bodhi tree in Bihar, northern India, which were passed on through word of mouth via the Orally Transmitted Teachings for hundreds of years, until they were finally written down as Sutras.*

The Lotus Sutra *is named after the lotus flower, or water lily, which holds an important symbolism within Buddhism. The lotus grows and can only flower in water that is almost stagnant, dark and thick with mud and algae – these are its ideal conditions providing nutrients for the organism to flourish. The lotus is chosen as a symbol of transformation. The stagnant, muddy pond represents suffering, the material from which life can grow – the key is transformation. Transforming suffering into joy, poison into medicine, pain into happiness is the foundation of Nichiren Buddhism. That is not to say we have to go looking for suffering, nor accept suffering as a positive or favourable condition. A person's life does not have to be defined by their pain, but their own set of struggles and painful circumstances can be used for growth.*

The Lotus Sutra declared that every person has the potential and indeed the right to become happy, to become Buddha or achieve Buddahood, in this lifetime. The sutra also contained the controversial declaration that women have an equal right to Buddhahood as men, which flew in the face of cultural convention at the time. The patriarchal militaristic government of thirteenth-century Japan had control over every aspect of civil life, including religion. The mysticism of reincarnation meant individuals accepted their lot and engaged in devout ascetic practices in the hope of being reborn with higher social status in the next life. This suited a totalitarian regime that depended on keeping their population impoverished in order to fund political battles elsewhere. Famines and natural disasters were devastating the lives of Japanese inhabitants, while the ruling elite turned a blind eye.

Nichiren's ethics stood in direct opposition to the state-approved Tendai school of Buddhism at that time. When he approached the leaders of Japan and asked them to consider the teachings of the Lotus Sutra he was considered too radical and seen as a threat to the state. He was an activist who set about challenging and remonstrating with the government and powerful priests who had remained in command of the country for centuries. He wrote letters to heads of state, and began converting followers of Tendai to a new and radical practice. His efforts were seen as an uprising and were met with bloodshed – his supporters were violently oppressed and he was almost executed himself before being exiled to a small island. His writings survived and now chanting Nam Myoho Renge Kyo *is an international movement.*

The story of Nichiren, his determination to perceive truth and to relieve suffering, struck a chord with me. There was enough suffering in my background and childhood for me to want to do something about it. I already had my suspicions that the state authorities didn't have my best interests at heart, let alone the interests of those in more dire straits than me, and the political system didn't have human happiness built into its foundations. As a teenager I began engaging in environmental activism and the anti-war marches around the time of the allied invasions of Iraq and Afghanistan. I became particularly interested in non-violent direct action; I learned about a children's theatre in Palestine who were supporting trauma survivors to break through sectarianism, and read books about civil disobedience. Chanting was opening up a new perspective. At meetings I heard the terms 'cherishing one's life' and 'dialogue through friendship, peace through trust'. I was invited to see myself and all other human beings as precious Buddhas, with the potential for great joy and happiness. I was introduced to the notion that world peace could come about by transforming our collective karma.

I chanted at weekly meetings for over a year before I finally decided to join in fully and get my own Gohonzon, an object of devotion to sit and chant in front of every day. I decided to transform my own set of painful circumstances and one of the first things on my list of personal battles was my financial karma. I had almost dropped out of my Fine Art degree because, among other reasons, I had always struggled with money. There had never been any family money to fully support me and I was amassing a hefty student debt. The financial pressures of working part-time minimum wage jobs were impacting on my studies. I almost crashed out of art school when I went on a student exchange programme in Paris, which left me with maxed-out credit cards and heavily overdrawn.

Depression and anxiety were never far away by then and alcohol had become a crutch. Chanting helped me start to transform anxiety and despair into resourcefulness and pragmatism. I decided to take time off from my degree to take stock and get myself into a less financially precarious situation. It was during that gap year a sequence of events led me to auditioning in a lap-dancing club. When I got the job it was exhilarating, but I also had to immediately focus my time-management skills. I was already earning a full-time wage working at a restaurant during the day, so figuring out how to work two jobs while getting enough rest was a challenge. It was exhausting, but the extra income from working at night meant I was now earning enough to pay off debts, save money and enjoy things like going for an expensive meal or buying my very own bed with a brand new mattress for the first time. Sleep became a precious commodity and eventually the split shifts weren't sustainable. After a couple of months I called in sick one too many times at the restaurant, but by then I was earning more than enough as a dancer and I could say goodbye to minimum wage for a while.

About six months in I found myself feeling conflicted about lap dancing. Although the first club I worked in was relatively well run, I didn't actually know this until I'd started working elsewhere and had a few different clubs to compare it to. While the money was better than minimum wage, the actual working conditions of the clubs were getting to me. Right from the start I'd never been completely comfortable with the business model, which I eventually learned was the same across the industry – we didn't get paid a wage by the clubs but instead had to pay them a house fee every night to work there. In some clubs we also paid a commission at the end of the night on what we earned (either a percentage of our earnings, or an arbitrary amount roughly decided by a manager at the end of the night), and we could be fined for calling in sick or breaking the rules.

The threat of being sacked was used like a cattle prod, a continuous reminder of how little power we had since there were no official employment contracts. It was a different working environment to any other minimum wage job I'd been in, where I'd show up and slog through eight hours for a fixed pay packet at the end. In a lap-dancing club we were sold the premise of freedom, of 'self-employment' – the idea was that we worked for ourselves. But ultimately the clubs had women working for them, under conditions closer to employment (being told what to wear, how to behave, when to work and whether or not we could leave the clubs early on a slow night), but without any employment rights. Dancers were working eight-hour shifts with no guaranteed wage at the end, gambling their time and money (paying the house fee always felt like placing a bet to me); all the while the club was making money every time someone walked through the door, bought a drink or went into the VIP room.

Certainly the earning potential was a lot higher than any other job I'd done, but we were not treated with enough respect in return for our hours of sitting in an empty club, propping up the business. We were the reason the place even existed – the customers literally only turned up to spend time with us. Yet this was not reflected in the business model; instead of being seen as business partners or contractors we were treated like walking, talking ATMs. The customers were often treated better than us. The stripping part was great, I had no hang-ups about taking my clothes off and being on stage as a sexual entertainer; there were moments at work that were truly life-affirming and euphoric. But once I'd worked at a handful of different venues it soon became apparent that they were run by people who didn't seem to give a fuck about my welfare, and weren't open to conversations about how the business was structured or how it may be improved to support workers. I loved my job, but disliked the places I had to work in.

I remember the first time I revealed at I was a lap dancer during a Buddhist meeting. I'd kept it under my hat, mainly because of an expectation that I would be met with disapproval or shame, but the reaction couldn't have been further from what I'd anticipated. No one gave the slightest hint that I ought to be ashamed or stop what I was doing, no one stigmatised or othered me; there was nothing but compassion and acceptance in the room. It felt like there was a total understanding that I would either use the challenges of being a lap dancer to fuel my own personal growth and create value in society, or that I would do it some other way. Being a lap dancer wasn't the problem; it was whether I would transform my karma or not.

Being an artist, activist and Buddhist gave me three powerful sets of tools for reimagining the world as a better place. Art school opened my eyes to the visual and material world, the built environment, the public and the private, and the narratives of aesthetics; being an activist uncovered the political world, the hidden agendas, corporate interests and the authority of media; and being a Buddhist revealed the nature of suffering, the power of compassion and kindness, and the endless capacity for transformation. This meant working in a strip club was not just about earning cash to me, there was endless opportunity for learning and growth.

One of the most useful tools I learned from the practice of Nichiren Buddhism was the concept of the ten worlds, or ten life states, on a spectrum from pain and suffering – the lower worlds – to happiness and Buddhahood, or enlightenment. At the bottom are Hell, Hunger, Animality and Anger, states characterised by despair, greed, foolishness and ego, all traits that I became very familiar with while working as a lap dancer. Higher up the spectrum are Tranquillity, Rapture, Learning and Realisation, which are characterised by calmness, playfulness, observation and self-discovery, all of which absolutely applied to working in a strip club as well. At the other end of the spectrum, the two remaining life states – considered to be higher states of consciousness that lead to enlightenment – are Boddhisattva and Buddhahood. A Boddhisattva is a Buddha in training, a life state of strong compassion and empathy for others. Buddhahood is the final stage, an amalgamation of all the others into a state of truth, wisdom and awareness, also described as enlightenment. Bringing my Buddhahood to work, being wise enough to transform suffering into joy, seemed like a pretty radical idea to me.

Working in a lap-dancing club I encountered all ten life states. The club with all its animalistic and greedy energies was the muddy pond, the perfect conditions for me to transform. I didn't need to identify with anyone's suffering, instead I had the potential to transform it into joy. The value I was creating wasn't just the cash I was making, but the energy I was changing. I would chant every day before work, or I would chant quietly in the toilets to get me through a bad shift; every time something shitty went down I would chant to process and transform it. My main priority was always to make money and not go home with less than I started, so of course I chanted primarily for cash. But I also found myself chanting for protection, to have a good shift, to cherish my colleagues. Supporting and encouraging my fellow sisters in the changing rooms, making people laugh, offering a shoulder to lean on or a temporary state of pleasure, no matter how fleeting, became about as important as getting paid. I started to work with the determination to see and meet every one I spoke to as the Buddha himself.

I couldn't always be a Buddha, in fact I rarely was. There were so many obstacles and challenges; there were alcohol and egos, and layers and layers of debasement. Scratch the surface of the sex industry and you'll find all the lowest energies competing for dominance, exhausting and exploiting those who find themselves in the muddy pond, gasping for oxygen. The first dancer who ever taught me how to give a lap dance,

Catherine (not her real name), took her own life several years later. I met her on my first night, doing a working audition at my first club in Glasgow. She always seemed nervous, and was extremely paranoid that one night someone from her hometown might walk into the club and recognise her. She came from a small village outside the city and was living a double life. Her family didn't know she was a lap dancer and she was terrified of them finding out. When we worked together she would avoid the entrance and whenever customers walked in she would remain out of sight until she was satisfied that she didn't know them. She had a coke habit and spent a lot of time on her shift in the DJ's office, and would come out with all this chemically enhanced confidence.

I never really knew Catherine all that well. She drove us all to Newcastle one weekend for a work trip. Scottish strippers would regularly pile in cars together and head to the stag capital of the UK to work, and being in a different city meant she could relax. There is a moment seared in my memory when she was dancing on stage to a Missy Elliott song, totally lost in the performance. She wasn't the best dancer in the club or anything, but in that instant she occupied her role with a purity that I'll never forget. She was tiny and slight, like a bird, with bleached blonde hair, a deep fake tan and amazing eyes. She used to wear a neon pink fishnet mini dress that glowed under the UV. She was at the front of the stage at the tipping rail (not that anyone in Scotland tips) sitting on her haunches and leaning back against the pole. She mouthed the lyrics of the song 'between my thighs' and when the beat kicked she dropped her knees open revealing a flash of her neon pink G-string, and she did this thing with her hand, sort of using it like a fan on her crotch, before her knees came back together and she turned away. The whole move only took a few seconds, but the stripper aesthetics were unmistakable and flawless. In that moment, unfettered by her fear of being found out, she found her flow and was utterly present.

Although we weren't that close, news of her death was devastating. I'd already left Scotland by then. The club we both worked at had changed management and I'd lost touch with any of our mutual connections. One night while I was visiting Glasgow I bumped into the old club DJ, who was now working as a doorman elsewhere. He told me right there and then that Catherine had hung herself. I had to compartmentalise what he'd just said so I could carry on with my night but I knew it was awful. I knew that her precarious balance of work, fear and addiction meant she was vulnerable and isolated. Without the support of a community to help her process the emotional demands of her work she tried to outrun them. The social stigma of being identified as a stripper and all the degradation that comes with it can be too much to bear for some – not least in a village where residents all operate within the same moralistic social system, gossiping about each other at coffee mornings or at the local supermarket. In such places the facts do not take precedence over personal judgement. People's feelings and assumptions about women who work in the sex industry as dirty women, whores, disease carriers, women with negative social value, unworthy of love and acceptance, probably contributed to Catherine's fear of being outed as a stripper or, heaven forbid, being labelled as a sex worker. The thing I'll never know is if she died while her family and neighbours were still in the dark, or did she commit suicide as a reaction to being found out. I never knew how much support she had or how many friends she could rely on, but I suspect that she found herself isolated from any kind of peer support network. She wasn't the only stripper in Scotland tortured by stigma – I met so many over the years with similar patterns of fear, carrying their shame around like excess baggage.

The residents of Catherine's village, like folk anywhere, were conditioned from day one to believe that sex workers are the worst kind of people, and that the very lowest misfortune to befall a person, particularly a female, is to become a prostitute. Hooker jokes literally use sex workers as punch lines; they are endlessly objectified in mainstream pop culture as victims and plot devices. I was raised to think the same way as everyone else. When I started to experience appalling conditions, abusive managers and exploitative business practices I remember having the feeling that perhaps the evidence was correct. Maybe I was doing something wrong, maybe the negative experiences were my own fault because, after all, I was going against everything I'd been taught. I was a lap dancer – what did I expect? My early hesitations and observations about poor treatment of dancers could have so easily conjoined with my internalised shame, confirming the core societal beliefs that women who behave like sluts are not deserving of respect or dignity. My life circumstances were different to Catherine's but not so different that I couldn't relate. Perhaps if those Buddhists hadn't seen past the shame and simply acknowledged me as a human being with a set of challenges and opportunities for growth, my life may have gone very differently. Had I not found support from a community who were accepting of my choices, would I be here? When I think of Catherine's death now I get a strange, eerie feeling, and think, 'There but for the grace of God go I.'

2

LICENCE TO STRIP: A HISTORY OF SEXUAL ENTERTAINMENT

I'm part of show business, I always have been. There's a
lot more to it than just presenting nude girls, you must
entertain as well.[1]

—Paul Raymond

Present day sex industry regulations can't be divorced from
the past; they have evolved from a sequence of historical and
cultural developments. In all law-making, shifts in public attitudes can influence regulations for a generation, and often
there isn't an opportunity to challenge or update the standards
set by one particular law for many more generations to come.
Stripping – like all other licensable activities controlled by the
state, such as gambling, drinking alcohol, live entertainment
and even public protest – is a hotly debated civil liberty.

In virtually all cases relating to civil liberties and personal freedoms of the individual, the argument given for state regulation is one of public protection.

Sex work laws as we know them in the UK date back to the Contagious Diseases Act 1864, an act that was intended to control the spread of sexually transmitted diseases among soldiers returning from the Crimean War.[2] Garrison towns around the country where warships docked became hectic areas where prostitution was prevalent, and the spread of venereal infections was unstoppable. Rather than focusing on the responsibilities soldiers had towards their health and therefore their country, the logical (and misogynistic) conclusion at that time was to fixate on the health status of the women who serviced them. Thus it was written into law that women were accountable for the sexual habits of the 'noblemen' fighting for their nation.

The Contagious Diseases Act 1864 turned prostitutes into legal pariahs and gave local doctors, police and magistrates aggressive new powers. They could arrest and detain any women suspected of prostitution, perform barbaric physical inspections (given the lack of hygiene in medical practice it was quite likely that some women actually contracted infections this way), provide treatment with or without their consent, incarcerate them in asylums for three months, and add them to a list of 'identified' prostitutes created for the purpose of official monitoring. Not only that, but the law did not legally define the word 'prostitute', leaving the door wide open for abuses, so it wasn't long before any woman could be accused and subjected to the violence, stigma and intrusion engendered within the law. When 'innocent' middle-class women found themselves victimised by the law this became a major motivation for early feminist movements. This 'middle-class' feminism has become a well-repeated trend throughout history, which will be explored further in Chapter 7, The Victimhood Industry.

Of course, the sex industry did not begin in 1864. There is a rich history of sex work laws chronicled in Eric Berkowitz's 2012 book *Sex & Punishment: 4000 Years of Judging Desire*. According to Berkowitz, there have been periods of regulated sex work throughout European history, including licensed brothels ordained by the church and/or state:

Christian ambivalence about prostitution reaches back to Saint Augustine himself, who . . . condemned all sexual desire as unclean and wicked . . . There was nothing worse than a prostitute, but Augustine also saw that if they were pulled from circulation, men's lust would seep everywhere and pollute the world. Prostitutes were damned but their souls were to be sacrificed for the betterment of good society. Nearly one thousand years later, the influential theologian Saint Thomas Aquinas had the same outlook: 'Prostitution in the towns is like the cesspool in the palace: take away the cesspool and the palace will become an unclean and evil-smelling place.' Taking this thinking one step further, the church and city authorities concluded that so long as there was a need to clean out human muck, they should make some money in the process. Thus was born the licensed brothel, a factory of evil serving the common good. By 1358, the Grand Council of Venice would declare that prostitution was 'absolutely indispensable to the world.'[3]

In Southwark, London, a small, gated graveyard, nicknamed Cross Bones Cemetery by a cult following of artists and conservationists, contains the buried remains of women who worked as prostitutes in the early red-light district along the south bank of the River Thames. During the medieval period, the area now known as the South Bank was outside the jurisdiction of the City of London. Long before Parliament was founded in 1801, the Bishop of Winchester, Henry of Blois, permitted the licensing of brothels during the twelfth century; the church then collected taxes from the licensed premises. The sex workers who were licensed to work in the brothels or 'stews' in the 'Liberty of the Clink' became known as the Winchester Geese; historical accounts suggest this was for their method of baring their white breasts to passers-by to attract custom.

While this history of licensing provides us with a useful context for understanding legalisation today, we also see how sex work laws have been shaped by religious patriarchy. Aquinas' medieval rationalisation of the sex industry as a necessary evil to contain dangerous male urges no longer holds up as a 'good reason' for doing sex work today. Identifying male desire in this way is treacherous territory, and it's no coincidence that church and state benefited financially – this version of male sexuality as hapless and inevitable not only justifies a history of profiting from women's work, but also a history of failing to hold abusive male behaviour accountable. Sex workers' rights are not built around this logic; radical feminists who insist that decriminalising the sex industry would legitimise abusive patriarchal attitudes are clinging on to an outdated paradigm. Present day sex workers are not choosing to go to work for the service of male desire, any more than they were in the twelfth century. They are doing it for *their own* benefit, to survive, put food on the table and a roof over their heads.

WORKING THE STRIP

Although there's a common historical context, the legislation governing striptease and sexual entertainment originates from a very different path to prostitution laws. Despite the natural crossovers, the different forms of sex work have always been somewhat separated in law. The history of striptease licensing in the UK really only begins in the 1930s with the arrival of the Windmill Theatre, Britain's first and oldest strip club, famous for having remained open during the Blitz, and immortalised in the 2005 film *Mrs Henderson Presents*.[4] After buying a cinema on Great Windmill Street, Soho, business owner Laura Henderson modernised the building and renamed it. After a series of unprofitable business ventures, Henderson and her manager Vivian Van Damm hit upon the notion of the *tableaux vivants*, one of the earliest allowable forms of striptease in public. Inspired by the permissiveness of the Folies Bergère and Moulin Rouge cabaret theatres in Paris, featuring nude dancers, Henderson and Van Damm decided to offer nude entertainment; but the uptight, shame-laden post-Victorian British attitude towards all things sexual (at least in public) meant this was strictly forbidden. According to the film, Henderson was desperately sad about the death of her only son, who had been killed in combat during the First World War while still a teenager, without ever having had the joy of seeing a naked woman. Legend has it that Henderson used her feminine powers of persuasion to convince the Lord Chamberlain to allow nudity as long as the performers were not moving. By drawing a comparison to the paintings and sculptures in the National Gallery she argued that a nude person standing stock still on stage, like a living statue, was no different to fine art.

The position of Lord Chamberlain is an extremely power-ful role within the aristocracy. As the head of the royal household, the Lord Chamberlain is charged with private matters pertaining to the monarch. It is normally a lifelong position served by a Parliamentary peer who acts as the primary channel of communication between the sovereign and the House of Lords. The Lord Chamberlain's office organises royal ceremonial activities including the State Opening of Parliament, but for 230 years between 1737 and 1968 was also given the power to grant licences for theatrical productions, effectively making him the royal entertainment manager. Gaining the royal seal of approval for nudity on her stage was a huge breakthrough for Henderson, as well as for freedom of expression in general from the heavily repressed Victorian period of sexual inhibition.

Thanks to Henderson's trailblazing activities as the matriarch of the Windmill Theatre, its trademark *tableaux vivants* became a runaway success. Performers could appear naked only if they were static so arranged themselves in scenes or *tableaux*, curtains would fall and lights would black out to allow them to appear and reappear without breaking their pose. A revolving floor was built to allow for the models to be viewed from every angle, and male performers were also included in the mix. No sooner was the new style permitted than dancers and theatre producers elsewhere started to push boundaries, giving rise to variations including the fan dance – in which a naked dancer could move on stage as long as their nudity was covered with the use of huge ostrich feather fans, and for a final few moments at the end of their routine they could reveal what was underneath as long as they stood motionless in a pose. The Windmill was a lucrative venue, and was soon surrounded by a throng of copycat businesses, all jumping on the bandwagon to tap into the brand new permitted market-place.

While the new rule authorised by the Lord Chamberlain applied to public theatres and stages, it didn't cover the activities of private members' clubs. The elitism of private members' clubs dates back hundreds of years, continuing up to the present day; the Garrick, Carlton, Athenaeum, White's and the suggestively named In & Out military club are all prestigious institutions for British aristocrats, politicians and other figures of imperialism to gather and commune in a traditionally men-only environment. The Garrick Club still does not permit female members to this day. Gentlemen's clubs have long provided the tabloid media with plenty of material for the great British tradition of scandalising the non-traditional, non-monogamous habits of high-profile aristocrats and celebrities. Members' clubs have appeared in many other forms too; Molly houses (gay brothels known for their non-binary sex workers) are some of the best examples of spaces where laws that governed the rest of the public were thrown out the window for a certain privileged elite who could afford to conduct their sexual proclivities behind closed doors. Unsurprisingly, the sex industry has a closely intertwined history with the gentlemen's club. One particular private members' club, the Raymond Revuebar, became a huge hit thanks to the arrival in Soho of a new charismatic businessman with very modern ideas – Paul Raymond.

❦

I worked at the Windmill for one night. When I moved to London in 2010 I was looking around for a good club to work in – I already knew my preferences by that time, large brands and corporate chains weren't for me. I wanted somewhere with character and a sense of history; the Windmill had that in spades. I'd seen from their website that auditions were held every weekday afternoon. I got my swag on and rocked up in a black leather biker jacket, skin-tight black leggings, winklepickers and a white 'Make Love Not War' T-shirt.

The audition process was grim. I was the only dancer to audition that day and the female manager auditioning me seemed more annoyed than welcoming or interested. She showed me into a dank changing room some-where in the warren-like basement that had no windows and very little airflow. She told me to get undressed down to my thong and high heels, and to wait in the dressing room. I followed her instructions and waited for maybe fifteen minutes, shivering in the cold. I'd cycled eight kilometres to the club and felt my stomach growling for the lunch I had in my bag. I was losing energy fast so finally caved in to my body's needs. When she eventually returned to the room she was met with the sight of me, naked apart from a black thong and clear plastic heels, shovelling mouthfuls of pasta from a Tuppaware box. I didn't expect the look of disgust that spread across her face. 'Well you can put that down,' she said, which I did while probably stifling an eye-roll. She then asked me to stand up straight, which I did, spin around, which I did, and then she said, 'OK, you can put your clothes back on now,' leaving me alone to get dressed and quickly stuff some more food in my mouth before she could catch me eating again. When she came back she told me I could start on Saturday night, and that the house fee was £60 (which I thought was reasonable for central London).

When I turned up for my shift the staff at reception were so dis-organised that I went straight downstairs without paying my house fee. The changing rooms were segregated into a hierarchy of dancers: new girls, dancers who had been there longer, and the veterans who had been there for years who looked me up and down with a similar disdain as the manager who had auditioned me. I was shown into the correct changing room by the house mum, a small Chinese lady, whose job it was to micro-manage our every move, even down to where we placed our belongings. It was a rule that when we were ready to go out into the club, all our clothes and makeup had to be neatly packed away in our bags so that the chang-ing room didn't become messy. I'd never seen that level of control before.

I had high expectations of the oldest strip club in the UK. The venue was a huge converted theatre space, with VIP booths up in the circle bal-cony, and an incredible stage; but there weren't that many customers and, as per usual, there were too many dancers. One of the girls told me that Saturday nights are tough to make money, it's normally mid-week that wealthy clients come in and spend more. I already knew my working-class roots jarred with entitled businessmen, and so I wasn't convinced I'd found 'my' club. The atmosphere at the Windmill that night was tough;

dancers would wait by the main doors for customers to enter, at which point there would be a kind of scrum. Sometimes two or three dancers at a time would stick to a client like glue until they were turned away, but sometimes the strategy paid off. I saw a customer walk in and just let himself be dragged into VIP for a couple of hours by the first two girls that grabbed him at the door.

The Windmill, like many other clubs in central London, was a hard hustle. Too many dancers all competing for the spoils created the kind of environment that attracts a specific type of client; entitled, arrogant and egotistical. Some men go into strip joints knowing they have the upper hand, especially those who are familiar with the economics. They know we've had to pay the club to work, so we are starting from a deficit. That night I experienced all the worst elements of male behaviour that strip clubs are so easily associated with. I approached a crowded table of clients celebrating a stag party with a stunningly beautiful woman of colour who was also working that night. One of them said to me, 'Tell your friend to go and speak to my mate.' I leant over and gave her the tip off, and when I returned to my potential customer he said, 'Nice one. He hates black girls.' It was sickening. I spent hours hustling from table to table, having my time wasted by dudes who were clearly enjoying the position of power they found themselves in. Having finally secured a private dance with one, he pretty much coerced me into giving a full-contact lap dance and letting him stroke my arse and thighs. I consented because in truth I actually prefer giving full-contact dances, so it never feels like a violation, but I took a risk by breaking the rules of the club on my first night. It was a perfect example of how consent is undermined time after time by the economic context of the business model the industry is built on.

I got too drunk that night. Customers kept buying me drinks as a strategy to keep me talking to them for free, and I didn't yet have the confidence to say, 'I'd rather have a glass of water and you can give me the cost of a drink as a tip.' I spent a fair bit of time in the changing rooms, trying to suss out the dynamic of the club, and found that they served us sandwiches and biscuits at 1 a.m. to keep us going until closing; a bizarre detail given the reaction when I was caught eating during my 'audition'. I didn't make it to the end of the night, which would have been 4–6 a.m. I was climbing the walls with frustration and decided to cut my losses. I packed up and sailed past the front desk with a smile, breathing an internal sigh of relief that I'd got away without paying the house fee. When I got home I found a dress and a bottle of perfume were missing from my bag. I was too pissed to remember if I'd left them out of my bag in the changing room, but when I went back the next day to retrieve them they were long gone.

I sat on that experience for a while, trying to understand it. I was new to London, and felt out of my depth. I'd had similar experiences before at big name clubs and they all left me feeling the same way: anxious and insecure. I'd got on better in smaller clubs with fewer dancers and a sense of camaraderie. I didn't like the feelings that came up when I found myself having to hustle – comparing myself to other girls and fixating on all the ways I wasn't 'good enough'. My ego didn't cope well in an environment where I had less control over each moment-to-moment interaction with a customer. My anxiety levels reacted like clockwork, and alcohol was readily available to self-medicate with. A good night at work was *validating, but a bad night at work debilitating; I responded by becoming even fussier about where I worked.*

One of the nagging doubts that night left me with was about karma. As a Buddhist I couldn't help making the connection between losing my dress and perfume with not paying my house fee. I felt I had been spiritually punished for being sneaky. It took me a while to fully see the bigger picture; that over the years I have given so much to the industry in general, not just my money but my time, labour and energy; that clubs take and take from us while washing their hands of any duty of care. I don't have a modicum of guilt about my house fee anymore. The one night I worked there I felt the energy and culture of the club, almost like it was coursing through the building itself. It wasn't a good environment to be doing sex work in.

When Paul Raymond entered the central London scene in the early 1960s, thirty years after nudity had been legitimised on Laura Henderson's stage, public attitudes towards sex had shifted dramatically. His appearance coincided with the free love movement, Women's Lib and birth control; the swinging sixties was a decade of significant cultural challenges to the social foundation of heterosexual marriage, and Raymond was in the right place at the right time to capitalise on the new era of libertarianism. As portrayed in the 2013 film *The Look of Love*,[5] he came to epitomise the prevailing spirit of male chauvinism of the period, living up to the stereotype of a philandering millionaire. He presided over his business empire as a publisher of soft pornography and men's magazines, as well as investing in a property portfolio in Soho that was eventually worth hundreds of millions of pounds. His commercial dealings and personal affairs earned him the tabloid epithet 'the King of Sleaze' as he became widely known as the man responsible for bringing the sex industry to Soho.

The epicentre of his domain was the Raymond Revuebar – London's most iconic of gentlemen's clubs, and the jewel in the crown of his profitable kingdom. From 1958 to 2004, the venue was billed as the 'World Centre of Erotic Entertainment', and to this day, its original neon sign, carefully preserved as a reminder of Soho's seamy past, still flashes its tantalising promise of 'Personal Appearances of the Worlds Greatest Names in Striptease'. The Raymond Revuebar eventually fell out of fashion and went out of business in 2004, but after a few changes in management, the club was reborn under a new identity in 2011. The Box is now one of London's most prestigious nightclubs, regularly playing host to Hollywood actors, Saudi princes, international oligarchs, and even members of the British royal family, including Prince Harry. The club takes full advantage of its notorious past and still profits hugely from striptease and sexual entertainment, thanks to the preservation of its sexual entertainment licence. Prices start at £1,000 per table on weeknights.

By the end of the 1960s there was another change in legislation. The Theatres Act 1968 marked the end of the Lord Chamberlain's reign as national censor of live entertainment;

it has been the job of Parliament ever since. Censorship of public theatres had been in place as far back as the 1700s and among other reasons was originally intended to protect royal and governmental administrations from political satire. But by the mid-twentieth century theatre was diversifying, different forms of entertainment like cinema and TV were mainstream and censorship in theatre was no longer good for business. The Theatres Act 1968 was a major development and represented a loosening of the grip held over the public for centuries by dictating the political and social commentary they may or may not be exposed to. Under the Act, theatres were finally allowed to present ideas and images that had previously been outlawed – including nudity.

The Theatres Act hugely boosted Raymond's business enterprise. Having already exploited the lack of censorship permitted in private members' clubs, he was then free to open more venues that fell within the legal category of public theatre, offering nude entertainment. The lifting of the striptease ban meant that venue owners took advantage by quickly organising their venues into theatres to cater for the booming trade in spectators. Raymond's biggest venue, the Revue Bar, was patronised by many of London's high-flying elite, both male and female, making Soho the zenith of nightlife in the capital. Frank Sinatra, Richard Burton, Peter Sellers, Judy Garland and the Beatles were among the list of stars to patronise the club. Among the many theatres and venues he operated, Raymond also bought the lease on the Windmill Theatre, which by this time had reverted back to being a cinema. He restored it to its original purpose as a strip club, before he sold it on to the Ovide family, who ran it until the SEV licence was lost in 2018 (after an undercover investigation found the venue to be in breach of their licensing conditions).[6]

The lasting memory of Soho throughout the 1970s and 1980s as a bustling red-light district endures today, despite attempts to erase its past and gentrify the area. A thriving red-light district grew up out of a neighbourhood that had been neglected and condemned. Strippers and sex workers toiled in close proximity to each other and the strip clubs, backstreet bars, theatres, porn cinemas and brothels were standard fixtures vying to attract a certain type of audience. The stereotype of the seedy John, wearing a grubby mackintosh and feeding his appetite for sexual encounters, became a stalwart feature of the era. It was this very stereotype that fed the public imagination, leading to much hand-wringing by a British middle-class housewife, Mary Whitehouse, who became known as the face of censorship. Whitehouse and her supporters lobbied hard for restrictions on the distribution of obscene material, and for a return to 'decent, modest, family values', something of an uphill struggle against the anti-establishment zeitgeist of the 1960s.

A web of laws that governed prostitution and pornography emerged; the Obscene Publications Act 1959 revised guidelines on pornography for licensed publishers to work within (although the underground porn trade often escaped restraints) and the Sexual Offences Act 1956 had firmed up the regulations on prostitution, clarifying the specific definitions of offences such as pimping and procurement. It took another forty-seven years before the Sexual Offences Act 2003 amended regulations around sex work: testament to the lack of public concern for sex workers' lives and livelihoods.

However, when it came to stripping, sexual entertainment slipped through the net. Besides the Theatres Act 1968 there wasn't much written in the law about striptease. It is worth bearing in mind that while London had a burgeoning sex industry and a progressive outlook, the rest of the country didn't have such a visible sex trade. Strip clubs, or venues designated specifically for the purposes of striptease entertainment, were actually relatively rare around the UK up until the arrival of lap dancing in the 1990s. Legs 11 opened in Birmingham in 1996; the Truffle Club opened in 1999 in Glasgow; the Western Bar in Edinburgh was established in 1974, possibly one of the earliest examples of a strip venue outside of London, although it wasn't until the 1990s that they built private dance booths and introduced lap dancing. Clearly, only larger cities had populations big enough for a viable night-time economy that could sustain public striptease as a regular business. While there is little documented evidence of the private activities that went on behind closed doors, there is no question that there is an untold folk history of striptease up and down the country in working men's clubs, the back rooms of pubs, and anywhere that groups of punters could gather to consume sexual entertainment. While the tradition of strippers in East End London boozers is somewhat better remembered, there is no reason to believe that pubs around the country weren't also cashing in on the trend.

It wasn't until the early 1980s that there was a concerted effort to identify and authorise sex-related businesses on the high street. The Local Government (Miscellaneous) Provisions Act 1982 for most part deals with local bylaws at an extremely pedestrian level – controls on public highways, the erection of pylons and signal towers, rights and restrictions on land belonging to local authorities, bathing and boating, public sanitation and mixing concrete by the roadside, to name a few examples. Part II Schedule 3 of the Act, titled Control of Sex Establishments, determined the right of local authorities to inhibit the spread of businesses dealing in erotica through the use of licensing. The Act defined sex establishments as sex cinemas and sex shops, selling porn and 'sex articles', but says nothing of striptease; critically, it also contained a legal loophole that was to be fantastically exploited in later years. Paragraph 7 of Schedule 3 declared that:

The appropriate authority may waive the requirement of a licence in any case where they consider that to require a licence would be unreasonable or inappropriate.[7]

Importantly, this law essentially *left it up to each local council to decide* whether a sex establishment was desirable in its jurisdiction or not, and to decide whether it required a licence. Without a national policy it was very much down to the discretion of councillors whether a strip club, sex shop, peep show or porn cinema may or may not be granted a licence. Providing waivers to business owners who probably ought to have a licence meant the ruling was wide open to varied standards, favours and abuses. Once again, without a legal definition of striptease as a licensable activity, and the Theatres Act still permitting nudity on public stages, regulating strip venues remained a grey area and it was simply left to economic forces to shape its popularity and sustainability. Throughout the 1980s and 1990s strippers had become commonplace in pubs and clubs around different parts of London; Soho, King's Road and Shoreditch were known for offering striptease shows. The Local Government (Miscellaneous) Provisions Act 1982 meant it was really up to each individual London borough to decide whether to ban it. Without clear rules, whatever was good for business was considered permissible.

⌁

I worked at the Box for a brief spell in 2015, courtesy of connections I'd made through the East London scene. Some strippers manage to straddle the two very different worlds of strip clubs and cabaret. One of them was Barbie who formed her own Burlesque troupe, the Dirty Darlings. They were given a regular spot on Tuesday nights at the Box, and I was invited to perform with the troupe. The venue had a small club upstairs in the attic of the building, with a smallish stage and a pole mounted in the middle of the dance floor. The idea was that we, the Darlings, would be part of a floor show at the beginning of the night and then work the floor, selling private lap dances to the crowd for the rest of the night.

It was a real thrill to be working there, knowing the history of the venue. The changing rooms had the original 1960s wallpaper, with a brightly coloured flowery design, which must have been from the Raymond Revuebar days. There was a crazy buzzing atmosphere backstage, some real divas were working there. I got to work with Reuben Kaye, who went on to be an international cabaret superstar. I also got to watch the head-lining acts on the main stage downstairs, which really did blow my mind. The Box offered contracts to international performers to perform runs in London for weeks or months at a time. Buck Angel, the 'dude with a pussy', had me questioning everything I ever thought about gender. A London-based performer, Mouse, was famous for her 'human fountain' rectal squirting routine, and her ability to smoke a cigar with her vagina. One night I watched a Pocahontas act themed around masturbation, which climaxed with the female performer balancing her entire body weight on the elbow of one arm while also anally fisting herself and doing the splits. The Box really were making the most of their SEV licence, and part of me wondered why some other strip clubs were so strictly controlled and micromanaged by their local authorities. The Box operates with the exact same SEV licence as a strip club, yet there are other venues where strippers have to dance one metre away from customers, and a performer spreading their legs or touching their own genitals during a lap dance might result in them being fined or fired. It appears that despite the licensing regime being the same, the entertainment permitted varies wildly from one local authority to another, even venue to venue. But while wondering how the Box were putting on sexually explicit shows while other regular strip clubs were totally restricted, I looked around at the audience. Premier league footballers, Hollywood actors, members of the Saudi Arabian royal family and the cream of London's elite were piling through the doors. It was a far cry from the crowd of middle-aged dads found in a typical strip joint. It would seem that sexual entertainment is only considered problematic by local authorities if it happens in an actual lap-dancing club.

I was working in the upstairs club one week when I saw someone who looked familiar, standing in the shadows a bit away from the dance floor. He was wearing a Russian-style fur hat, so I sidled up to him aiming to use the hat as a conversation starter. As I got closer I suddenly realised how I recognised him – it was Usher. By this time I was in his personal space and he was waiting for me to speak, but I didn't want to be syco-phantic, so tried to play it lowkey. I squinted my eyes and said, 'Do I recognise you?' He nodded his head. I said, 'Are you maybe a bit famous?' He nodded again and smiled. I smiled back and then I simply reached up to give his hat a stroke but not before a middle-aged white guy who looked like he had been trained in combat appeared out of nowhere like an assassin. Within a split second, Usher's private security detail made an assessment that a lingerie-clad stripper in a nightclub was not a physical threat to his client and backed off. I gave Usher's hat a friendly rub (it felt *fantastic by the way), offered him a lap dance which he politely declined, and then moved along.*

Trying to sell a lap dance in that place was difficult. The music blared so loudly that it was impossible to have a cosy chat, and there wasn't really a proper area for private dances. It wasn't a big earner, but since we were charging £50 a dance it was possible to earn a couple of hundred each night, sometimes more if we were lucky. I bagged £500 one night dancing for a group of people in one of the party rooms. They were all wasted, writhing around on a four-poster bed while one of them just kept handing me £50 notes from her designer clutch bag, gleefully tucking them into my garter belt. I also managed to make a professional connection with a wealthy guy who lived in a nearby penthouse flat on Rupert Street, who organised raucous private parties and would regularly book me to perform striptease shows for his elite crowd.

There were normally five Darlings performing at a time. We had to arrive at 9 p.m. for a rehearsal, and then wait around for a couple of hours before the club opened. We were asked to bring matching black out-fits and given matching chokers to wear as part of the brand. The import-ant thing about this arrangement was that we all got paid £50 to show up, and then anything we made on top was ours to keep. Being actually paid a set fee for turning up instead of having to pay a house fee was a huge step in the right direction – and being told what to wear was fine by me as long as I was getting a wage for it. It was a pretty good set up, for all of a couple of months. But when one night we were all sat down to have a new payment structure explained to us, my heart sank. We'd still get paid a fee, but the club would now get a cut from our lap dances (which they had the power to do since plenty of customers paid for every-thing using cards, meaning our payments went through their card machines), and if we earned over a certain amount we wouldn't get the £50 fee. There was a convoluted, sliding scale that reminded me of the shit they do in strip clubs, which left me feeling confused and undermined.

I walked away after that night. The Dirty Darlings residency at the Box didn't last long. I'll never know exactly whose idea it was to intro-duce a commission structure, whether it was Barbie or the venue. The lasting impression left me with a bad taste in the mouth. Like the Wind-mill, the Box had its history woven through the fibres of the building. Raymond's spirit was in the walls and we were all touched by the Invis-ible Hand of his economics – never satisfied, he was still groping around for more.

It wasn't until the late 1990s with the arrival of lap dancing that the picture of striptease legislation in the UK began to really take form. Lap dancing is a sub-genre of striptease and an art form in its own right. The emergence of pole dancing as a sport and fitness trend is testament to the skills practised by many professional strippers, and pole schools across the land now offer chair-dancing classes as well. There are con-flicting schools of thought around the origins of pole dancing depending on whom you ask (it's a good measure of whore-phobia whether or not a pole artist tries to distance the discipline from strip club culture). Chair dancing – a trend of choreography using a chair as a prop – is a close approxima-tion of lap dancing, which without question derived from strip clubs. Lap dancing first appeared in New York in the 1970s at the Melody Club, which introduced audience participation and called it 'mardi gras', before it quickly migrated to the west coast where the Mitchell Brothers O'Farrell Theatre adopted the idea. The increasing availability of VHS video technology meant that sex cinemas and pornographic maga-zines were less profitable, so a new concept was required to compete with the comfort of viewing pornography at home. Lap dancing, and in particular full-contact lap dancing, fitted the bill perfectly.

Once again we have to return to Soho, London, for the story of how lap dancing arrived on the UK scene, and unsur-prisingly it was the ruthless business dealings of a handful of male industry operators that resulted in another shift in legis-lation. The emergence of lap dancing is really a tale of two clubs and their commercial rivalry, within the context of a murky and largely unregulated night-time economy. The two venues which sparked a growth industry, and still to this day are among the biggest names in striptease entertainment, Stringfellows and Spearmint Rhino, would eventually have to join forces and fight for their right to survive under the hellfire of feminist outrage. But in the mid-1990s they were embroiled in a battle as they vied for the custom of London's wealthiest clientele.

Peter Stringfellow was a contemporary of Paul Raymond who also became a tabloid celebrity and household name, thanks to the endless media fascination with his private life and public persona. He didn't shy away from attracting attention and courted plenty of media coverage; he notably made large donations to the Conservative Party, and lived up to his papparazzi stereotype by stepping out with women half his age and sunbathing in a thong. Stringfellow hailed from the north of England and had been successfully running discotheques throughout the 1970s and 1980s – one of his earliest business triumphs came about at the age of twenty-two when he managed to book the Beatles to play at a church hall in his hometown of Sheffield – and he had a strong foothold in the world of night-time entertainment.

Despite his success, he was on the brink of bankruptcy when he visited a topless table-dancing club in the US and decided to break into the striptease industry. He first introduced table dancing to his New York nightclub in 1990, before bringing it to his London club, Stringfellows, in 1996. The Covent Garden club is still in operation today. One of the significant things about Stringfellows is that it never set out to be a lap-dancing club. The venue advertised the performers as a 'cabaret of angels' offering table-side dancing, which initially was topless only. Unlike the Raymond Revuebar, Stringfellows was not a members-only club; it was open to the public and therefore operated under different licensing bylaws set by

City of Westminster Council. By the end of the twentieth century, Stringfellow had cornered the top end of the erotic entertainment market in central London. He distanced himself from the backstreet striptease clubs and peep shows, which offered a more furtive experience, and in many ways didn't even consider himself in the same industry. Stringfellow was aiming to *legitimise* his strippers by calling them 'angels' and keeping their thongs on.

Spearmint Rhino is probably the most well known lap-dancing club in the world, thanks to the development of their global brand. John Gray founded the company in the US in 1989 before deciding to launch internationally. There are now sixteen clubs throughout the UK, US and Australia. The history of the club chain is loaded with controversy, from John Gray's history of fraud (for which he earned a prison sentence) to the split with his UK business partner Simon Warr (who went on to form the rival chain Platinum Lace in 2012). A cursory Google search reveals endless press coverage of contentious allegations, painting a picture of a ruthless businessman.

There are multiple angles from which the inner workings of a corporate lap-dancing chain can be viewed; the tabloid press feasted on accusations of scandal and vice in clubs, while women's rights campaigns have condemned and attacked the commercialisation of women's bodies. Business analysts have admired the astonishing economic growth of lap dancing,

based on applying the same branding and marketing principles of, say, a burger chain to the sex industry. Regardless of
the morals or ethics involved in women selling sexual entertainment to male clients, it is irrefutably true that a lot of
people made life-changing amounts of money from the company, and a great many of them were the women dancing in
the venues. It is also true that when Spearmint Rhino arrived
in London it changed the entire culture of stripping in the
UK, with ripple effects still being felt to this day. It looks to all
intents and purposes as though John Gray had a limited but
clear set of ambitions for his international launch – to open as
many clubs as possible and make as much money as he could,
no matter what it took.

Spearmint Rhino opened their flagship UK venue on Tottenham Court Road in November 2000. Although it was
within walking distance of Stringfellows, it was located on
the boundary of a different London borough. This meant the
new club was regulated by Camden City Council, while
Stringfellows continued to be regulated by City of Westminster Council. Thanks to the degree of autonomy given to
councils by the Local Government (Miscellaneous) Provisions
Act 1982, Gray was able to procure a waiver from Camden to
provide full nudity in his new club, despite being less than a
mile down the road from his competitor. Thus commenced a
period of antagonism during which the two giants of erotic
entertainment battled it out to become the market leader. One

story in particular leaps out as an example of the intense competition between the two businesses.

In preparation for opening up shop, Gray had sent a couple of dancers to work in Stringfellows as spies, gathering information on their business model and pricing scale. It proved to be a clever strategy: Spearmint Rhino entered the market with a business plan that directly rivalled Stringfellows, and it worked. Not only did he have customers queuing up to get in, he also had Stringfellows' 'angels' queuing up to work there and bringing their loyal client base with them. During the first few years of business rumours were flying that Spearmint Rhino was a venue where 'anything goes'. Because regulations were so vague, and lap dancing hadn't even been described in law yet, the club was essentially a frontier land where the spirit of the Wild West proliferated, earning the brand a reputation and kudos that attracted clients from far and wide. Stringfellow, furious that his rival was dragging down standards, reacted by sending one of his longest working, most loyal and trusted dancers over to work undercover at his rival's venue, as part of a clandestine plan to catch them out.[8] Legend has it that she was making so much money at Spearmint Rhino that she never went back. Stringfellow's next move was to send in a couple of private investigators to gather evidence of what was really happening; this plan soon proved to have more of an impact. Stringfellow shared his findings with the London Metropolitan Police, whose own investigations soon revealed that some dancers in Spearmint Rhino were performing blow jobs and hand jobs in the private booths.

When this information hit the local and national news it quickly became a focus point for radical feminist abolitionist campaigners. However, it wasn't enough to pull the plug on the business. Camden Council responded by revoking the club's licence and then reinstating it once they were satisfied that the club had 'cleaned up their act'. Eventually, Stringfellows had to concede to market forces by offering fully nude dances, convincing the City of Westminster licensing authority to provide him with a nudity waiver also. The cloak and dagger routine had all the markings of a 'Carry On Stripping' farce, and no doubt may be turned into another feature film once enough time has elapsed to allow for the art world to tastefully reappropriate the material. But as with many other similar narratives, it's easy to forget that lost within the titillating comedy are the lives and livelihoods of thousands of women. The realities of their work and their ability to transform their lives by becoming financially independent are almost always overlooked in favour of focusing on the unruly antics of male king pins.

It was almost a decade after Spearmint Rhino opened before legislation was reviewed and updated to curtail the activities of British lap-dance clubs, but not before the industry got a huge boost in the mid-2000s. This came in the form of the Licensing Act 2003, a piece of legislation drafted under the Labour government of Tony Blair and Gordon Brown that was intended to boost the night-time economy. Like Raymond before, who had been well placed to benefit from the Theatres Act 1968, Gray, Stringfellow and many other bosses of newly opening strip clubs were in the right place at the right time. The Licensing Act 2003 relaxed and stream-lined rules around night-time entertainment, making it a lot easier for businesses to apply for a Public Entertainment Licence. A PEL is needed for providing any sort of live music or entertainment, and under the new Act a PEL could be essentially bought from a local council without much difficulty. This became another loophole; strip clubs were opening up all over the country with a PEL, the same licence required for opening a karaoke bar or a live music venue. Between 2003 and 2009 there was a booming trade in striptease across the whole of the UK. At one point there was a new lap-dancing club opening every week throughout the country. And every venue that opened was replicating the extremely lucrative business model of *charging dancers to work*; a business model that was more or less risk-free for business owners, which became incredibly well established throughout this period.

Councils were granting PELs to strip clubs, along with nudity waivers, no doubt for a number of reasons. At the very least, the Local Government (Miscellaneous) Provisions Act 1982 gave every council the democratic right to make their own minds up. Waivers came at a price, meaning councils could generate extra income on top of licence fees by charging strip clubs a 'nudity fee'. Another explanation, besides licences and waivers, is that a profitable and functioning business creates jobs and wealth benefits the whole community. The creation of jobs and incomes takes pressure off state welfare systems. When it was a matter of fostering economic growth in their own area, there didn't seem a good reason for councils not to allow strip clubs to open. It is also possible that some councils simply weren't aware of the activities and impacts of striptease businesses and simply rubber-stamped their licence applications without giving it too much consideration.

The late 1990s and early 2000s are remembered for their staggering economic growth, as the deregulation of banking created rapid upward mobility. Before the global economic crisis of 2008, investment bankers in London would regularly spend vast sums of money in strip clubs, often claimed as a business expense under the category of corporate entertainment. Strip clubs near the City of London banking district were patronised by *Wolf of Wall Street* types, drinking and partying to excess. Alongside the Gordon Gecko style spending culture, was a newly emerging lad culture. The 'Ladettes' of the 1990s were part of a zeitgeist in which women and girls found that using their sex appeal was a totally legitimate way to get ahead. Lads' mags created lucrative careers for glamour models – Jordan a.k.a. Katie Price became a household name – and stripping was starting to become seen as gainful employment. British girls growing up in the 1990s were exposed to a pre-internet mainstream pop culture diet of Britney Spears and the Spice Girls, which was more sexually suggestive than it ever had been. However, the increasingly sexualised milieu back then became too much for some women to bear.

Object is a women's rights organisation, founded in 2004 by Dr Sasha Rakoff. Among their list of complaints, which includes their opposition to reproductive surrogacy and transgender ideology, one of their top priorities is ending commercial sexual exploitation. Their website states in their own words:

> 'Lap dancing' or 'gentlemen's' clubs are known as Sex Encounter Venues [*sic*] under the Policing and Crime Act 2009, but may more accurately be referred to as Sexual Exploitation Venues. They are establishments where men gain sexual satisfaction and/or feelings of superiority by viewing exploited women displayed like slaves for sale – prostitution may also take place. SEVs profit from the sexual objectification of women. We OBJECT. [9]

Object soon joined forces with other feminist organisations such as the Fawcett Society, the Women's Support Project, the Lilith Project as well as a number of high-profile journalists and politicians to begin lobbying for an end to the growing industry of lap-dancing clubs. They cited research purporting the harmful wider social impact of lap dancing on women, such as the Lilith Report, which has long since been debunked (see Chapter 7, The Victimhood Industry). Despite their inaccuracies, reports claiming that lap-dancing clubs were linked to higher rates of sexual violence landed in the media, causing a national outrage campaign that still continues to this day. Countless books and articles were published on the topic, which boosted the careers of many feminist writers and journalists. Their entire take on strip clubs was simple: commercial sexual objectification is harmful to women everywhere. Strip clubs were now easily identifiable, having opened on the high streets of most cities and towns across the country, and became a straightforward target.

From 2003, when lap dancing really started to pick up trade thanks to the Licensing Act, until 2009 when the Policing and Crime Act set out to curb it, radical feminist campaigners rallied around the call to ban stripping in the UK. By November 2008 enough momentum had built up for a debate to be held in Parliament by the Culture, Media and Sport Committee to discuss lap dancing.[10] Representing the pro camp were members of a newly formed organisation called the Lap Dance Association (LDA), very few of whom were actual lap dancers but industry operators and club owners. Having come under serious attack, it looked as though longstanding rivals Stringfellows and Spearmint Rhino were now collaborating to save their companies (though despite their purported alliance, at the beginning of the plenary session to examine witnesses, Peter Stringfellow insisted on making it known that he was not a member of the LDA, and was attending in his own capacity to represent his own businesses and no one else's). Also in attendance was Chris Knight, an executive from club chain For Your Eyes Only, and Kate Nicholls, the LDA secretary. Witnesses who were calling for lap dancing to be banned completely were Sandrine Levêque from Object, and Nadine Stavonina de Montagnac, a writer and ex-dancer, who offered her own personal experiences of poor treatment and exploitative business practices. As the only person who had actually done the job, De Montagnac's was the only voice of an actual (former) lap dancer heard in Parliament that day.

The LDA made two grave errors in their approach. One was their failure to include any dancers' voices on their panel, no doubt lending credence to the idea that dancers were being controlled by clubs. Nicholls, the only female voice on the pro-stripclub panel, and unfortunately occupying the traditionally female role of 'secretary', seemed to compound the problem by saying:

We did not bring any dancers here today to give evidence to you, but we do have some of our dancers in the audience. They are extremely concerned about some of the issues that have been raised in the media and the way they have been portrayed. If you want us to arrange a meeting with them we would be happy for you to talk to some of our existing dancers.

The quote has the uncomfortable effect of making lap dancers sound like chattels, at the beck and call of their overseers. The other mistake was to take the tack that lap dancing was not sexual, claiming their clubs were just a bit of fun. Stringfellow tried to liken his dancers to women in skimpy outfits at the local disco, or to David Beckham posing in Calvin Klein underwear. The evidence submitted to Parliament that day by Stringfellow and the LDA was unsophisticated compared to the steadfast and articulate feminists, especially given the gravitas of the environment. Ultimately, they were poor advocates for their industry. The basic tone of their testimony was summed up in a memorandum they submitted to the Committee:

Our criticisers [sic] have obviously never visited a lap-dancing club. The reality is that, if they had, they would realise that although the girls take their tops off, it is definitely them who wear the trousers.[11]

One thing the LDA did achieve was to remind the Committee that local authorities *already had the power* to manage the licensing of strip clubs under the Local Government (Miscellaneous) Provisions Act 1982. The LDA were not opposed to the idea of empowering local communities to decide whether they wanted a lap-dancing club, no doubt based on the rapid industry growth they had seen. It seems that Parliament agreed; rather than banning lap dancing altogether, an attempt at a compromise was reached with the passing of the Policing and Crime Act 2009, which simply *updated* the 1982 Act. Local authorities were finally given a clear licensing regime for sexual entertainment that outlined several key distinctions.

The first thing the law did was create a legal definition of sexual entertainment, and effectively made it illegal without a Sexual Entertainment Venue licence. This had an overnight effect on the industry as many clubs operating with only a Public Entertainment Licence were suddenly required to obtain a new type of licence on top of their running costs. For business owners who had only envisaged the fast money that could be made in the short-term, this added a level of administration and uncertainty wasn't worth the bother, so they simply shut up shop. The law also gave local authorities more guidance on what conditions could be attached to the SEV licence. There was a sense in which the welfare of dancers ought to be upheld, and so licensing conditions could include things like provision of showers and clean drinking water for dancers (but said nothing of the business model that failed to recognise their employment rights as workers). Licensing conditions could also restrict the visibility of clubs by preventing them from advertising and promoting themselves publicly. Chapters 3, Gatekeepers of Desire, and 5, What's Wrong With Regulation?, will take a closer look at licensing conditions and make sense of the implications they have for dancers, bosses, customers and wider society.

Possibly the biggest effect of the Policing and Crime Act 2009 was to simply inform councils (and the public) that they were, after all, in charge of the sex industry within their own jurisdictions. This meant in practice that councillors were suddenly required to respond to the growing contempt of residents, whose concern about the spread of lap-dancing clubs had been thoroughly piqued by the incessant press coverage over the past five years. Mainstream radical feminism saw to it that if anyone had been unaware of a lap-dancing club in their area, they were disgusted about it once they were. Middle-class homeowners were more likely to have a problem with any threat to property value and future investment in their area. Lap-dancing clubs became symbols over which class warfare was fought.

Once the law was passed in November 2009, Hackney City Council was the first local authority to attempt an outright ban on SEVs throughout the entire borough. However, once the successful fight back campaign found that a handful of the clubs in the area had the right to continue trading under grandfather laws, Hackney became a test ground from which a new policy arose: the nil policy. New laws often result in case law – this means testing new legislation through the court system to see how well it stands up in practice. Since the Policing and Crime Act 2009 essentially reasserted the powers that local authorities always had, which included the power to expel strip clubs from an area, Hackney then put this power to the test in 2010 by attempting to revoke all SEV licences in the borough.

Licensing law is not like criminal law: decisions are not made by judges and juries; instead they are made by panels and committees of councillors. Licensing authorities have a democratic duty to their population to involve citizens in the decision-making process via public consultations. A decision to revoke licences and close down an entire business sector cannot happen without first putting it to the public. When Hackney launched a public consultation to obtain views on the matter of SEVs, they had expected a groundswell to respond in support of club closures. The results showed, however, that local residents were overwhelmingly in support of the clubs. So the court of law – i.e. the licensing authority – was required to concede to the public.

Hackney's experiment became case law for all other councils; if they tried to simply revoke SEV licences, clubs elsewhere could point to the test case in Hackney as proof of their right to trade. But a compromise was sought, and arrived in the form of the nil policy. Since it would be undemocratic to shut down existing businesses, it could be made almost impossible for new ones to open up. SEV policy was therefore designed and rapidly reproduced by other councils, which created a complex and hostile environment for SEVs. Local authorities had the right to set a limit to the number of SEV licences in the area, which could be a limit of nil (not including any pre-existing licences). Any future applications for SEVs could be automatically vetoed, and existing SEV licences would be required to pass through more stringent renewal processes each year. In most cases, particularly outside London, councils simply reverted to a policy of allowing existing clubs to stay open (so long as they held the correct licence) and disallowed any new clubs from opening. If SEVs weren't going to be closed, they were about to feel the squeeze of an ever-tightening licensing regime of enforcement and scrutiny.

Much to the dismay of feminist campaigners, the Policing and Crime Act 2009 did not completely outlaw strip clubs. The only way to ban something effectively is to criminalise it, and that may have seemed a step too far for lawmakers at the time. While the 2009 Act has dramatically reduced the number of strip venues in the UK, and placed heavy responsibilities on SEV licence holders, a stronghold of remaining clubs continues to trade. The picture of striptease regulations in the UK since 2009 resembles a game of cat and mouse. Abolitionist campaigners are no closer to giving up on their mission to rid the world of strip clubs than club owners and licence holders are to letting go of their business model. The clubs that continue to survive are the brand name chain clubs – the big players who can afford to keep throwing money at their problems by hiring lawyers specialising in licensing law. A monopoly has grown up out of the bubble, as smaller independent businesses can no longer compete with the heavyweight corporate venues, and the industry becomes more homogenised by the year.

From a sex worker's point of view, the Policing and Crime Act 2009 has done nothing to improve dancers' working conditions – clean drinking water and showers are a poor sub-stitute for long-term welfare packages, living wages and employment rights. Legislation at present may well keep the industry in check regarding its wider social impact outside the clubs, but it has failed to protect female workers inside the clubs. For the best part of a century the history of striptease regulation has been a story of business owners competing for revenue, a public split between those who endorse the venues and those who disapprove, and legislators struggling to keep up. Feminist campaigns, laws and business models are not built around the needs and demands of the workforce, and as long as the employment rights of workers in the sex industry go unacknowledged, exploitation will continue. Throughout the timeline, voices of dancers have been absent from the narrative. The history of striptease is a chronology of women silently watching from the sidelines while bosses, legislators and radical feminists make decisions about their welfare without their input. This is what has to change. If the industry is to overcome its misogynistic heritage, there cannot be another repeat of the day in Parliament when Peter Stringfellow stood up to defend his right to earn a living from the sex industry, despite having never been a sex worker himself. As much as strippers' voices needed to be heard that day, they need to speak out now more than ever.

———

Sometime in 2007 I worked the opening weekend of a new club in the north-east of England. I heard about it from a couple of dancers I'd become friendly with who were sisters. I used to stay at their flat when I went down for work weekends in Newcastle. Like many other dancers, they would eke out a tiny bit more income from offering their home as accommodation to travelling strippers, which became one of the ways we built community and solidarity among ourselves. The older of the two sisters had got the gig of house mum for a new club that was set to open in the neighbouring town, so she set about rounding up new dancers for them. Her mum lived locally so she offered me a place to crash since we'd become quite good mates by then.

The opening weekend of a club is always hyped up as this huge money-maker, like cash will just be falling from the sky. I used to watch a TV show when I was a kid called The Crystal Maze; *teams used to run around doing challenges to try and earn gold and silver tokens. At the end they would all get into this giant crystal dome and stand on these huge fans blowing air up from under their feet. The gold and silver tokens were released into the dome, getting blown around by the fans, and the contestants had to try and grab as many as possible. Stripping sometimes reminded me of that – I could imagine a bunch of women in lingerie, jumping around in the* Crystal Maze *dome, with Richard O'Brien doing the commentary. Like always, the opportunity of earning impossible amounts of money was tantalising bait. 'Chasing the money' is what keeps us travelling to new cities, looking for new clubs. It was always a popular topic in the changing room, and rumours of making crazy money were a continuous motivation to keep going and tolerate ever-increasing levels of bullshit.*

There was only one word to describe the new club: rough. It felt like Ibiza in the 1990s, a regular nightclub that had been quickly adapted as a lap-dancing venue. The lighting and sound were terrible; there was no stage and instead, a pole had been put up on the dance floor, which had a hard, tiled surface, increasing the risk of injury. Backstage it was utter chaos. No one had a clue what they were doing. The house mum had no experience or skill at managing people, and it turned out she hadn't been the only one who'd been offered the same gig. There were three or four house mums sort of vying for control backstage, and the stress levels in the changing room were unbearable. Predictably there were far more girls than the club needed, all paying house fees. There were no contracts to speak of, no training or dialogue between dancers and business owners, no clear instructions being given. I twigged on to some drama backstage about one dancer, who was five months pregnant and showing, being told she couldn't work. She was furious because she'd been told on the phone that she could, and obviously had made the journey to the venue with all her gear. Her friend who'd come with her, who was also a dancer and had come to work that night, was caught in the middle – not wanting to miss the opportunity of making money but not wishing to seem unsupportive either.

The client base was mainly local men, working-class blokes who liked to drink, dance, chat up women and have the occasional punch up. I grew up in a working-class northern town, so they were a familiar crowd to me. Some were genuinely grateful that a strip club had opened, and I don't remember anyone really abusing their position of power. In fact it looked like none of them had any power to abuse, for the simple reason that none of them really had much money. We had all been mislead by the promise of mountains of cash, because in reality the majority of customers who went in there didn't have the kind of disposable income that makes our job worthwhile.

That weekend was a bit of a low point. I'd been dancing less than a year and was still navigating my way through the industry. There were pitfalls everywhere. This was one of the clubs that popped up purely to exploit a market that had suddenly emerged, and it was a good earner for them. The business had clearly been cobbled together to take advantage of the genius model of charging men who wanted to look at naked women, and then charging the women even more to dance for the men who wanted to look at them. Anyone with the initiative and capital could turn up at the local council and buy a PEL, rent a venue, stock a bar full of booze, put some staff on the door, pay their mate to DJ, put the word out among the local strippers that there was a swimming pool of money to dive into, *and watch the money roll in. It was another kind of gold rush, and of course many women did well out of it. I made several hundred quid that weekend, more than I could make working a minimum wage job. But we never got to see that swimming pool of money that we had created.*

Reflecting on that weekend I could well understand why feminist campaigners would want to shut strip clubs down. The template of charging dancers house fees started by the big clubs in London was clearly a money-spinner, so suddenly people were replicating it all over the country. It preyed on precarious women in provincial towns without many other employment options, requiring them to hand over their own cash first in order to get their high-heeled foot in the door. I could see the debasement at the core of it all, and it didn't surprise me in the slightest to see feminist campaigners up in arms. But I couldn't shake the feeling that we needed to demand our workers' rights, before they demanded to put a stop to it. On the one hand, it looks like women being exploited by male customers, but on the other, it looks like workers being exploited by late capitalism. And I know which version I felt more exploited by.

3

GATEKEEPERS OF DESIRE

> It used to be the case that if you wanted a political
> critique of desire, feminism was where you would turn.[1]
>
> —Amia Srinivasen

The current business model of the strip club industry is built
on wage theft. The system of charging dancers to work was
effectively born twenty years ago, when lap dancing arrived in
the UK at the turn of the twenty-first century and strip clubs
became high street brands. Before Spearmint Rhino landed in
London, lap dancing had already unofficially arrived in East
End strip joints and backstreet venues, but the corporate
branding that lent Spearmint Rhino an air of professionalism
helped legitimise the business model. Before lap-dancing clubs
changed the shape of the industry for good, strippers used to
get paid an actual wage to perform in venues. But the tables
have turned so dramatically that there is now not a single SEV

left in the UK that pays dancers even a nominal fee to turn up for a shift.

The model has proven so successful that it has saturated the entire commercial field, and clubs now have a structure that relies entirely on the ability to charge workers fees, percentages, commissions, and even fines. This is despite the fact that many clubs elsewhere in Europe pay dancers a fee to show up, on average around €30–50 at the beginning of their night and then take a commission from dancers' earnings thereafter. A significant portion of a strip club's revenue comes from dancers themselves, meaning that charging dancers to work enables venues to survive economically regardless of whether they can attract customers or not. Dancers are placed in a strange hinterland, not quite customer, not quite worker, not quite business partner, but always denied their employment rights. Over the last twenty years working conditions in the UK have steadily deteriorated, from a boom period when profits soared to a present day marketplace that resembles the Hunger Games for strippers.

Working in a strip club means having to negotiate an astonishing number of hurdles, but many of them are hidden and systemic. What is seen at surface level – customers' wandering hands, a boss who abuses their power, financial exploitation – are not singular problems, at least not in the way they are normally characterised in the mainstream. They are all symptomatic of a broken legal framework, which has failed to protect strippers as workers and grant them employment rights. The most serious obstacle of all is their inability to access the same legal due process that workers in other industries can use to tackle workplace abuses and leverage reform.

Workers' rights for people selling sex and sexual services continues to be a confusing and cyclical sticking point. Mainstream narratives remain frozen around the horrors that preside in the public imagination, much to the frustration of the sex workers' rights movement, who are asking for those narratives to progress beyond the divisive nature of the argument over whether anyone has the right to buy or sell sex. The real question to ask, according to sex workers, is 'should people selling sex have workers' rights?' For sex workers on the ground right now the answer is undoubtedly yes; it's for good reason that the phrase 'Sex Work Is Work' has become a mantra for sex workers to organise around. It seems like a no-brainer to them that as a group they could use their employment rights and protections as a tool to crowbar safer business practices into their industry and defend themselves from exploitation and harassment, if only these powers were enshrined in law.

Sex workers aren't the only ones demanding change. In recent years, workers at Uber, Deliveroo, Pimlico Plumbers, as well as other independent contractors in the gig economy, have been embroiled in long legal disputes to establish the correct classification of worker status for people doing precarious work.

Strippers are set to become the next group of workers to join a collective battle to establish their correct employment status and begin taking back control. Anyone who is denied their labour rights at work can be thought of as a victim of gate-keeping, sex worker or not. The authority to grant such powers to workers lies with several key players.

In the case of strip clubs, it is not merely club bosses and staff; policy makers, licensing inspectors and local police can all otherwise be thought of as gatekeepers too. Managers and bosses run clubs; local authorities regulate them; UK law shapes local policy; laws are written under the influence of popular public opinion (the tone of which, regarding sex work, is currently dominated by mainstream feminist journalism). In this chain of command, the two groups at the bottom of the pile are dancers and customers. Customers are not included in this list of gatekeepers, which may appear counterintuitive to the argument put forth here. At first glance it may seem that strip clubs have only ever evolved as a response to male desire. On the other hand, it could be argued that they have evolved to exploit male desire as well as female labour. In this respect, customers and dancers are not too dissimilar, in as much as what unites them is their joint lack of power and resources to challenge the exploitative business model. The only power customers may have to challenge exploitation is to avoid the industry and refuse to patronise it – a common enough response although it doesn't do much to improve the lot of workers left behind. Within this structure, both groups are left to navigate one another's respective needs – the dancer's need for money and the customer's need for gratification, in whatever form it presents – by entering into a transactional relationship, which may or may not be a productive arrangement for both parties.

It is not the message of this book to claim that customers are benign innocents, or victims of the sex industry themselves. On the occasion that this transactional relationship fails and customers mistreat workers, particularly when they have the economic advantage to do so, the regulatory and economic environment is set up to protect the interests of an abusive customer above the interests of dancers. One can point to any instance of customers harassing, coercing or injuring sex workers and instantly conclude that abolition is the only solution. However, the reality is not so simple. Perpetrators of violence and abuse operate in particular arenas. They understand the relationships of power they have with their victims, and know they are generally safe to abuse the most vulnerable women within society. It's logical that women who are criminalised and stigmatised, who do not have access to state protection and work in a largely deregulated market that does not afford them basic employment rights, make the easiest targets. It's therefore imperative to open a clear pathway to rights for workers; further criminalisation has no benefit to an already precarious and at-risk group, and serves merely to drive the industry deeper into the shadows of the criminal marketplace, where violence and coercion are more likely.

Imagining the strip club as a marketplace may sound like a novelty to some, but for those who operate and work in strip venues there is nothing novel about it. There are various market forces that have a direct impact on how clubs are managed, how customers consume and how workers perform their labour. Changes in legislation, public attitudes and economic trends have all taken a toll on the industry. One way of better understanding the current problems in the existing industry is by making historical comparisons to previous business practices. The sex industry has always been adapting to social changes, reinventing and reforming how sexual labour is performed for maximum profit. But the question of who is genuinely profiting versus who is performing the labour is pertinent to the future of the industry.

THE GOLDEN DAYS OF STRIPPING

Jo King is a stripper icon whose career began in 1978. She later went on to found the London Academy of Burlesque, and in 2008 she was invited to perform at the Burlesque Hall of Fame's 52nd Annual Reunion Showcase Legends night in Las Vegas. She was the first British performer to be given the accolade. According to *Time Out* magazine, 'We've long pointed out that nearly all burlesque roads in London lead back to uber-doyenne Jo King.'[2] It is commonly suggested that King is responsible for establishing the neo-Burlesque scene in the UK. During a research interview for this book she spoke about her early experiences of stripping.

> Back when I started I was a Burlesque Striptease Entertainer – that's what we were called then. Throughout my career I created over a hundred of my own acts, dancing and removing my clothes, entertaining both men and women. In the 1970s and early 1980s I performed about six to eight spots a night travelling from one club to another in London's West End. I had to pass an audition and the venues paid between £6 and £10 per spot, cash in hand, paid on the night – I was responsible for my own tax and insurance.[3]

King describes working conditions as varied but for the most part performers were treated well. Dressing rooms were provided backstage and refreshments were available. When asked what could go wrong at work, she answered, 'drunk customers, but security was always pretty tight. I have always been able to use my sense of humour to calm a situation, but if that didn't work, club security would have a word, and, if necessary, escort them from the premises.' Same as any other pub or venue then. King was self-employed in the true sense, free to come and go, free to wear what she liked and perform with her own unique style and flair, if that was what venues wanted. She would be booked by venues directly, or by agents who would organise gigs for her. Some agencies would take a booking fee from venues, some would take a cut from her earnings; some, seeing an opportunity to increase their margins, would of course take a cut from both parties. According to King, 'venues, payment structure and attitudes changed constantly'. However, one thing never changed: King was always working for a fee, agreed in advance of her gigs.

Another stripper legend, this time hailing from Scotland, is the indomitable Gypsy Charms, who has been part of the industry for over two decades. She worked at the Western Bar in Edinburgh's infamous 'pubic triangle' strip club district, before co-founding the showgirl troupe French Fling, as well as performing and producing acts on the Scottish cabaret scene and creating shows during the Edinburgh Fringe Festival, including 'The Illicit Thrill' and 'Ask A Stripper'. She began stripping in 1998 when she was working as a fitness instructor at a local gym and her male boss, another stripper, introduced her to the industry.

> I started off in the bookings. It was the private shows, the parties in the backrooms of pubs, working men's clubs, social clubs, sports clubs, nightclubs – anywhere with a bar really. Dancers with more experience used to take me on bookings with them, and show me the ropes. It was all about solidarity and mentorship in those days. There was a grouping of us

that used to work together and it was all word of mouth. And it was money upfront, or there's no show.[4]

Charms would be booked to perform for stag dos, birthday parties, retirements, gentlemen's evenings, even fundraisers. A common event was the formulaic smokers' evening. 'There would be a stripper, a comedian, a band, and maybe another kind of act like a magician or something. Sometimes there would be a whip round, which is where the tradition of strippers jugging in pubs came from.' Jugging is a dying practice among strip venues, most common in East London strip pubs. Dancers walk among their audience with a glass, normally a pint jug or some other container, to collect tips from viewers before performing on stage, usually £1 per show. While on the one hand the practice may appear demeaning for dancers, it becomes a lot less demeaning when it in fact ensures payment for the skill and labour of performing on stage, whereas in many clubs, dancers are expected to strip on stage without pay, as part of their regular shift.

Charms would be free to create her own routines and the more effort she put in the more likely she was to get booked again. Word got around that she was a brilliant performer, and she became a popular act. Bookings were normally informal, last minute phone calls – one dancer might have a work phone to take jobs, whose number would get passed around between potential clients. In turn, she would have a number of trusted stripper friends she would call on to accompany her on the job.

Importantly, there was a sense of safety among performers:

> It was drummed into me really early on from other dancers to never work on my own. We'd either work together in pairs or groups, or if you were performing alone you took a 'driver', usually a bloke, who looked big or mean enough to act as some kind of security. It could be a mate, or a boyfriend, or someone I would share a small cut of my fee with; my husband used to come on jobs with me. I would never, ever perform on my own, I wouldn't feel safe walking into a job without someone else.

Charms explained how strippers would self-organise and locate their own methods of safety. They could work together, and if a job didn't feel safe they could turn round and walk out, moving on to the next gig.

Another member of stripper royalty is Keri Gold. An Essex-born, bubbly, buxom blonde, with a reputation as a showgirl and exhibitionist, Gold is the epitome of 1990s glamour. Gold began stripping in the mid-1990s and went on to form a dance troupe, Diamante Dolls, choreographing and touring shows for cruise ships, as well as finding fifteen minutes of fame on ITV's *Britain's Got Talent* performing a chair-dance routine and flirting with Simon Cowell. Gold has been stripping for almost her entire adult life, and has seen dramatic changes over the twenty-five years she has been performing, having worked in every type of strip establishment imaginable, from pubs to lap-dancing clubs, agencies and private parties. She mentions one particular venture, Olympia Moments, which was a self-organised enterprise run by dancers themselves.

> There were three dancers called Ulrika, Max and Lady Jane who got together and started a night themselves. It was once a month, and I was at the first party and nearly all of them after that. Those nights were amazing to work. The organisers would meet up in advance and plan it all, and they created some real magic.[5]

Olympia Moments was started by a group of women who'd found themselves growing tired of ever-changing conditions, no job security, mass sackings of dancers by venues who wanted to change their roster of performers, and poorly organised gigs by agencies who didn't care about the experience of performers or clients as long as they were getting their booking fees. So a small number of them took matters into their own hands. They had a list of email addresses of all their favourite clients carefully cherry picked over several years; they would find a pub or venue with a function room to hire and just do it themselves.

Honestly, those parties were the best nights I worked, they really were fun. The clients were always the pick of the crop, they were the most polite, respectful, friendly customers. The parties would always have a theme, there would be a choreographed group show in the middle of the night, like a pantomime. A lot of effort was put in, we'd decorate the space with props or balloons, and there were snacks for punters. We'd make our money doing lap dances in private. It was £20 for a dance, and we all had the same boundaries when it came to touching. They could touch our boobs, but nothing else. And it was better that way, everyone was happy to stick to the same rule, no one was offering anything extra so we were all equal, it was teamwork.

Gold explains how the dancers remained in control of the event, and it was a lucrative enterprise.

I always had a target amount that I wanted to earn and I always made it easily. The ratio of dancers to customers was amazing, there were always more blokes than there was of us, so they would be queuing up to get dances. Sometimes the dance area was just behind a sheet that we'd put up for privacy. We all did a floorshow that we didn't get paid for but we were happy to do it. We all paid £20 towards the costs of running the night, but it was all really transparent where the money was going. It was to pay for the hire of the venue and whatever props or food we needed. There was a real sense of camaraderie, everyone looked out for each other.

In 2014 a small limited edition book was self-published by artist and Senior Lecturer of Photography at the University of East London, Julie Cook, and her husband Paul Davies, Senior Lecturer of Architecture at London South Bank University. Simply titled *Olympia Moments*, after the name of the 'company', the book documented the OM adventures several years after the events finally came to an end. Among the regular patrons of OM, Cook and Davies were so well known on the strip scene that Cook and her camera gained the kind of unprecedented access to the world of striptease that many photographers can only dream of. Cook had earned the trust of East London's stripper network, having previously published a beautiful book of photography, *Baby Oil and Ice,* 2002, also a chronicle of East London strip pubs. Cook and Davies cut an unusual shape as frequent customers of the strip bars, but they were long-term followers and fans of the dancers, and formed lasting friendships with many. Their body of work is a cherished homage to the creativity and labour performed by many of these women. Davies writes in *Olympia Moments*:

The dancers might have taken their clothes off for our entertainment, but the gentlemen kept their trousers strictly buttoned up. Control was absolutely in the hands of the girls, and as far as they were concerned there were strict limits, admittedly set more around the basis of value for money than artificial morality. There were no silly three-feet rules at an Olympia Moments party; that, after all, was the added value the dancers were providing and I don't think I've ever met a dancer who was not anything but entrepreneurial.[6]

Between Davies' description and Gold's testimonial, they describe a business plan where dancers remained in command of their own work. They chose their customers on an invite only basis, set their own prices and boundaries, literally built their own working environment (in the sense of constructing the workspace and private dance areas according to their own requirements) and maintained a supply and demand ratio that worked in their favour. This, incidentally, is what full decriminalisation looks like: sex workers pitching in together for safety and creating the working environment that best suits their economic needs. When strippers were able to book their own venues, organise their own parties, invite their own guest list (effectively screening their own clients) and manage their own workspaces, they were not at the mercy of club owners as gatekeepers.

The example of OM is probably one of the best ways of understanding the difference between legalisation and decriminalisation, and how the two legal regimes actually play out in reality. The Policing and Crime Act 2009 was an attempt at regulating the stripping industry, but it had the effect of shifting power in the workspace away from workers and straight into the hands of licence holders. The effort to clean up the industry made unofficial parties such as the OM monthly nights illegal. Under SEV law, anyone wishing to provide sexual entertainment now requires an SEV licence. After the law change, venues such as the pubs used by OM, or the social clubs from Charms' days of working the bookings, were no longer confident to book strippers or allow private parties, for fear of breaking the law. Dancers now have less choice and less power as a labour force; they can no longer build their own workspaces and must make do with dancing in the remaining venues regardless of how they are run, how much the house fees are or how crooked their bosses may be.

Local authorities are the gatekeepers of licensing; they regulate how many licences are granted and who gets to have them. Since most councils in the UK have adopted a nil policy on SEVs, vetoing any future SEV licence applications, this makes it virtually impossible for strippers to get together and open their own venue – it is now unfeasible to hope for any new licences to be granted. This means that the remaining 150 or so SEV licences left in the country are now like gold dust. This in any other industry would be called a monopoly; in this case one that has actually been sanctioned by the state. Legalising strip clubs has disempowered workers, making them more precarious by lack of choice. Licensing has produced a system of gatekeeping that denies workers their right to self-determination. The licensing regime of strip clubs in the UK is a perfect example of the failure of legalisation.

———

I don't know how I became so interested in employment law. Maybe it's because I've been doing some form of paid work since I was thirteen. Maybe it's because by the time I was twenty-two I was already exhausted from the number of terrible minimum wage jobs I'd had and the hours I'd spent pulling pints, pouring coffees or bleeping groceries through supermarket checkouts when I needed to be studying. Working on minimum wage I'd already experienced some pretty humiliating conditions – long hours, crap uniforms, unavoidable chores, all in return for an hourly rate of pay. But I was the kind of person who would actually read an employment contract before signing it, so by the time I became a stripper I had a sharpened awareness of my rights as an employee. When I started stripping I couldn't get my head round what I was seeing, and couldn't understand how the business model had ever been allowed.

Becoming a stripper was my first venture into self-employment. I did my first audition in a Glasgow club when I was nineteen, before I had any idea how strippers earned money – I assumed they got paid by the hour or by the night, like in every other job I'd done up to that point. I kept asking how much I would get paid, but they were cagey about it, avoiding the answer. It was a red flag to me, so I sacked it off and forgot about the idea for a while. It was another three years before I came back to it. A mate's girlfriend explained to me how it all worked and allayed my misgivings. She described the set up, the house fees and rules, and reassured me that I would earn decent money. That turned out to be accurate; I made consistently good money in my first club, and the house fees there were very reasonable. We'd pay a door fee of £12 when we arrived, and then at the end of the night the club would look at how many customers had been in, and charge us all a fair commission based on how busy it had been – this was capped at £40. Private dances only cost £10 but that was an easy sell, and because the atmosphere of the club was relaxed customers were happy to spend.

There was only one night when I left with minus £12. I remember sitting in my kitchen telling my housemate – he said, 'That's rough.' I guess it just made me more determined to work harder and improve my sales skills. I'd done sales jobs before; when I was on a gap year I had worked for a while in the kids' department of Harrods, demonstrating and selling magic toys. I would be paid a daily rate, and, if I hit a sales target, I got a bonus commission. I also worked as one of those charity fundraisers who stand on the street and get people to sign up for regular donations. I got paid an hourly rate for that, but I had targets I needed to try and hit, which were reviewed regularly by the company to make sure I was in the right job. Stripping was a sales job, no doubt about that.

Before stripping I'd only ever done jobs where I got paid an hourly or daily rate, so it was a big change to pay money upfront, and then work without any guarantee that I would even make anything. I had to adjust quickly, and if I didn't like it I knew where the door was. So I sucked it up, and got on with it. I made £130 on my first night, which was a revelation. It was three times what I would have made for an eight-hour

*shift on minimum wage, so of course I wasn't thinking about the econom-
ics or the business model straight away. But then it sort of dawned on me
slowly, week by week, as I encountered more and more rules and levels of
control that it felt more like employment, even though I wasn't getting paid
by the hour. There were so many rules, some of which were so dumb, but
the more we were bossed around the more irate I got.*

*The long dress rule before midnight was always laughable. We'd have
to wear these special stripper gowns, which had to be long enough to go
past the knee – but were skimpy enough to reveal most of our flesh
anyway. There was this weird pretence of class and respectability, like the
symbolism of being a 'good girl' if the dress goes past the knee. And then
suddenly at the stroke of midnight we could all come out of the changing
room in lingerie sets and start swinging from the chandeliers. These ideas
were all clearly straight out of the male imagination, and a misogynistic
one at that.*

*I took huge issue with the fact that we had to arrive at a certain time,
and couldn't leave early if we were having a bad night. I was working
another job in a restaurant during the day when I started dancing, so I
had to balance my energy levels – every extra hour of sleep counted. As
far as I was concerned if I was self-employed that meant I was free to
leave if the club was quiet – why would I waste my time sitting in an
empty club when I had to wake up in the morning? It incensed me that I
wasn't allowed to leave the building without permission from management. Nothing felt more infantilising to me than that. Dancers who had
worked there longer had more sway and so there was lots of favouritism
going on. It wasn't a work environment that respected my time and agency*

and I felt that frustration right from the beginning. But no matter how much I resolved to just put my head down and work hard, the indignation never left me. The business wouldn't exist without us, we were the reason customers were walking through the door in the first place. I would sit in my first club and look around, thinking about how the bar staff and door security were getting paid an hourly rate, managers were getting a salary, but we were paying *the club, and yet still being treated like employees.*

When I began working in different clubs, travelling to new cities and countries, I encountered more and more situations that triggered my resentment. As I worked my way up into the 'high-end' branded club chains, the house fees became higher at which point being bossed around and told what to do, how to behave, what to wear, felt more deplorable than working in 'lower-end' backstreet dives. It felt seedier to me to be paying exponentially increasing amounts of money to be micromanaged by managers whose salaries were literally coming out of my wages. At one club we had to sign a 'contract' telling us what to wear, how to behave, and also contained a list of misdemeanours (using our phones on the club floor or chewing gum). The worst of it was that throughout the night we had to comply with some humiliating 'promotions' laid on by the club for customers. When the DJ played the Austin Powers *theme tune, no matter where we were sitting or whom we were talking to, all dancers had to get topless for the duration of the song, no exceptions. Another song instructed us to give a customer a free lap dance. It was like something dreamed up by some* Carry On *film scriptwriters, and it was clear that none of the dancers liked doing it and it was hard to see how customers could enjoy watching us doing something we weren't totally comfortable with. I didn't last long there – and from what I've heard since, neither did their terrible promotions.*

Another club were coercing us into performing more free labour by promoting their brand for them. Management would take us out of our shift and out onto the street to hand out flyers and attract business, something I was deeply uncomfortable doing, as were many of us for obvious reasons. Social stigma makes us vulnerable, and I quickly felt that when we were outside a sports stadium being harassed by a group of football lads. Being forced to parade around in public wasn't my only beef; having worked occasionally as a model I also knew that the club didn't have the right to use my image to promote their business for commercial gain without my consent, which should normally come in the form of a signed model release contract. I never saw such a document, and when I took it up with management it was clear they had no intention of respecting my right to either anonymity or reimbursement. I didn't last long there either.

I've often wondered who these people are that wind up owning and managing strip clubs. It's clear to me now after many years that the only people who can happily step into a role that so blatantly overlooks our freedoms, bodily autonomy and rights in the workplace must have narcissistic traits. I could never get over the fact that there was a club in the West End that had chosen the name Gaslight of St James! Over the years I've formed some working relationships with a few of the more reasonable characters, but the power relationships were by no means equal. For the most part management roles are taken by men, who have never performed a striptease or traded sexual labour in their lives, and don't expect to. This imbalance means those relationships can never be fully reciprocal, not without a shared, lived experience of what it actually means and feels like to strip.

The thing I've never understood, though, is why managers would continue making business decisions without consulting us. It seems clear, in any industry, that if you have happy workers you have a profitable enterprise. Forcing us to do things we didn't want to do, like flyering without pay, was unlikely to reap healthy rewards for the business. Making us dance on the pole if that is not our forte, forcing us to wear certain items of clothing that we don't feel comfortable and attractive wearing, taking off our tops when a certain piece of music plays like well-trained Pavlovian pooches – all of these decisions were counter-productive. Having regular meetings with dancers, asking for our feedback, listening to our points of view, taking a creative approach to management may have yielded magnificent results. We may not be experts on running a business or managing a bar, but our time, labour and specific skillset are exactly what the customers are paying for – we are experts in selling desire. That is our specialism.

I remember a conversation I had with a customer at the bar of one of the dodgiest joints I'd ever worked in. I was having the classic conversation that strippers love to have, the number one topic of conversation when we are bored and the club is empty: what would a stripper-run club look like? I asked him what he thought, and he said simply, 'Variety. You'd want all your dancers to be different and unique, all with their own personality.' It occurred to me there and then that what we were actually selling to customers was a holiday from their regular lives. An experience, a suspension of disbelief, a temporary state in which desire is explored and pleasure is allowed. I looked around and thought about how the club was run on control and subservience — and it struck me that it was some kind of miracle that anyone could find any sort of temporary state of self-actualisation in such a place. But then again, perhaps these were exactly the right conditions in which such a need might present itself.

If only strip club bosses could see what we see. If only they could empathise with us in the way we can empathise with our clients. But then again, narcissists aren't known for their empathy. A workplace where bosses can never relate to the labour being performed by workers, or simply choose not to, is not going to create a valuable and sincere environment. Without the right support to do so, we are permanently swimming upstream to create value and meaning in our own work at any given window of opportunity, if indeed that is what any of us want to do. For the majority of dancers I've met, though, the primary value they want to create is the price of their labour. They want to make money, to get paid. For any of us that is value enough.

⌐ ⌐

Emily (not her real name) works, at the time of writing, in a central London strip venue in a prominent location catering to a crowd of tourists and international businessmen. There is a good chance of footfall, but considering its location and expansive interior it is rarely full of customers. She likes the club, though, as it feels familiar to her. 'You know when something just feels comfortable because you've got used to it. Like if you still smoke the same brand of cigarettes as the one you first tried when you started smoking? It's like that. It was the first club I worked in.' Emily started stripping in her early twenties to support herself, and has worked on and off for nine years. She used to work full time until she took a break for a few years. 'I got burn out, I was getting a drug habit. But now I'm sober and dancing again.' The club is not an easy environment to be in while she is in recovery, but she is managing to make it work. She had been sober for three months at the time of interviewing her for this book.

She said, 'One of the things I liked when I started was doing promo for the club. There were two different ways of doing promo, and the one I liked was when we would get taken to fancy places or events to promote the club – like the football or the boxing, we'd be the ring girls and wear a branded outfit. Or we'd dress up nice and go to conferences or even charity galas.'[7] When asked if she got paid to promote the club, she explained, 'Sometimes we got paid, sometimes we'd get a discount on our house fee, or the club would give us dance vouchers or drinks tokens; it would depend on the job.' She went on to describe the other kind of promo, the one she didn't like:

Managers would come and ask us mid-shift to do promo for the club. They would take us out to members' clubs and bars around London to approach customers and entice them back to the club. Girls I was on promo with were worried about people thinking we were prostitutes and the whorephobia made me very uncomfortable. On the whole, though, I felt more vulnerable because it was sneaky tricking guys into coming back to a strip club when maybe they genuinely thought we were interested in them. Sometimes they became angry once we arrived back and realised they had to pay for our time, it was embarrassing. And then we'd get into trouble with management for not keeping them there. We'd get a reduction on our house fee, but we'd lose our time on the club floor while we were out when we could have been making money.

The house fee at Emily's club is £55 for an evening shift. Dancers have to arrive at 9 p.m., otherwise it's an extra £10 for every hour until last entry at midnight. It's £20 for a day shift, which starts at 5 p.m. 'You always have to give £5 to the house mum as well, even if she's not in that night.' The price of a lap dance is £20, or at least that's what customers are told by security staff on the way in. 'Once customers are in we say that it's actually £20 topless, or £40 fully nude – that's called a naughty forty. When I first started dancers would say to me, "Charge £50 for a dance, don't undercut each other." But then I would see those same dancers who said that to me undercutting their prices later in the night.' The idea is that dancers are allowed to charge what they want for a dance, but as this isn't properly communicated to customers on the way in they are often left confused and suspicious by dancers all offering different amounts.

'A dance lasts about four minutes,' says Emily, 'so I found a good way to make money. I'd offer customers ten minutes fully nude for £100 and they think I'm doing them a deal, so they usually go for it. But then management have cottoned on to that and they've just introduced a new rule that we can't do ten-minute dances in the open dance room. We have to take them into the VIP room, so they can get their cut.' The new ten-minute VIP package according to the club's latest rule costs the customer £70; the dancer is charged 20 per cent commission so she receives £55. For the same amount of time and labour the dancer will now gets £55 instead of £100. In order to get their cut of £15 the club have taken £45 out of the dancers' pockets.

Fifteen minutes in VIP costs the customer £150, if paid in cash (this is despite the new ten-minute package for £70 – in theory the customer could buy two ten-minute packages, giving them twenty minutes for £140). Emily has to pay a fee of £45 as rent for the room, called a *sit down fee*, and so she gets £105. If the customer pays by card, the club adds on a surcharge of 20 per cent to the price bringing it up to £180. Emily still gets the same £105. For an hour in VIP things get really complicated. The room rent for an hour is £150. If the customer pays by cash, she can charge £500 or £600, or in fact she can charge whatever she likes, since dancers are tech-nically in control of setting their own prices. So if she charges £500 cash she will keep £350, if she charges £600 she will keep £450. However, things get really murky if the customer is paying by card. The club uses the £600 price as a starting point to add on 20 per cent, bringing the price to £720. But they then use the £500 price point when paying the dancer, from which the £150 room rent is subtracted, leaving Emily with £350 out of the £720. For the same amount of time, labour and effort Emily loses £100 because the customer is paying by card and the club has the EFTPOS machine.

The pricing strategy seems intentionally convoluted to keep workers constantly perplexed, and anyone who questions the system is met with contempt by staff. According to Emily, 'Dancers aren't supposed to question the prices. One of my friends got sent home and suspended for two weeks because she wasn't happy about something the club was doing, and tried to ask the managers about it.'

One of the benefits of having a VIP room is greater control for the club. Management can keep track of dancers' movements and monitor the time spent in there. Should a dancer and client run overtime by a few minutes, the club can charge the dancer for another fifteen minutes' worth of rent if they so wish. The threats of fees and fines tend to keep dancers in a state of anxiety, which is not usually the atmosphere clients are looking for. Top tier VIP is another great earner for the club. There are mezzanine booths up on the balcony with a great view of the stage, in which the customer must spend a minimum of £1,000 and they have to buy a bottle. So if they are spending by card, they can pay £720 for an hour with Emily, plus a bottle of champagne or their favourite tipple, for £300. Once again the dancer only gets £350 from the transaction. When asked what happens in VIP, Emily says, 'Nothing more than the dance rooms. We dance, we strip, we talk about whatever the customer wants to talk about, let him think he's in love for an hour or so. We're not allowed to touch, those are the rules of the club.'

If customers want to tip dancers on stage, they can purchase fake tipping dollars from the club – the fake dollar bills cost £1 each, with the obligatory 20 per cent surcharge if paid for by card. The dancer picks up her tips after her show and when she cashes them in at the end of the night the club keeps 50 per cent as commission. So a customer using their card pays £1.20 per tip, dancers get 50p. When customers are using an international credit or debit card they are required to fill out a form and provide ID, a level of admin that takes time. When the party is flowing, customers don't want to do admin so they use the ATM instead. Unsurprisingly, it's common practice for strip clubs to have an ATM inside the premises for clients. 'The ATM wasn't working for weeks and that was a nightmare,' Emily says.

There was one occasion recently when I had an American customer, we were chatting and getting on fine. He didn't want to come to VIP but he said he wanted to tip me £200 for my time and to continue sitting at his table for a bit. I took him to the office to do the card payment. Suddenly the price was now £280, which is more than the 20 per cent surcharge. He was like, 'Where did that number come from?' and the staff member just shrugged and said, 'That's how much it costs.' He looked at me and I said nothing, but then he asked her, 'How much does the dancer get from that?' She said nothing, he looked at me again and I said, 'Well, we do have to pay the club a commission from card payments.' Then he just changed his mind, and said he wasn't going to pay anything. We both left the office and he stood there and told me I was being exploited and I needed to join a union. I just had to grit my teeth and smile; I earned nothing from the time I'd spent with him.

The club has a hierarchy of staff working in the venue: dancers, chip girls, waitresses, bar staff, managers, security and DJs. Chip girls earn a salary and a commission from the amounts of money that is charged through the club's card machines, so they have an incentive to keep adding a mark up on prices. Chip girls can only enter their role of employment once they have earned their keep as a waitress for one to two years. Waitresses aren't paid a salary at all, and instead work for tips and a commission of drinks sales. This means they can often interrupt the dancers' work by hustling for the attention of clients, and their spending. Club rules strictly forbid dancers from taking customers' numbers, but the same rule doesn't apply to waitresses – they can text a client and invite him into the club to see her, but if a dancer gets caught doing the same thing she can be sacked for violating the club's licensing conditions.

Clubs are often set up in such a way that various different roles are all essentially working in competition with each other, and this competition is felt most acutely by dancers who have had to pay the club for the privilege of grafting in their building, and whose actual earnings are incrementally poached by those with more economic power and control over them. When everyone in the team is stuck in the individualistic pursuit of chasing sales, it's no wonder that the club doesn't see much return business. The toxicity of such an environment is the perfect breeding ground for favouritism, bribery and inconsistent workplace practices. Dancers might curry favour with certain managers or bar staff, they may tip bouncers to turn a blind eye; the entire system is based on the simple principle of 'looking out for number one'. In this case to have any power in the strip club means being a gatekeeper to other people's ability to perform their role and earn money. Within the hierarchy of gatekeeping in a strip club, licence holders are at the top of the chain since they have the ability to run and manage their business however they see fit.

Emily doesn't seem to mind that much about paying house fees and commissions, and compares her work to other forms of self-employment. 'It's like taxi driving. Taxi drivers have to pay to work, they've got to get their licence and pay a percentage of their earnings as well.' Emily's comparison is fair; there are many other self-employed roles that come with a 'cost-of-entry', so to speak. Market traders have to pay for their pitch; hairdressers frequently pay rent for their chair in a salon; barristers have to pay rent and bills to their chambers. However, this is as far as the comparison goes. In a free market, gaffers do not tell traders what they can sell on their stall, how much to charge, and what they can and can't wear while doing it. Hairdressers are free to charge what they want for a haircut and decide how long it will take. Barristers are free to set their own hourly rate, and can come and go freely – their chambers do not tell them what time to start and finish their shift, nor do they have to ask permission to go home early during a quiet spell. Nonetheless, the comparison with taxi drivers is meaningful; in recent years taxi drivers working for major industry leaders Uber and Addison Lee have mounted legal claims to demand their rights as gig economy workers.

THE MICRO-ECONOMY OF A STRIP CLUB

House fees and commissions are not the only examples of gatekeeping in strip clubs. When dancers begin working in a club it is common practice to require them to sign a type of contract, or a 'code of conduct', which, rather than being a mutual agreement between two parties, is a list of rules made up by the club that apply in one direction to exert control over dancers' behaviour and comportment. Club rules can vary wildly from club to club. Some rules are informed by licensing conditions, such as 'no touching' between dancers and customers, implementing a 'three-foot rule' which compels dancers to keep a physical distance of around one metre between herself and her client during a private dance; while other rules may be entirely arbitrary, made up on the spot by managers who can abuse their authority. Some club rules may be at odds with the objective of making an income and club bosses may find the restrictions on their licences to be harmful to their business model, and so choose to ignore them, or find workarounds. If an individual stripper decides to flout the regulations in private to suit her own personal needs, she may tip a member of venue staff to look the other way. Even the rules of one particular venue can vary from dancer to dancer, while these private micro-economies may shift and evolve from one night to the next.

One of the most common rules encountered in strip clubs requires all dancers to perform a stage show at least once during the night for free; that is to say the club does not pay them or give them a discount on their house fee in return for their labour. The reasoning offered is that dancers are given an opportunity to 'advertise' themselves within the marketplace of the club, and attract attention of would-be customers. This is convenient for the club, since they can provide customers with a steady flow of unpaid entertainment, regardless of whether they spend anything more than the price of entry and a drink from the bar (with both of these streams of revenue going directly to the club). Clubs may have strict rules about stage shows, with rotas for dancers to stick to. The club may have a system to allow dancers to miss or change their slot if they land a customer in VIP, but it's just as likely that they may be fined if they miss their slot. Dancers may be required to perform in the order they arrive to work that night, and the club may charge dancers a fee if they want to skip their stage show. Other rules can include no chewing gum, or no using mobile phones on the club floor, even before any customers have walked in; there can be complicated protocols about queuing to talk to a customer, like a taxi rank system that favours some dancers over others.

There can often be rules about shifts, requiring dancers to work a minimum of three nights per week, for instance. If she wants to work a shift which is a better earner, say a Saturday night, she has to work a Monday, a slow night, as well. Moonlighting is also forbidden, which means strippers can't choose to work at a different venue each night. Instead they are expected to remain loyal to one venue, despite the fact they do not receive a retainer or any kind of guarantee of future employment from them. There may also be rules about dress codes. The most important weapon in a stripper's arsenal is her outfit.; it is her primary mode of self-expression and the main way to stand out and get noticed. It is particularly egregious then that some clubs have rules about outfits: long dresses until midnight, 'fantasy nights' which involve costumes, or no thongs or bare buttocks on display.

There are countless other tiny ways that management can choose to exercise authority over dancers – deciding when to permit cigarette breaks, or whether a dancer can go out for a snack. Most venues will never let dancers go out for a dinner break, the logic being that if she leaves the premises she is free to perform extra services for clients. It is of course possible to give a quick blowjob round the back of the bins, but it seems like a leap to organise a business decision around the very slim likelihood of it ever happening. One venue in West London introduced a new rule for dancers that required them to get a token from the bar if they needed to use the toilet or go back into the changing rooms. Dancers also had to carry clear plastic purses so staff could instantly identify what was being carried, to prevent them from keeping cash tips. Some clubs cannot bear to allow strippers to earn cash tips from customers, from their stage show or even just as a show of appreciation, without being able to take their cut.

For strippers the gatekeeping begins before they are even offered a place in the club. Audition processes can vary and are often highly discriminatory. Dancers can be rejected based on age, race, body type, breast size or hair colour. In some venues dancers are frequently told that they must lose weight, and can even be refused shifts on the basis that they have gained extra body fat. Some club operators have a preference for women who have had breast augmentation surgery, and fulfil a certain stereotypical look. Apologists for strip clubs will often say they have a brand to maintain, and choosing per-formers based on their image is not that different from other entertainment industries. But stories about shocking instances of discrimination in strip clubs often go under the radar.

Sasha Diamond is a stripper and theatre performer, and easily one of the most talented pole dancers in the UK. Her pole skills are breathtaking, and she regularly teaches pole classes from her own studio and at several of London's pole schools. She is also a woman of colour whose experience of working in strip clubs tells us how failing to protect workers enables the kind of inequality that echoes an era that most of us in twenty-first-century Britain would like to imagine was over. Diamond explains that she began stripping in a big name lap-dancing club in central London. 'You had to be really prim and proper to work in those large clubs, you had to have all your hair and nails on point, your outfit had to be perfect. As a black girl I could never have my natural hair, that would be deemed inappropri-ate. I had to wear a wig or a weave, and be like Black Barbie.'[8] She spoke of many incidents of discrimination.

There was this other African Australian girl, she was a bit braver with her outfits. She looked like an eccentric mermaid, but nothing more unusual than any of the white dancers. When head management came in to inspect one night, she got shouted at and sent straight to the dressing room and shamed for looking different. She was upset, but no one knew what to say, we all knew it had nothing to do with her outfit, and they had the power to do that.

More worryingly, Diamond describes systemic prejudices over the years that she had no way to fight.

I always had to work harder for the same money. When we start dancing in a club the first rule you learn is to ask for the money upfront. You take a customer for a dance and he pays £20 at the beginning. But customers would often complain, like they'd say, 'Well, you haven't danced yet, how do I know if it's any good?' I never felt entitled enough to insist so I would do the dance and then the customer would walk out without paying. That happened to me many times. There's nothing you can really do then because the club will just say I should have got the money first.

When it came to auditioning for clubs things weren't much better:

I've been told by some venues that they aren't looking for 'my sort' or that they have enough black girls already. I went to one major West End club to audition and after I came off stage the manager body-shamed me, telling me I need to lose weight – which is ridiculous because I train at the pole every day. Even one of the house mums thought that was out of order because she pulled me aside and said come back in three months. I ended up working there, but I remember when the owner came in with his entourage he treated me like shit but was nice and friendly with all the other white dancers. I've been racially abused by customers more times than I can remember, and management just do nothing.

Diamond recounts example after example of being sidelined and marginalised by clubs and customers alike, so often that it eventually became reason enough for her to exit the industry.

WHO ELSE GETS A SAY?

There are two other groups who also arguably fall into the category of gatekeepers, since they wield so much influence over popular opinion and policy making: radical feminists and media executives. The combined power of these two stake-holders – the resolute conviction of the SWERF agenda amplified by the pervasive grip over public opinion held by media outlets – culminates in almost universal control over wider public debate about sex work. It's not news that conditions for many sex workers are unacceptable; the received narrative in the mainstream is that the sex industry has become synonymous with exploitation. SWERF campaigners use examples of abuse as further proof, ensuring that when the public think of a stripper they think of an abused woman, rather than a worker.

Sadly, the threat of radical feminist campaigns prevents sex workers from whistle-blowing about their poor working conditions, knowing that to do so will create more evidence to be weaponised against the industry. As Mac and Smith write in *Revolting Prostitutes*:

> A sex worker may describe a bad day at work as a labour-rights violation, sexual abuse, or simply a shitty day at work. Regardless, their testimonials are not merely symbols to be interpreted by non-prostitute feminists, especially not as part of a rallying for the criminalisation of their income. Current workers are the experts on what *current working conditions* in the sex industry are like. It is frustrating to sex workers when the exited or non-prostitute perspectives are centred, and our voices are treated as optional extras.[9]

Within the ideology of radical feminism that identifies all forms of selling sex as gender-based violence, the conclusion is drawn that the *only* way to help a sex worker is to help them leave sex work. An 'exited' woman is therefore someone who has successfully left the sex industry, and whose voice is celebrated within mainstream feminism as a survivor. The cacophony of voices and opinions that favour the narratives of survivors who have exited the industry over those who are *continuing* to survive in it creates a racket in which current sex workers' voices cannot be heard. This means some of the most mendacious business practices continue to go unchecked by those who are best placed to call them out.

When public policy grows out of dominant narratives, we can call this gatekeeping. Perhaps the true definition of sex workers' marginalisation is the inability to control their own narratives in the public imagination throughout history. The ultimate form of gatekeeping comes down to whose voices dominate public discourse, and the volume at which they are transmitted; there can be no doubt that sex working voices are spoken over time and again in favour of radical feminists and exited women. This form of gatekeeping is possibly the biggest obstacle that sex workers have to overcome in order to establish their labour rights, since their lack of voices in the mainstream means being unable to control received narratives about their work. There is little hope that exploitation of sex workers can be tackled until sex workers themselves, rather than non-sex workers, can win greater control over political dialogue.

It is easy to read through this seemingly endless list of atrocious workplace abuses and draw conclusions like 'shut them down then' or 'do a different job'. It is precisely this logic that supports efforts to shut down strip clubs and eradicate the sex industry altogether. Despite the rather damning reflection of strip clubs in this chapter, it is not the intention of this book to see venues closed down. Shut-them-down logic does not address the fundamental point that sex workers are made more vulnerable precisely because they can't access their labour rights. Being denied basic employment protections makes workers vulnerable to exploitation in any industry. Breathing down workers' necks like overseers in a dystopian purgatory may sound like grim working conditions indeed; however, there are increasing comparisons to be drawn with workers in other industries; in recent years the online conglomerate Amazon have been making headlines for their arcane use of deplorable employment practices at their warehouses, euphemistically called 'fulfilment centres'.[10] However, shut-them-down logic does not extend to Amazon; we have never seen high-profile celebrity petitions to shut down the online retailer for the protection of their staff.

Shut-them-down logic also fails to acknowledge the invisible reality that for a stripper the ability to earn £350 per hour may be empowering to her. Having to put up with appalling work conditions, performing free labour for the club or being infantilised by paternalistic rules may all be worth it in return for landing a client in VIP for the night; for her that might be a straightforward transaction she is willing to enter into. Cries to shut them down completely disregard any value created by dancers' labour, whether financial, creative or otherwise, and ride roughshod over the countless individual narratives and personal choices made in challenging circumstances. There is nothing restorative about this approach; shutting clubs down does not unlock workers' access to power and justice.

While sex workers' lack of rights creates vulnerability across the entire sex industry, if we look specifically at strip clubs in the UK it is evident that licensing authorities have a huge role to play. Rogue operators exist in all industries, but in this instance rogue operators are given a free pass because the legislation itself does not recognise the labour performed by workers. Authority in the workspace has been given to venue operators instead of workers, and authority over the venue operators lies in the hands of the state. Strip club bosses and managers are answerable only to their regulators. At present the only actors with any power to introduce change and reverse the culture of exploitation are local licensing officials and police, i.e. the state. But if the state is failing in this role, then who is responsible for scrutinising the business practices of licence holders? The answer to this question ought to be obvious – dancers themselves should have the power to scruti-nise and take action against bad players. No one understands their own workplaces better than those who work in them.

4

IS STRIPPING SEX WORK?

> The ELSC wish to self-identify using the term 'stripper'
> to draw a distinction between the work they do and
> other types of sex work. While the ELSC stands in total,
> open and honest solidarity with other sex workers and
> sex worker organisations, and has no resistance to the
> term 'sex work', for the purposes of campaigning on
> issues that specifically affect strippers in the UK the
> ELSC remain committed to the definition 'stripper' to
> describe what they do for a living.
>
> —East London Strippers Collective Manifesto[1]

The term 'sex work' was coined in the late 1970s by activist,
writer, theatre maker and sex worker Carol Leigh, a.k.a. the
Scarlot Harlot. Leigh worked closely with a group known as
Call Off Your Old Tired Ethics (COYOTE), which focused
specifically on the plight of prostitutes and the systemic

violence they faced then (and still face today). In 1978 she attended a conference in San Francisco held by an organisation called Women Against Violence in Pornography and Media. She intended to act as an ambassador to help feminists better understand the lived experience of women selling sex and sexual labour. But she attended a workshop on prostitution and heard the term 'sex use industry' as an attempt at a terminology. She felt embarrassed and objectified by the phrase. It was problematic in the sense that it failed to recognise any sense of agency or consent among women selling sex. She hit upon the term 'sex work industry' shifting emphasis away from the customer and onto the work of the provider, thus enshrining a sense of autonomy for herself and her colleagues as 'actor and agent in the transaction'. She used the term in her 1980 one-woman theatre production, *The Adventures of Scarlot Harlot*, but it didn't appear in print until 1984. In 1987 another publication, *Sex Work: Writings by Women in the Sex Industry*, popularised the term. Leigh published her essay 'Inventing Sex Work' in 1997 as part of an anthology of essays, *Whores and Other Feminists*, edited by Jill Nagle. In it she explained:

> The usage of the term 'sex work' marks the beginning of a movement. It acknowledges the work we do rather than defines us by our status.[2]

'Sex work' is used as an umbrella term for all workers in the sex industry. There are different ways to sell sexual labour, and the rapid technological advances in the last half-century have seen to it that many forms of sex work are here to stay. Sex work includes all forms of sexual performance – stripping, web-camming, selling online content (nudes and video clips), pornography – as well as the more traditionally thought of forms of sex work such as escorting, prostitution, professional domination and BDSM role-play. There are also less well-known types of sex work – sex chat lines via phone or text – or the more relational style that involves transactional relationships like sugar-babying, i.e. carefully curated arrangements with clients who pay an allowance in return for a short- or long-term commitment.

The phrase has entered the mainstream lexicon so success-fully that it has been adopted by major NGOs such as the World Health Organization and Amnesty International. Sex work is defined by the WHO as:

> the provision of sexual services for money or goods. Sex work-ers are women, men and transgendered people who receive money or goods in exchange for sexual services, and who con-sciously define those activities as income generating even if they do not consider sex work as their occupation.[3]

Definitions of sex work start to become wider when the con-cept of survival sex work is introduced. Money or goods may be anything of value to the person engaged in the exchange – housing, drugs, food, protection are all things that can be traded for sex. In 2018 investigative journalist Ellie Flynn made a documentary for the BBC about the rise of landlords offering housing in return for sexual favours, in response to the UK housing crisis.[4] According to the documentary, more women are trading sex for a place to live and more men are emboldened to offer such arrangements under austerity cuts that leave greater numbers of people with no financial security. Some of the more strident campaigners for sex workers' rights assert that sex work is born out of traditional socio-economic factors that leave women financially dependent on male breadwinners, and even widen the definition far enough to argue that marriage is the original form of sex work. It's no coincidence that COYOTE formed out of a group initially called Whores, Housewives and Others.

By the time the phrase sex work came along, the sex workers' rights movement was already well under way. In the mid-1970s a highly politicised lobby began forming in California and Europe demanding rights for prostitutes, flying in the face of glaring social stigma and inequality. The movement in Europe included the French Prostitute Collective, which formed out of a series of sex worker-led church occupations. Selma James, the American feminist, writer and social activist, said of the time:

I was in France in 1975 just after the famous prostitutes' strike that launched the modern sex workers' movement in the west: women had occupied churches first in Lyon and then all over France to protest police arresting and fining them while doing nothing to stop murders and rapes. They formed the French Prostitute Collective and proclaimed: 'Our children don't want their mothers in jail.'[5]

James went on to be the first spokesperson for the English Collective of Prostitutes (ECP), one of the longest running sex worker-led organisations in the UK, also founded in 1975. ECP have become one of the leading advocacy groups for sex workers' rights in the country, campaigning for the full decriminalisation of sex work, the right to recognition, safety and resources, and for the provision of financial alternatives to prostitution so that no one is forced into sex work because of poverty.

ECP work tirelessly to raise awareness and challenge policies that severely and unfairly impact women in sex work. On their website they outline some of their demands:

- Protection from rape and other violence.
- An end to police brutality, corruption, racism and other illegality. Prosecute police who break the law.
- No zones, no licensing, no legalised brothels – they are ghettos and state pimping.

- Self-determination. Sex workers must decide how we want to work – not the police, local authorities, pimps, madams/managers who profit from our work.
- Rights for sex workers like other workers; the right to organise collectively to improve our working conditions, a pension, and to join trade unions.[6]

When it comes to understanding the lived experience of sex workers in the UK, there are few organisations as well equipped to explain the safest conditions for all sex workers, including strippers. Which is why, as much as possible, the advocacy of groups like ECP must be at the heart of all policy decisions about sex work.

IS STRIPPING A SEXUAL SERVICE?

Strippers who resist the term 'sex work' have a hard sell on their hands, particularly if, under the WHO definition, sex workers include people who 'do not consider sex work their occupation'. While the actual work of stripping may have changed dramatically over time, from the fondly remembered vintage tassle-twirling routines much celebrated by icons of neo-Burlesque like Dita Von Teese, to the twerking, hustling and emotional labour performed in present day lap-dancing clubs, the core essence of what's on offer remains the same: nudity and sexuality. Striptease entertainment did indeed have a more theatrical bent to it prior to the arrival of lap-dancing clubs. Performed on a stage and viewed at a distance by the audience, it could be argued, as it regularly is by members of the Burlesque community, that striptease on stage is not sex work, but instead performance art.

This critique falls apart, however, when applied to lap dancing. Gone are the nipple-pasties and *tasteful* diamante under-things that 'leave room for the imagination', replaced by a more graphic code of signifiers. Strippers perform eroti-cised dance routines; they wear outfits made of practically nothing designed to provoke the pornographic imagination of onlookers. Bodies are cinched, sculpted and augmented to reveal a hypersexualised gender stereotype. They may some-times dance with a pole and bring an impressive repertoire of athletic tricks to their performance; but unlike most contem-porary Burlesque performers, they spread their legs wide open. They reveal primary and secondary sexual organs in exchange for money, or the possibility of earning it. Everything they do is sexualised and the suggestion of sex is thoroughly embedded in the artifice.

This clarification explains why nudity in Burlesque and cabaret does not carry the same licensing obligations as lap dancing. Live displays of nudity within a context of artistry, theatre or humour aren't necessarily performed with the primary purpose of sexual arousal. It may be an incidental side effect should a member of a Burlesque audience be aroused, but as long as it is *tasteful* it isn't *licensable*. This is why nudity, partial or otherwise, is allowed in public bars and in theatres, while lap-dancing clubs and SEVs carry with them the stigma that comes with the servicing of sexual arousal.

Many strippers will be at pains to explain that a lap dance does not involve penetrative sex and is merely a performance. The principal purpose of a lap dance is actually quite variable; the gesticulations and simulation of sexual positions may be accompanied by elements of fondness, affection and companionship, as well as humour and artistry. But, from a *bystander's* point of view it is almost impossible to argue that the purpose of a lap dance is for anything other than the sexual stimulation of the viewer. A lap dance is a short and intimate interlude, which normally lasts four to five minutes (the length of one song). The client remains seated while a dancer performs a striptease in close proximity, moving between their legs, straddling their lap, grinding and body-rolling, and where contact is permitted, engaging in consensual touch. There is the potential for the client and/or the dancer to become sexually aroused during the performance; the dancer may occasionally feel a client's erection through their clothes, if performing a full-contact lap dance. The answer, therefore, to the question 'is stripping a sexual service?' is inevitably, yes.

IS STRIPPING WORK?

What lap dancers and other performers have in common is the wider sense in which none of their roles are traditionally considered to be *real* work. There is a deeply shared discomfort at the idea of a stripper (or any sex worker for that matter) performing sexual labour without a smile on her face, since the idea that she may not be enjoying herself is anathema to consumers. This creates a strange double bind for strippers; in order to appease the collective unease of her audience she is compelled to do the emotional labour of making her work look effortless, as though she is performing out of an innate need for self-expression and would happily do it for free. She cannot reveal her inner state, her personal trials, her anxiety about money or job security; to do so would break the spell of the fantasy that she is horny, sexually available and concerned only with the needs and desires of her clients. Historically, this façade has allowed a confusion to grow around stripping; if it doesn't look like work, then it won't be recognised and treated as such. Comparisons can be drawn with other forms of labour; models, actors, musicians, cabaret artists and comedians are also similarly viewed as non-jobs by audiences, and whose labour is also widely exploited by producers and consumers alike.

It is well worth asking what it is about lap dancing that sets it apart from other forms of performance, and why it is *not* socially accepted in the way other forms of labour, such as modelling or acting, are. One explanation for this lies within the Policing and Crime Act 2009. One of the clear outcomes of the legislation was to legally define 'sexual entertainment' with a precision that had not been offered previously. According to Section 27 of the Act, sexual entertainment is defined as follows:

(1) In this Schedule 'sexual entertainment venue' means any premises at which relevant entertainment is provided before a live audience for the financial gain of the organiser or the entertainer.

(2) In this paragraph 'relevant entertainment' means—

(a) any live performance; or

(b) any live display of nudity; which is of such a nature that, ignoring financial gain, it must reasonably be assumed to be provided solely or principally for the purpose of sexually stimulating any member of the audience (whether by verbal or other means).[7]

The law has very effectively carved out a definition of sexual entertainment that leaves no room for debate. The words 'ignoring financial gain' are important here. A lap dancer, or even a customer, might argue that the sole purpose of a lap dance is to earn money, or pay a lap dancer for her time. However, once the exchange of money is no longer the main intention, it's hard to argue why a performer would be removing her clothes in a sexually suggestive manner if it weren't for the purpose of arousal. Legislators have cleverly obfuscated the main purpose of the work – to earn a living – by writing this out of the legislation.

It's an interesting thought experiment to use the definition of sexual entertainment, as outlined in the Policing and Crime Act 2009, to evaluate whether other jobs fall under the definition of sex work. If a photographer takes a photo that is 'solely and principally for the purpose of sexually stimulating any member of the audience', could that be described as providing a sexual service? What about a producer of video pornography who never performs but works long hours on a shoot, is this sexual labour? Would a driver who accompanies an escort on a job and waits outside until the end of the booking for safety be defined as a sex worker? The answer from the sex working community is a resounding no. Performing sexual labour doesn't include performing labour alongside or in association with sex. In which case it is the person providing the *sexual* labour who has the right to define as a sex worker, and no one else.

While I was travelling through Australia on a working holiday visa, I wound up working at a club in Sydney called the Petersham Inn. It was an eye-opener to see how strip clubs could actually be reasonably well run in a country where the sex industry is a functioning and accepted part of the night-time economy. The Petersham Inn was a perfect reflection of the relaxed attitude towards sex work that I encountered over and over again while I was travelling in Australia on a work holiday visa.

The Petersham Inn was a suburban pub, my favourite kind of place. Strippers only performed there at weekends, the rest of the week it was a regular bar. The clientele were working-class men with a bit of money to throw around, rather than the wanker bankers of the central business district. The place was a true man cave. There was a food hatch serving classic pub grub, live sports on TV, and an indoor smoking area and betting room. There was a back room with a bar, stage and private lounge where the stripping went on from Thursday to Sunday (the club owners were smart enough not to have any TV screens in the back so the strippers didn't have to compete with sports matches for the clients' attention). There were also topless barmaids at the weekends serving drinks. There was a relaxed atmosphere, but that didn't spill into an overbearing sense of entitlement – the place was too lowbrow for that. Customers were free to wander in and out of the stage area and watch the strip shows at will. The stage was a raised floor in the middle of the room with massive armchairs all the way round, and the private lounge for lap dances was a communal VIP room with white leather seating. It all felt very social, everything was a shared experience and done in full view of everyone else. This was unlike any venue I'd worked in the UK – almost every British strip club has an aura of intimidation, in line with how much they are stigmatised. Bouncers would often scare potential customers away at the *door, which was infuriating to us dancers and always seemed counter-intuitive to the purposes of making an income for the club.*

The business model at the Petersham Inn worked well. There were no house fees, the club took a straight 20 per cent commission on anything we earned — no weird sliding scale fees or hidden charges — so we always knew where we stood financially. Dancers could make money there in a number of different ways. You could do regular shifts as a stripper that involved earning tips from stage shows and private lap dances, or selling time in the VIP lounge. Topless waitressing was another option. Dancers could also earn a commission from selling printed tipping dollars to customers (for tipping dancers on stage). I discovered after a few days that the club were doing discount deals on large bundles of tipping dollars; meaning they were actually helping us out by getting the currency flowing round the room, and absorbing some of the costs by offering a small concession on big transactions. They weren't then passing that loss onto us, because our commission stayed at 20 per cent; this was the first time I'd encountered such a reasonable business strategy, and the club shot up in my esteem. They had the right idea, and understood the tipping game well enough to know it was a group activity. Once a few players get the game started then everyone wants to participate in the tradition of throwing the paper notes and watching them 'rain' on the dancers. Stage shows could be lucrative because the club had managed to create a healthy tipping culture there.

Stage shows have always been my strong suit since I love the audience interaction, and find it easy to earn tips this way. This club was ideal, it was so laid back that I could step off the stage and wander into the

crowd, sit on people's laps and invite them to tuck dollars into my costume. One night, while I was performing a final show towards the end of
my shift I encountered a bald man with a thick northern accent, sitting on
his own with a stack of tips on his table, wearing shorts and a Hawaiian
shirt, and wearing obnoxiously thick-framed glasses. He looked like a
cross between Moby and Heston Blumenthal. His interaction with me
was coarse and comical, but I came away with his entire stack of tipping
dollars. It's always the weirdos I meet at the end of an otherwise unevent-
ful night that catch my attention.

I went back to his table after my show, and it didn't take him long to
proposition me for sex. For some reason I didn't walk away. Between his
bizarre communication style and the dissonance between his down-at-heel
appearance and his overly self-assured manner, maybe the familiarity of a
fellow northerner, I intuitively felt he was harmless. My instinct told
me that his façade of confidence and swagger belied the depth of his
vulnerability – I felt like I already knew the true character of this male
gargoyle, I'd already met him a thousand times before. At that moment I
had nothing better to do than to see where this interaction could lead, and
so mainly for my own entertainment I followed up his crude proposal with
a straightforward answer, 'That can be arranged.'

Throughout my years of stripping my boundaries were held in place by
whorephobia. My feelings about prostitution and full-service sex work
were heavily associated with shame and stigma, although rationally I had
very little resistance to the concept of it. As I was growing up I don't
remember women talking about it much, but the men around me were the
ones with strong opinions. As a sexually inquisitive teenager I visited the

red-light district of Amsterdam out of sheer fascination with all things libidinous, and I considered the idea of being paid to have sex a completely valid prospect. Earning money for something enjoyable seemed very reasonable. My first boyfriend explained to me, 'All those girls are on drugs and controlled by pimps.' An excessively slutty Halloween costume one year earned me a huge row from my older brother, and a guy I was infatuated with at college did some of the loudest slut-shaming of all. These voices stayed with me, echoing around my psyche for years into my adult life.

I remember the first time I heard myself referred to as a sex worker. When I began stripping I lived in a shared house with two guys who both seemed mildly proud to be living with a stripper, as though it kind of earned them some kudos. One of them worked in the finance district, and his weekend began on Wednesday and ended on Monday – Party Marty was his name. After a few months of stripping, he said, jokingly, 'When are you going to invite your fellow sex workers round then?' Until then, I think I'd only ever seen the term 'sex worker' written down, so when I heard it in person it got my attention. He wasn't using the words as a slur or insult, so perhaps that gave me the psychological space to integrate the language; I've never felt any resistance to the term 'sex work' since.

After that early trip to Amsterdam I'd always privately reserved for myself the possibility of selling sex. Studying feminist discourse in college revealed to me the conflict between opposing camps of women who felt differently about the sex industry. There were those who identified with the lusty power and self-agency of sex work, and then the others who saw it as nothing but a patriarchal construct that places women in a position of subservience and victimhood. I could see both sides, but I identified more with the pro-sex camp, having had a taste for the lusty power of sex work myself. Becoming a stripper meant I was solicited for sex more regularly than ever; this wasn't a new thing – I'd been solicited plenty of times simply walking down the street. My internal conflict about sleeping with customers for extra money came to a final conclusion when I brokered a deal with myself. I knew that I could but only under certain conditions. I would need to feel safe, and the payment would need to be worthwhile. £1,000 became the amount fixed in my mind that I wouldn't go beneath. Whenever I was asked the question, 'How much for you to come to my hotel room?' my reflex response was, 'It starts at four figures.' It became a solid boundary. Most customers couldn't afford or weren't willing to spend that much. Throughout my dancing career I was in a privileged enough position of financial security that I always had the choice to walk away. It came very close to happening on a couple of occasions, but circum-stances conspired to get in the way each time.

When I reeled off my stock response this time, I forgot that the con-version rate in Australian dollars meant the four figure minimum was in fact a reduction of my usual 'rate', and I slightly regretted not starting at $1,500. But by this point I didn't care that much. I felt safe and the extra money was convenient. He gave me his address, and I saw on Google Earth that he lived only five minutes' walk from where I was staying – it felt like circumstances were conspiring this time to aid things along. I asked a close friend to buddy me (I knew to do this from listening to other sex worker friends over the years), sharing the name, address and phone number of the client, and what time I would be back.

I arrived at the front door of a beautiful townhouse, it was a hot night and he opened the door in his underwear (clothes are pretty optional most of the time in Australia). The first thing he said was, 'I thought you weren't coming.' His personality had changed dramatically and his machismo was as absent as his clothes. He seemed smaller now in his private habitat, his vulnerability was amplified. His house was messy and lived in; there were a couple of wetsuits laid out on the floor. I quickly learned that he was a diver, and he bizarrely showed off his shaved legs to me in a jocular fashion. He offered me champagne but I told him I'd rather have tea, and being a fellow Brit he was delighted to make me an Earl Grey. He got $1,000 in $50 notes out of his freezer, and put them in a glass, explaining that he kept his money in there 'for safety'. He hinted that he was renting the house from some dodgy people, but I wondered if he was just exaggerating for effect. He was a talker and raced through multiple subjects, his job in the army, how he was about to retire after thirty years, how all the lads in his regiment thought he was gay because they never saw him chasing women, how $1k was nothing to him, how his ex-girlfriend was incredibly beautiful and (like me) taller than him, how healthy he thought I looked, how unhealthy he thought most people were. Some of his boyish exuberance returned and he revelled in having my full attention; he wasn't that interested in hearing my opinions on anything, so I could just sit back and let him talk. It was easy.

After maybe half an hour he asked, 'Do you wanna come upstairs?' I followed him up the wooden staircase. He asked me if I liked Simply Red and without bothering to wait for my answer, he started playing a DVD of Simply Red in concert. Not Simply Red at their peak in the early 1990s, but Simply Red circa 2010, with a middle-aged Mick Hucknall *crooning around a stage. My brain instantly lurched to the scene in* American Psycho, *where the protagonist waxes lyrical about Whitney Houston's album before murdering a prostitute in his flat. I didn't sense any danger, but there was a tiny voice in my head saying, 'Is this how I die? Like in a Brett Easton Ellis novel?' Like clockwork my go-to coping mechanism for dealing with potential harm was my dark sense of humour, not that my safety was something to be glib about. I'd purposefully kept my phone switched on and in my hand, making sure he saw me text my friend, as a symbol of my connectivity to the outside world, which obviously isn't a failsafe method of self-protection. It wasn't the first time alone behind closed doors with a male I'd only just met, and yet I was suddenly very aware of my own welfare. Not because I was afraid; in fact being in New South Wales meant that I was probably as safe as a sex worker can ever be. But suddenly all the stereotypes of prostitutes fed to me in books and films came alive in my imagination.*

When it came to performing the deed itself, the issue of safety was in fact completely reversed. As soon as foreplay began the physical connection and touch of another person sent him into such a deeply relaxed state that he simply passed out. I didn't know what to do at first, sitting motionless on the edge of his four-poster bed, expecting him to wake up again any moment. I was amazed; he was actually at the mercy of a stranger in his house and it seemed astonishing to me how safe he must have felt with me to fall asleep. Once I heard him snoring I quietly crept out of the house, looking at all the things I could have robbed, with Mick Hucknall still warbling in the background.

I learned several things from the encounter. Some of it had felt like work: when he was performing oral sex on me and the stubble on his chin was agonising, I'd tried to guide his head towards a better angle but he wasn't getting the message, which wasn't terribly different to some of the bad sex I've had with people I'd met on dating apps. I also knew some dancers would see me as a traitor, while others would offer me high-fives. When I retold the story to my co-worker the next day, she congratulated me on such an easy gig. I also learned I had no guilt or shame, no sense of stigma anymore. It felt every bit as reasonable as it seemed on that first trip to Amsterdam when I was seventeen. I also considered myself incredibly privileged to earn a grand compared to anyone who has traded sex for a place to stay or something to eat. In the end, I thought . . . my body, my business.

~ ~

STIGMA AND RISK

Sex work carries risk. For some sex workers the burden of risk is too heavy: evictions, police raids, arrests, deportations, travel restrictions, visa denials, social services investigations, loss of child custody, confiscation of earnings by the state, bank account suspensions, tax investigation, social exclusion, inexplicable gaps in regular employment, risk of violence, sexual assault, prison sentences and criminal records are just a shortlist of the devastating consequences that may beset those who take up sex work, no matter their level of choice and agency. Being a sex worker means having to negotiate risk at every turn; the levels of risk vary from worker to worker, depending on their levels of privilege and access to protection.

Strippers do not have to navigate the same risks as, say, a street worker. A stripper is not at risk of arrest or prison time since her work is legalised, and she works in a licensed work-place. However, the stigmatising of lap-dancing clubs over the last decade has led to increasing levels of state intervention and scrutiny. In August 2018 Strathclyde Police and Home Office immigration officers raided a lap-dancing club in Glasgow, Seventh Heaven, descending on the venue during business hours.[8] Twelve uniformed cops swept through the club to carry out a 'licenced premises and welfare check' which consisted of taking dancers one by one into the club office, while still dressed in their work lingerie, to be inter-viewed by police. Personal details were taken, and even dancers' tattoos were recorded for identification purposes. Dancers were understandably disturbed by the swoop; the heavy-handed approach towards a legal business is indicative of a shift in public perceptions towards strip clubs as harmful sites of violence and coercion. Examples of police raids show how strippers who work in a legal and regulated industry can occasionally experience similar levels of persecution to those of other sex workers. Social stigma has engulfed strip clubs so deeply that lap dancers are perceived to be an at-risk group who require police intervention, even though no trafficking victims were found that night.

Stigma has a cyclical set of consequences for a person's life. The first problem of stigma is silence – stigmatised people don't talk. They hide secrets from friends and family. This leads to isolation – stigmatised people don't reach out for help. They don't seek out support and lack peer networks. Isolation increases vulnerability – isolated people are more likely to be victims of violence. Isolated and vulnerable people who are lacking social support and connectivity are directly in harm's way. Sex workers are at a higher risk of violence, rape, sexual assault and murder than any other social demographic, and among them queer, trans, people of colour are the most at risk of all.[9]

The cycle of stigma perpetuates itself, particularly when the harms of the sex industry remain the narratives that ubiquitously dominate headlines, film plots, TV dramas and political debate. These narratives pervade our collective consciousness, ensuring that when we think of the sex industry, we think of harm. A story about a sex worker raising a family, putting food on the table, paying for education and escaping poverty is not a newsworthy story unless it has a violent sub-plot as well. Violent narratives merely begin the cycle of stigma all over again – a headline about abuses in a strip club, or assault against street workers, without any interrogation of the circumstances that lead to vulnerability, further stigmatises sex work. If we fail to appreciate what makes people vulnerable then we fail to break the cycle. And if we contribute to stigma, we contribute to harm.

WHOREPHOBIA AND THE WHOREARCHY

The word used to describe the stigma that applies to sex work is 'whorephobia', i.e. the pervading belief that people who sell sex and sexual services are fundamentally bad and/or broken people, victims of circumstance in need of corrective treatment. Public policy that seeks to restrict the spread of lap-dancing clubs and limit their wider social impact could be described as whorephobic. Strippers experience whorephobia along with others working in the sex industry; they risk being socially ostracised and frequently encounter problems when trying to integrate into daily life. Lap dancers who want to open business bank accounts to deposit their incomes are turned down by banks whose policy excludes people working in the adult entertainment industry. In parallel with full-service sex workers being arrested for carrying condoms, strippers can be detained and refused passage of entry by border control officials for carrying Pleasers – the brand of plastic shoes known for their notoriously high heels that have become synonymous with stripping and sex work – in their suitcases.

For some sex workers the burden of stigma is too much to bear, and so one typical response is to try and repackage it as something that doesn't apply to them. This is called the whore-archy, a systemic problem within the sex industry where people who do some of the more privileged and safer forms of sex work, like stripping or webcamming for example, assign a sense of value to their own work by demeaning and devalu-ing other more perilous forms of sex work. If they don't touch their clients or provide full-contact services, known euphemis-tically as extras, then they don't have to carry the can of stigma; they can pass it on. Saying, 'I would never do X', or 'I don't have to do Y' doesn't solve the problem of stigma, it incubates it. When strippers keep their distance from full-service sex workers they are unfortunately contributing further to whorephobia.

One instance of the whorearchy in practice occurred in London in 2010. Just a few months after the Policing and Crime Act 2009 was written into statute, Hackney City Coun-cil, immediately attempted to shut down all the strip clubs in the East London borough by revoking all their licences. It was mooted in the local press as a radical solution to the 'problem' of SEVs, although it seems more likely to have been part of an effort to gentrify the area in the lead up to the London Olympics 2012. Huge development investments were being made in the district and the Queen Elizabeth Olympic Park in neighbouring Stratford was well under way. Strip clubs probably weren't part of the future vision. But despite taking a hard-line abolitionist approach, Hackney City Council were not expecting the backlash that followed.

A coalition of support rapidly emerged in favour of the clubs, including a surprising formation of dancers, local business owners, neighbouring residents, lawyers, trade union activists, and some high-profile advocates. A public consultation found overwhelmingly in favour of the venues, followed by another that returned the same result. Strippers engaged in trade union activism and joined the GMB to begin organising to protect against potential job losses. Greater London Assembly member Andrew Boff appeared in a short documentary titled *Hands Off*, filmed and produced by filmmaker Winstan Whitter,[10] speaking in support of the clubs. James Goff, executive director and founder of Stirling Ackroyd, an estate agency that had profited hugely from the exponential economic growth in Hackney, attended a licensing hearing and spoke eloquently in favour of the local strip clubs. Goff, who had become well known as one of the key figures responsible for the financial expansion of Shoreditch, told licensing officials how important the venues had been during the early days of his business and argued that without the strip pubs he would not have been able to meet with speculators and bring new investment to the area. It seemed unfair to suddenly expel them after the tremendous escalation that had happened around them, especially since some of them were family-run firms established by previous generations. Even the local vicar of Shoreditch Church, Rev. Paul Turp, spoke in favour of the clubs to the BBC calling for the clubs to remain in operation as a safer option, compared to the alternative unlicensed, unsafe spaces he had seen in the area previously.[11]

The campaign to save the clubs quickly gathered pace and was steered by dancers themselves. Lily La Fleur, Jennifer Richardson and Edie Lamort were all Shoreditch dancers; they lent their support to the clubs and provided a voice for dancers themselves. Lamort, in particular, became thoroughly involved in the struggle to defend the SEVs and protect local dancers' jobs. According to Lamort, 'I was trying to reach out to other groups and businesses – members of the kink community, Torture Garden, big Burlesque nights. The feeling was that if the clubs got shut down then who would they come for next. But it was difficult; no one wanted to be associated with lap dancing.'[12]

The campaign culminated in a public demonstration outside Hackney Town Hall, with dancers calling for an end to the persecution and threat to their workplaces. One of the few organisations that did turn out in support was the English Collective of Prostitutes. However, when one of the venue owners heard that ECP were planning to attend the protest, dancers working in their venue were forbidden from taking part. Lamort explains, 'Dancers were told by club bosses that they weren't to show up to the picket line. The fear was that if strippers were seen alongside prostitutes it would simply play to the council's point of view. The risk of losing their licences was very real, so the club owners were terrified of anything that might make them look worse.' Despite this act of solidarity, strippers themselves were not only fighting to overcome the stigma attached to their work, they were also prevented from standing alongside women who were similarly stigmatised.

This is an important example of everything that can go wrong within sex worker organising and advocacy. When dividing lines are drawn between groups of sex workers in the form of control in the workplace, it takes an extraordinary level of solidarity to put one's own livelihood on the line for a higher set of principles. The Hackney strippers were already so precarious as a group, their jobs so at risk, that their boss was able to leverage further powers, controlling their own campaigning strategy to save their own jobs.

In the end, the Hackney strippers' campaign was successful. After an expensive and fraught legal appeal, four venues' licences were reinstated under so-called 'grandfather laws', meaning they were able to draw upon historical precedent to argue that their licences pre-dated the new Policing and Crime Act. Many venues that didn't have the retrospective licences had to shut down, leaving only a handful to enjoy less competition and new powers as a monopoly. Throughout the campaign to preserve licences and the media circus that ensued, workers' rights were not addressed or protected; the focus was entirely on keeping the clubs open. Divisions between the organising camps of the sex industry left the pro-stripper lobby disunited and without a coherent coalition of voices demanding rights for workers. The dancers who had lent their time and effort to this cause were not rewarded with job security. In the years that followed house fees went up, working conditions deteriorated, jobs remained precarious and dancers had no more power in the workplace than before; Edie Lamort was eventually sacked because her boss didn't like her new haircut.

The control exerted over the Hackney dancers is only one example of the whorephobic culture that has grown within the lap-dancing industry. Whorephobia among strip club owners was never as clear as when Peter Stringfellow spoke in Parliament in 2008, claiming that his strip club had nothing to do with sex, saying, 'I do not want anybody coming into my club thinking they are going to get a sexual encounter.'[13] While it sounds like a preposterous statement for the owner of a strip club to make, there is a very simple logic behind it. Offences pertaining to organising sex as a commercial business carry heavy punitive fines; brothel-keeping carries a punishment of up to seven years in prison. It stands to reason then that the operators of strip clubs may distance themselves from any-thing that would at the very least cost them their licence and livelihood, or at worst land them in jail. It is not that lap dancers or even bosses are themselves inherently whorephobic, but as long as full-service sex work is criminalised strip clubs will fall back on whorephobia as the cost of admission to running a legalised business.

Strip club bosses are not the only interest group to resist the term 'sex work'. In the lead up to the Policing and Crime Act 2009, public conversation was intensely dominated by voices from the radical feminism movement, demanding a total ban on lap-dancing clubs. Radical feminists do not refer to themselves as Sex Worker Exclusionary Radical Feminists, or SWERFs, since the acronym does in fact contain the term 'sex worker'. A radical feminist may well refuse to use the term 'sex work' because doing so would be to acknowledge the concept of sex work *as work*. In July 2018 a Parliamentary debate was held to discuss the possibility of introducing new restrictions to online advertising of sexual services. During the debate, Jess Phillips MP interrupted Victoria Atkins MP to insist she use the word 'prostitutes' rather than the term 'sex workers'.[14] Sarah Champion MP, known along with Phillips for her staunchly radical feminist position on the sex industry, also added, 'Only one is true.' The fact that the term 'sex worker' cannot be tolerated by members of Parliament tells us a lot about how far there is to go before nuanced dialogue can take place at a government level.

Licensing officials, police, HMRC and immigration authorities have an equally hard time adopting the phrase, for similar reason to, although not as ideologically motivated as, the

SWERF agenda. To accept the concept of self-determination among people working in the sex industry would challenge an entire legal system that does not yet recognise their labour rights. Of course, whorephobia is not the only reason for strip club bosses to reject the term sex work; to recognise the working status of dancers would upturn their entire business model, which relies on misclassifying workers in order to maximise profits and minimise their liabilities as employers. This means, despite their ideological incompatibility, there is at least one thing that strip club bosses and radical feminists have in common.

***

I remember the day of the 2012 Olympic Torch Parade in London. I had a shift at the White Horse that afternoon, and the universe had so deigned it that the Olympic Torch was to be carried up Shoreditch High Street, right past the doors of the club. It was mental – I was having to push my way through the thronging masses, lining the streets for a two second glimpse of a flame, to get to my strip club shift on time. When I finally made it to Shoreditch High Street but I was on the wrong side of the street from the club, and still had a few hundred metres of pavement to push my way through. I looked at my watch and realised I had no choice, I was already cutting it fine. 'EXCUSE ME!' I shouted and fought my way through the line of union-jack waving punters who were fiercely defending their coveted places on the front row. I couldn't have cared less. I walked out into the middle of the parade route and marched up Shoreditch High Street, wheeling my bike which had become impossible to ride with this many people around. A nervous hush fell as I walked fifty metres right up the middle of the Olympic Torch Parade route to get to the strip club; the weirdest Olympic event ever. I held my head high as I approached the pub, and the crowd still staring in disbelief just stepped out of the way to let me get to the heavy Victorian doors.

Entering the pub that day was quite a reality shift. Stepping over the threshold of a strip club in the daytime is always a bit of a shock to the senses, even under normal conditions. Daylight is immediately swapped for a dark environment with flashes of bright coloured artificial lighting, and the everyday sounds of bustling urban life switch to booming R&B bass beats. But the day of the Olympic Torch Parade was especially strange; to go from the corporate carnival outside the door, literally a couple of feet away, to the sparsely populated dimness of a strip club in the afternoon was bizarre.

I was technically a couple of minutes late. Throughout my dancing career, of all the things that pissed me off about how strip clubs are run, it's the way management would use punctuality to discipline us. If I'm self-employed, as they keep telling us, why does it matter if I'm ten minutes late? I lost count years ago of the number of times I've thought 'if you want me to arrive on time, why don't you pay me a fucking wage then?' but to say so out loud would mean instant dismissal. There was no real recognition of our rights as self-employed performers. Being ten minutes late at most clubs could get you sacked easily, no matter how good you were at your job. It made my blood boil. I can always appreciate that running a business relies on staff turning up on time, but this was another type of control. It had less to do with the profitability of the club – and everything to do with sending out a message to do as we're told.

It didn't bode well for business that the club was so empty. For months we had all been anticipating the presence of thousands of visitors to the area to convert to higher earnings, but if anything the crowds were probably keeping our usual patrons away. The hordes outside were not our kind of consumers – families and tourists, children with dreams in their eyes waving their little nationalistic symbols, not lads on tour, stag dos and men in suits looking for louche entertainment. The club was dead that day, and it didn't change much throughout the tournament. I remember meeting one group with official lanyards round their necks – members of an Eastern European team were proudly showing off one of their male athletes. They sat at the front of the stage watching the stage shows, tipping their obligatory pound coins for each dancer's collection, but they didn't go for any private dances and left after about half an hour. I wondered if they had expected us to be more fawning and deferential to their muscle-bound hero. As the Olympics got under way the club got no busier, despite the months, in fact years, of expectations that the biggest international sporting event on the planet would provide a boost to the local economy. 'The sex industry always booms when the Olympic Games comes to town' was a much repeated mantra during the run up to the event. It didn't look that way once it was upon us. The massive campaign to shut down the strip clubs of Hackney, led by the local council and pushed for by feminist groups, had massively stigmatised the venues. The attention and press that the clubs had caught meant they were more easily identifiable to the public, associating them more with moral panic than private pleasure seeking.

Working as a stripper in East London during the Olympic Games wasn't working out to be as lucrative as we had all anticipated. An atmosphere of depression quickly set in, one that I was familiar with. I've always hated working under the expectation of earning exorbitant amounts of money; the job is hard enough without feeling that kind of pressure, and pressure always fucks up the chances of making any money. Clients can smell it. There is a unique ambience in a club when a group of strippers get their hopes up and start buying into the hype that they will finally bag that crazy cash payout, the dream that gets us all hooked, only to be brought back down to earth by the harsh reality of barely breaking even at the end of an eight-hour shift. Even the shiniest of baby-strippers, brand new to the job with the enthusiasm of a puppy, can become jaded and fed up.

Once the Olympics started up, I started to get itchy feet. The rumour mill started churning out stories that dancers were making good money over in the West End. It was the brand name chain clubs, Stringfellows and Spearmint Rhino, that were attracting the international big spenders. I'd left it a bit late to jump on that bandwagon, but I knew Stringfellows held open auditions one afternoon a week so I thought, what the hell, I'll give it a go. I'd already worked at Stringfellows in Paris before and I knew it was a very different vibe from East London, where I felt more at home. We had to wear long gowns for our audition, and there was a weird formula we had to follow for the audition – there were three poles on stage, so three girls auditioned at a time, moving in a clockwise rotation, so we would all have a turn on the pole at the front centre of the stage. We also had to strip in a format, first song fully dressed, second song topless but keep the dress on like a skirt, third song lose the dress. I had a classic stripper dress, cut away at the sides and held together with chrome rings – it worked best if I didn't wear a G-string underneath. I kind of didn't get the memo that full nudity wasn't required for the audition. So when I got to the last song I let my dress fall and heard a gasp . . . I looked around to see the other two dancers both still wearing thongs, while I was giving full frontal fanny. It would have been funny had anyone else in the room had a sense of humour. Judging from the reaction of the managers auditioning us, I may as well have cracked out a dildo and penetrated myself right there on stage. I wondered if they knew they were in a strip club, since they seemed so offended by the sight of a naked female body. I picked up my things and no one spoke a word to me as I left the club; needless to say I didn't pass the audition.

Experiencing whorephobia is not a walk in the park, and the occasional shaming from people outside of my profession for the choices I've made as an adult selling my sexual labour has left its mark on my psyche. But when it comes from the very people I work alongside in the sex industry, from managers and staff members in actual strip clubs, it's a distinctively awful ordeal. There have been many things about stripping that I got used to: the late nights, the boredom, the sore feet, the precarious income, the makeup stains on my pillows. But I could never get used to being shamed by people working in the same damn business as me. Witnessing whorephobic language or behaviour is incredibly common in strip clubs, and I've seen over and over how a seething culture of stigma has become ingrained in the way they are run. The whorearchy is alive and well in strip joints, and it's bullshit. Surely we can do better by now, can't we?

Niki Adams, spokesperson for ECP, explains that the question 'is stripping sex work?' is complex and risks becoming a distraction. It is pointless unless asked within the context of 'what are we trying to do together?' meaning it depends more on whether the intention behind the question is to divide and oppress or to unite and build solidarity. She goes on to explain, 'It's important who is asking the question. For us as sex workers the considerations and intentions are very different from those whose intention is to repress, to isolate, to push underground. We've always been navigating this oppressive regime, whether that be the criminalisation of full-service sex work, or the harsh licensing of stripping.'[15]

Adams is sympathetic to the reasons why any sex worker may choose to present an identity that increases their chances of social protection and acceptance, but she doesn't see how internal disputes can contribute anything positive to the developing discourse around sex work. The question of identity for sex workers has always been about power:

> We are constantly having to ask ourselves 'does this give me more power or less?' If women feel isolated, when our backs are against the wall, we may choose to try and present our experience in the most sanitised, respectable way possible to connect with other women, perhaps non-sex workers. That's a problem for the movement . . . We can't turn on each other because of what we decide to call ourselves. As long as the

intention is to bring us together rather than divide, it doesn't really matter what the language is.[16]

The key motivation for a stripper to assume a sex working identity, and all that comes with it, is solidarity. The term creates a buffer behind which all workers can exist, no matter their level of privilege. Sex worker advocacy relies on those with higher levels of advantage, who have the capacity to write books, attend universities and build strongholds of followers, to bring forward the experience of sex workers with less power who are most likely to face criminalisation and police abuse. As Adams states, 'I think those of us that are more in the public eye, our first responsibility is to make a way for others, to represent the experience of sex workers with least power.' Building a mass movement requires unity, and the global adoption of a shared sex worker identity no matter the range of privilege or risk is the first step in the fight against oppression, since it recognises a shared struggle.

The question 'is stripping sex work?' is loaded with multiple considerations, and it seems more important to think about who is asking the question; in every respect the real answer is – it depends who you talk to. Centring on the voices and intentions of non-sex workers seeking to eradicate the sex industry creates a political regime in which sex workers are constantly navigating stigma and forced to choose an identity that affords them as much power as they can glean, sometimes at the cost of other sex workers. Under this regime of oppression, strippers wishing to discuss the differences between their jobs and full-service sex work may be disparaged by the wider sex working community. In this context, the question 'is stripping sex work?' feels like a loaded gun. Dialogue cannot happen until this tension drops.

For strippers who identify as sex workers, the position in the workplace is not straightforward. For example, one of the licensing conditions applied to SEVs is a ban on advertising, which means club owners often rely on dancers developing lasting consumer relationships with clients. Dancers generally text their regulars letting them know their work schedules and inviting them to the club. But although swapping numbers with a client is now common practice, it can still be used as grounds for firing a dancer, as meeting or communicating with customers outside of work may be legally recognised as soliciting, a criminal offence under the Sexual Offences Act 2003.[17] A stripper's ability and willingness to identify herself as a sex worker depends on her proximity to risk and access to power. If doing so not only makes her job more precarious, but also incriminates her, then talking openly about sex workers' rights in the changing rooms may not seem worth the act of solidarity. According to Belle Knox, the so-called 'Duke porn star' (whose nickname refers to her choice to become a porn performer to pay for her $60,000 per year education at Duke University in the States):

The whorearchy is arranged according to intimacy of contact with clients and police. The closer to both you are, the closer you are to the bottom.[18]

It's useful to conceptualise privilege and risk as a spectrum. Knox is a key example of someone whose access to power and privilege as a white American citizen, studying at a prestigious institution, means she can choose to carry the stigma that comes with being publicly out as a sex worker. The same cannot be said for someone much less well resourced – as illustrated by the following hypothetical workers, whose circumstances determine their relationship to risk.

A Brazilian woman with a UK work permit may have chosen to work as a stripper, but her Catholic background means the sex industry is reprehensible to her family so she might hide this secret for fear of them finding out. She may feel so stigmatised that she doesn't reveal her job to any official authority or declare her income and over time becomes extremely anxious about having a 'double life'. Her fears of being outed to her family, investigated by HMRC and having her visa revoked all overlap and merge into a singular fear of *being caught*; whether this fear is substantiated or not, her anxiety further contributes to her silence. She may be sending some of her earnings back home to support family or funding her education to elevate her economic conditions, or simply to have a comfortable life. But regardless of her motivations, she is not likely to be attracted by the sex workers' rights move-ment since she simply has too much to lose.

A white, British-born, English-speaking, working-class strip-per, whose chosen work does not threaten to disrupt her life too much, can more comfortably reveal her job. But because prostitution is still heavily stigmatised by her friends and family she might have leveraged acceptance by reassuring them that she is absolutely not a sex worker. 'It's all a bit of harmless fun' and 'she's always in control' are the narratives she becomes attached to. The term 'sex work' is a threat to her personal relationships, so she won't assume the identity for fear of social exclusion.

Another white, British stripper who works to fund her degree, and has realised that sex work is her best economic option for the moment, may see things very differently. She is politicised, resourceful, tech-savvy, well informed of sex work legislation and aware of her human rights, whether or not they are observed at her club. She can conceive of herself as a participant in a shared struggle, whose radical demand for labour rights is adjacent to the wider demand for decriminali-sation. She may have to navigate the various risks that prevent her from using the phrase at work, but she has no problem assuming that identity outside her workplace in solidarity with less privileged sex workers than herself.

Full-service sex workers find themselves within a similar para-digm, even if they face a different set of predicaments. A migrant street sex worker who doesn't speak the language and is lacking structural support, or an addict whose treatment and housing are only offered on the basis that she abstains from prostitution, will be much closer to the arm of the law. But an independent escort who is well enough informed about the legal system to know she has the right to legal counsel or to refrain from talking to the police is in a far more privileged position. Any sex worker with access to the knowledge and resources required to defend herself in the legal system, or demand her labour rights, has unquestionably benefited from the work done by previous generations of sex worker activists and advocates – so much so that the term 'sex worker' demarcates privilege itself.

Sex workers fighting for harm-reduction and self-determination are creating the social and political spaces for dialogue to take place – and once again we see the sex working community doing the extra work, the heavy lifting of building their own platform to centre the voices and intentions of sex workers themselves. But the position is untenable: they are first required to show that they are all fighting the same struggle by assuming a shared identity, while at the same time trying to develop strategies for safety and empowerment, which relies on the discussion of their differences. Perhaps once it is built sex workers can use their platform to discuss their differences *and* their shared experiences without fear of being stigmatised for either conversation, regardless of what label they prefer to use.

5

WHAT'S WRONG WITH REGULATION? A CAUTIONARY TALE

The aims and objectives of this policy are therefore to promote; a. prevention of crime and disorder b. public safety c. prevention of public nuisance d. protection of children from harm e. improvement in the character and function of the city, or areas of it

—Westminster SEV statement of licensing policy 2012

Working at the White Horse was a laugh sometimes. Day shifts were pretty chilled for the most part, since hours could go by sometimes without a customer walking in. I mainly entertained myself by finding people to talk to. At some point they hired a new DJ, this young lad from South London with impeccable taste in music. In between the tired stage-show staples used by bored strippers who weren't bothered what they danced to he played amazing sets of progressive house; it was refreshing to be working alongside a genuinely talented DJ for a change. Being an audio-phile I soon found myself chatting to him about music. He was friendly and easy to chat to, a bit flirtatious but he knew the difference between flirting and harassment so never crossed the line.

One day I was doing an afternoon shift with Saskia, a veteran stripper who was still dancing in her forties, or her fifties, no one knew and it didn't matter because she was a legend. Customers who had known her for years still came in especially to see her, she was one of those salt-of-the-earth, part-of-the-furniture types who'd seen and heard it all. The White Horse was one of the few remaining pubs where we collected our tips in pint jugs before going on stage. We'd then go straight to the stage, leaving our jugs (sometimes full of money) in the DJ booth along with our purses and phones while we performed our stage routine. After we'd get off stage we'd then take the pint glass behind the bar to change up the pound coins for notes. The DJ was in a position of trust, and we never questioned that. Saskia, who had a keen eye on her money, kicked up a fuss that day; some cash was missing from her purse. As it happened, the pub owner was managing the bar that day, and while Saskia was brewing up a storm the young DJ pulled the juvenile move of pretending he'd found a note down the back of the sound desk, suggesting it had fallen out of her purse while she was dancing. It took them no time at all to check the CCTV. At the end of the shift he was called into the office, no doubt to be confronted with video evidence of his sticky-fingered actions. I saw him leave the building with guilt emblazoned across his face.

The news of the DJ thief spread rapidly and the changing room lit up with suspicion that he'd regularly been helping himself to our money pots. Most of us could remember that strange feeling recently, questioning whether we'd miscounted our earnings. I felt betrayed as I'd developed a friendship with him. It was a big enough story to keep the gossip mill running for a few weeks, though we never heard anything more of him. I understood at the time that the owner had told Saskia she could report it to the police if she wanted, but she chose not to. Most strippers want nothing to do with the cops – none of us wants a police officer looking down their nose at us, saying something that implies, 'well, you work in a strip club, what do you expect?' The pub owner could have also reported the crime to the police since the perpetrator was clearly captured on CCTV. They also chose not to, and it wasn't until later that the significance of this sunk in.

Having a crime committed in a venue would count against a proprietor when it was time for their SEV licence to be renewed; one of the things the council looks at is the police record of crime linked to the venue. Any regular bar would probably be able to report a crime of this sort without the pressure of having their licence so closely inspected. But with the deepest of irony, efforts to clamp down on crime and disorder in strip clubs were probably increasing the chance of crime going unreported. SEV licences are more precarious since the council are looking for any reason to revoke them. There's a hypervigilance towards adult entertainment that other venues don't have to work around. It feels like a weird double bind: you're damned if you do and you're damned if you don't. So we carried on like before, heads down; don't say anything because if you rock the boat we all drown.

Licensed venues are a good thing. At least that was the logic
offered by the vicar of Shoreditch Church, Rev. Paul Turp,
when speaking to the press about why he supported the campaign to save Hackney's strip joints in 2010. Without licences,
he said, the area would see a rise in illegally run venues such
as the ones that had blighted Shoreditch previously. 'It will
push the sex industry underground resulting in more women
working dangerously on the streets.'[1] His argument for legal,
licensed and properly regulated venues was clear: the alternative is worse. Over the years serving the community in
Shoreditch, Rev. Turp had seen for himself the direct consequences of a sex industry run by pimps and criminals, and he
argued vociferously for the council not to ban safely run venues
for strippers to work in. Disrupting the power held by abusive
pimps and managers is one clear objective of legalising the sex
industry. However, taking power away from a violent mob and
handing it to the state does not sufficiently reduce harm if the
state does not adequately protect workers who are most vulnerable to being victimised. There are many lessons to be
learned about sex work policy in the UK from looking at the
last ten years of strip club regulations.

The current licensing regime requires many strip clubs to
reapply for their SEV licence on an annual basis. By comparison, a personal licence, which authorises a *person* to sell alcohol, lasts for ten years. A premises licence, which authorises
the sale of alcohol in *designated premises*, lasts indefinitely (for as

long as the premises remain in use). This variation illustrates one of the many ways sexual entertainment is treated as inherently different to other forms of regulated night-time activity. In theory, annual SEV renewals are supposed to be important and necessary interventions, each time presenting an opportunity to scrutinise the duty of care a club has to its employees and customers. However, in practice it can go very differently.

Renewing an SEV licence is a long and convoluted process – it effectively means the club has to restart their business every year, since they are compelled to go through the same process they followed in order to get their SEV licence in the first place. A licence application must be submitted before a certain deadline, which is then followed by a period of consultation (normally twenty-eight days). During this period of consultation the local community gets to have their say; those in the know will understand this as an important window to either object to or approve of the existence of the particular SEV. Women's rights groups often use it as a platform to organise around, encouraging fellow campaigners to send template letters to the council that often use language speaking on the harms of sexual objectification and gender-based violence. Club bosses also have the chance to invite friends, neighbours, customers, and dancers themselves to write in letters of support to the council, defending their licence.

Camden Council's policy on SEVs has ordained that all

SEV licence renewals must 'go to panel', which means in practice that a decision cannot be made by one licensing official alone. The whole committee must be assembled for all the evidence to be heard and for everyone involved, which includes club bosses and/or their legal representatives, local voices and objectors, and generally anyone with the legal right, to have a say. A decision is really made on the grounds of who can put forward a better legal argument. Under licensing law, a licence cannot be denied on moral grounds. In practice this means the only objections to strip clubs likely to carry any weight are those indicating a breach of regulations in some form or other. In 2015 an objection was made against the SEV renewal of Charlie's Angels in Tower Hamlets, East London, on the basis that their overflowing bins were causing a public nuisance[2] (insert your own joke about taking out the trash). There are several different types of breach in regulations that can put a club at risk of losing its licence. This is not so different from a regular pub; selling alcohol outside of authorised trading hours, for example, or anti-social behaviour (excessive noise levels or illegal activities like gambling and drug-dealing being most common) can all result in the loss of a venue's licence to trade. But there is also another type of breach that focuses on the behaviour of dancers themselves, creating unnecessary stigma, and arguably doing more harm than good.

This is the strict rule that dancers may not touch patrons, which means full-contact lap dancing has been effectively outlawed. A full-contact lap dance involves a higher degree of intimacy than a non-contact private dance. While customers keep their clothes on, a lap dancer doesn't hold back from straddling their lap, pressing her body against them and indulging them with intimate touch. This is not necessarily sexual – it's often consistent with the human connection and physical validation sought from a massage therapist, for instance. Dancers are no longer allowed to place a hand on a customer's knee, shoulder or chest, sit on their lap or grind on their thigh, no matter what the level of nudity or, more importantly, consent is.

Enforcement of the no-touching rule leads to some bizarre, even farcical, situations; in some clubs dancers must perform a private dance behind a velvet rope, or on a special purpose-built podium (which of course enables club managers to impose fines on any dancers who are caught stepping one foot off the platform). Physical contact between strippers and their clients has become strictly forbidden in England and Wales under the Policing and Crime Act 2009, and over the last ten years of enforcing the new law, has become the latest taboo within a long history of legal obsession over the private sexual behaviours of consenting adults. Contact lap dancing itself is the intolerable act, the activity that cannot be allowed even inside a licensed strip venue.

The no-touching rule is intended for the benefit and protection of female workers. This sounds fair in theory until it is understood that these lap dances provided thousands of women with their bread-and-butter. The implicit reasoning is a little more complicated; a lap dance is close enough to a sex act to be forbidden as the basis for a commercial business under the terms of the Sexual Offences Act 2003. Legalising contact lap dancing would be a bit too close to legalising full-service sex work. Knowing that the no-touching rule has more to do with curtailing visible sex work in publicly regulated spaces somewhat undermines the argument for protecting workers – especially once we understand how the rule is used to scrutinise and vilify dancers. The story of Laura (not her real name) perfectly illustrates everything that is wrong with the regulatory procedure.[3]

LAURA

There is no clear trajectory for women who strip. For some it is a short-term stepping stone, for others it's a longer-term sideline to fund their ambitions, or provide an income for their families. For many it is a way out of poverty. Some dancers are able to carve a career out of stripping, and Laura is one of those known in the industry as a career stripper. She began dancing at the age of nineteen, and is still working as a stripper today at thirty-six. Her job has become integrated with her identity, and her passion for stripping reaches further than meeting her own needs; Laura is an active member of the East London Strippers Collective (ELSC) and the trade union branch United Sex Workers. She is doing a law degree with the aim of specialising in employment law, hoping to support women working in the sex industry. Her own story perfectly illustrates the current situation for strippers in the UK, in terms of how precariously positioned they are within the legal and business frameworks that regulate their jobs. She was happy to be interviewed for this book, but chose to be anonymous, since her work as a stripper remains as precarious as it ever has been.

Laura comes from a white, middle-class British family, with enough money to go round. She is well educated and could have done any number of different jobs, but as a fun-loving party-girl personality type, being a stripper was a choice to capitalise on something she was doing anyway – drinking, flirting and being the life and soul of every party. For her, dancing in the early to mid-2000s was an easy choice to make. The rise of 'raunch culture' opened the door for a new generation of women to make different kinds of choices, and Laura saw stripping as a perfectly reasonable option to monetise her labour. If she was going to do a job, she may as well enjoy herself and make a healthy profit.

Stripping was Laura's ticket to travel the world. She worked in Japan and Australia, declaring 'the highlight of my dancing career was working during the Melbourne Grand Prix'. Following the money, she became the kind of enviable globetrotter that many people might see as aspirational. As much as she worked and travelled, she spent along the way. Her earnings were used to pay for flights, accommodation, sumptuous food and a generous social life. Her contribution to local and international economies has not been insignificant. As well as sometimes making big bucks, strippers can also spend big bucks, and Laura is no exception. Not only has she worked in strip clubs, she's also made them a regular part of her own social life. 'They have kind of become my happy place. If I'm on a night out with friends, or on a date, or just looking for a new experience, strip clubs have always been my go-to suggestion. I've spent so much money on strippers.'

Getting an education was not something Laura neglected. She enrolled to do a degree in Politics and International Relations, and when she applied she was accepted at several of the most prestigious universities in the country. However, on arrival at university in the north of England, she soon decided the location wasn't for her as she was too far away from her earning potential in the top London clubs, so she quickly pulled out of her first term. In her own words, 'I made a decision there and then to study at the next most prestigious university that was as close to my work as possible.' She settled on a West London university, studying during the week and stripping on weekends and holidays. Unlike the majority of university graduates, Laura already had a well-paid job upon finishing her course. Still, she thought she would venture out and got herself a position in the City of London financial district as a PA for an investment firm. She was on a starting salary of £26,000, but she found that after tax deductions she wasn't taking home as much as she'd like, and was still moonlighting as a stripper on the side for a bit of extra spending money. Eventually the investment company closed, as did so many during the aftermath of the global financial crisis of 2008, and so Laura found herself dancing full time once more.

Then Laura's life took a different direction. In 2013 she quit dancing for several years to pursue a relationship with a partner whose income was big enough to support both of them, and started preparing for a new chapter as a wife and mother. A week before giving birth she was still actively involved with the ELSC, proudly showing off her baby bump at an event she helped organise alongside her fellow stripper colleagues. She became a mum at the age of thirty-two and all seemed well, until economic crisis hit again. The uncertainty of the markets meant that her partner's income could no longer be relied upon to support the family. After around eighteen months of struggling to make ends meet, Laura's decision to go back to stripping was no longer about meeting her own needs. She had a child to provide for, and the responsibility of being a parent kicked in. Stripping in 2017 was no longer as lucrative as it had been a decade before, but she knew she could still turn a better than average income. She had been out of the game for some time and it took a little while to regain the body confidence she had before giving birth; she threw herself into gym sessions to shift her post-partum body weight. Soon enough she got back into the routine of stripping, and making the most of the connections she had made over the years, she landed herself a place at a well-located central London strip club, Platinum Lace.

Platinum Lace, or PL, is a chain of strip clubs throughout the UK. The company director, Simon Warr, was previously a business partner at Spearmint Rhino before breaking away to open a separate chain of rival venues. To the untrained eye, there is little difference between the two brands – both have a corporate image with similar internal décor, huge gold-framed prints of topless women in the style of early 1990s soft-core porn. For the dancers themselves, there aren't too many differences in terms of working conditions either. Both clubs charge dancers house fees and commission; both expect dancers to conform to a strict regime of shift patterns, working hours and a heavily detailed list of rules. Importantly, both clubs frown on moonlighting, meaning a dancer cannot work at Spearmint Rhino one night and pop over to PL the next.

Initially Laura had to sign up to work four nights per week at Platinum Lace, their standard policy for dancers. Laura heavily relied on friends, family and her partner to provide childcare while she went back to working nights. Eventually, since she was friendly with the club bosses, they did her the favour of cutting her nights down to three per week. Shifts there are long and late, sometimes until 6 a.m. PL opens at

3 p.m. every day, and dancers can work day shift or night shift, sometimes putting in a double (when the club permits it). As a mum, working during the day was never really an option for Laura, so her nights normally began at 7 or 8 p.m. The house fee is £58 before 9 p.m., £88 after 9 p.m. They also take 20 per cent commission off everything the dancers earn, plus a list of prices for spending time in the VIP rooms that some might find convoluted and difficult to understand. According to Laura, PL is a pretty standard club when it comes to vacuuming up percentages of dancers' earnings. But they have a more relaxed style of management; Laura can take an hour off for dinner and nip out to Chinatown for a bite to eat if she likes. She is on good terms with her club, she complies with their requirements and in return she earns a comfortable enough living. She's pretty happy working there.

After six months or so of being back in business, personal circumstances and the breakdown of her relationship led her to make big life decisions. Dancing was fine as a temporary measure, but in the long term she wanted something better. She'd chosen her undergraduate degree knowing that at some point in the future she could convert it into a law degree with further post-graduate studies. She applied to go back to university, on a part-time basis, and gave herself a new set of targets. Her stripping income would now be used to invest in her own and her son's future; as she says in her own words, 'stripping is now funding my goals of qualifying as a lawyer and owning property within three years from now'. At this point Laura has a lot on her plate: raising a toddler, studying part-time, working three nights a week to pay rent and put food on the table, and any spare time she spends involving herself in activism and trade union meetings. The term 'superwoman' is not too far off the mark.

On 12 July 2018 England got knocked out of the World Cup semi finals. Strippers all over the country were poised to have a good night if they won, but once the result came in the jaded disappointment was felt yet again. Laura was hoping for a good shift that night, but she resigned herself to the likely drudgery that lay ahead. So she was pleasantly surprised when she had a customer go for a double dance and then a fifteen-minute VIP with her. He seemed very interested in her, asking her lots of questions about herself and her pursuits, he wasn't drunk or rude and didn't try to push her boundaries; he was the ideal customer. Little did she realise he was an ex-policeman turned private detective, hired by an opponent of the club to prepare a report that would end up used as evidence by the City of Westminster licensing sub-committee during the next licensing renewal hearing for PL.

Laura's mystery shopper turned out to be a retired cop called Stuart Jenkins. According to his own report, 'I am a former Police Officer having retired from the Metropolitan Police after completion of over thirty years' exemplary service. Throughout my police career the majority of my service was spent on specialist units engaged on proactive operations.'[4] These included firearms and surveillance officer, overt and covert licensing operations, investigation of serous criminal offences within licensed premises; he spent nearly a decade in total serving under the Clubs & Vice Unit, and is a Home Office qualified Crime Reduction Officer and Crime Prevention Design Advisor. It's reassuring to know that his impressive résumé of intercepting crime is being put to good use, hunting out strippers who have wandering hands.

Stuart Jenkins along with a colleague, fellow ex-police detective Nicholas Mason, visited Platinum Lace for the specific purpose of looking for breaches to their licensing conditions. His target? Catching dancers out for breaking the sanctimonious no-touching rule. He spent a total of £374 in pursuit of his aims; £30 entry for both men, £24 on bottles of beer, £40 for a naughty forty lap dance, £160 on fifteen minutes in VIP, and £120 on a lesbian dance. In his report he describes in salubrious detail his encounters with Laura,[5] and the various examples of bodily contact he experienced.

As she started to dance she forced my legs apart with her legs. She began to perform an erotic dance as before but this time there was physical contact as she ground her body against mine. Once she had removed all her clothes she brushed her breasts across my forehead; and rubbed my nipples through my shirt with her hands. She faced away from me and pushed her buttocks back into my chest, then sat down in my lap grinding her buttocks into my groin area. She straddled my upper leg and ground her buttocks on each of my upper legs in turn. At one stage she reached inside my shirt and pulled the hair on my chest. I asked her to stop this as it was painful which she did. At times she performed a floor show exposing her vagina and anus to me as she opened her legs wide.[6]

Laura wasn't to learn the identity of her mystery shopper for many months. She eventually found out when the club suspended her for a fortnight as punishment for breaking the rules. She said, 'The annoying thing is that his report went in as evidence during the public consultation period, but that was a long time afterwards so there was no chance of checking his statement against the CCTV which had been automatically deleted by then. But what's worse is that I don't even get a chance to defend myself, or argue that his statement is an exaggeration. I study law – why couldn't I examine the allegations myself? Parts of it were physically impossible for me to do . . . I never straddled him, we're not allowed to straddle customers, that's the number one rule. But the worst part was the rawness of his language, he made me sound predatory and violent.'[7] Laura's frustration at being unable to respond in person to the report became more deep-rooted as the case went on.

Stuart Jenkins' evidence wasn't the only documentation against Platinum Lace provided to the licensing board, as City of Westminster did a bit of investigating of their own. City inspector John Oddi, employed by Westminster Council, was asked by his line manager to view nine hours' worth of CCTV footage from PL and 'to document any incidences of potential concern, especially any breaches of the "no touching" condition'.[8] It took him thirty hours to watch it all and produce his report; one can only imagine what spying on lap dancers for the best part of a working week does to a person's mind. No doubt he was paid more than minimum wage for the trouble. In his findings, he recorded 454 breaches of the no-touching rule, out of which ten incidents were categorised as most serious. These included:

12/09/18 00.34.14 Two female performers and two male customers in one booth. Both performers indicate to the male customers the CCTV cameras. Both male customers repeatedly try to touch both performers who resist their attempts. The female performer places her left foot on the male customer's thigh and leaves it there for seven seconds.

12/09/18 00.36.22 The male customer holds female performer's left ankle using his right hand for two seconds which she doesn't attempt to move away.

12/09/18 00.38.38 Female performer straddles the male customer's right thigh and brushes her inner thighs against him for seven seconds.

12/09/18 00.38.50 Female performer repeatedly touches the inside of the male customer's thighs using her knees for nine seconds.[9]

It seems odd that an incident in which a customer tried to cop a feel but is fended off by the dancer has made it into the list of most serious offences. Much could be made of John Oddi's repetition of 'male customer' and 'female performer', as though somehow the gender divide must be continuously restated lest anyone forgets. Yet again the dehumanisation and objectification of the people being watched within the language of the licensing process is arguably worse, or at least just as bad, as any sexual objectification that radical feminists campaign against. When taken out of context, it can hardly be understood that these private acts between grown adults, who have lives, personalities, families, aspirations and vulnerabilities, could be anything other than grubby interludes or abuses of power. Such is the problem of viewing sex work through the reductive lens of the law: it disregards the embodied experience of the human beings at the centre of it.

❧

Around about 2016 a close friend and fellow dancer came to me to talk about something that was giving her anxiety. May (name changed to protect her identity) was working at the Kings Mead in East London; something had happened during a shift that seemed pretty shady, and she was unsure what to do. She told me that at the beginning of the night while the club was still pretty quiet, the dancers were taken one by one into the VIP room by some random guy and asked to fill out a form. The only vague explanation given was that it was 'for licensing'. May was asked to sign a template letter and provide her legal name and address. At the time she felt really uncomfortable, and the prospect of giving her identity on some kind of official paperwork triggered serious anxiety, so she barely knew what she was doing or understand what the document was for. Being American she couldn't help freaking out. Her immigration status was actually pretty stable so it wasn't likely she'd be booted out of the country, but the low-level worry that immigration services will always look for an opportunity to deport foreign nationals means that women like May are forever looking over their shoulder, particularly if their work in the sex industry comes to the attention of the Home Office.

Sitting in the VIP room with some dude who hadn't properly introduced himself or fully explained his objectives, she felt like her options were limited. She instinctively understood from the power dynamics that he was acting on behalf of the club in some way. If she refused to fill out the forms, or questioned their purpose, it was pretty likely she may lose her job there (like all dancers, negotiating the fear of being sacked is continual). May did not feel at liberty to query what was happening. She obediently filled out the forms while he drank from a bottle of beer. Unsurprisingly, she wasn't given a copy of what she'd signed, and left VIP feeling tense and uneasy, a feeling that only grew over the next few days. After talking it over a little with me, we were still unsure of what had actually occurred, until she received a letter in the post a few weeks later. The letter was from the council, acknowledging receipt of her signed statement in favour of the club's licensing renewal. Some of the details came flooding back and she remembered that she'd signed some sort of statement with words to the effect of 'I'm very happy working here. There are no problems with this club.' It turned out the dancers at Kings had more or less been coerced into signing a template letter in support of the clubs' SEV licence renewal application. Which of course they were all compliant with – for the same reason they pay fines for being late, or missing shifts, or keep their mouth shut when they report abuses or health and safety hazards in the workplace – because they had no workers' rights.

Conditions at Kings were some of the worst in London. I worked there one winter, when I needed to pay for some expensive dental treatment. There was not really any heating to speak of, apart from a single radiator keeping the booth by the stage warm so there was somewhere for customers to sit that wasn't freezing. The rest of the place was painfully cold, often for hours at a time until there were enough people to warm the place up with body heat. Sitting in those temperatures for long periods while wearing only lingerie isn't healthy, so some of the dancers would wear long cardigans. I took to wearing my woollen grey coat, which looked like a Vivienne Westwood knock-off that I found in a second-hand boutique. I was approached by one of the owners who told me to stop wearing it. I talked back, arguing that I should be able to keep myself warm like the other dancers. His demeanour changed from mean to menacing. His eyes darkened; he was clearly infuriated by a dancer arguing with him.

One of the things about Kings that dancers had to negotiate was the constant presence of either one or both of the two owners, whom we all felt were intimidating and unsympathetic. They would camp out at one end of the bar for the entire night, drinking with a small clique of cronies. When dancers presented their pint glasses to the group for tips during jug collections, 'friends' of the boss would usually rebuff them saying, 'It's OK darlin', I'm with him,' indicating to one of the men in charge of the joint, who would glower at any dancers with the audacity to ask the group for payment.

The changing room was a disgraceful space, overcrowded and dirty. The private booths were a shambles, the fixtures and fittings were all filthy and broken, the threadbare, beer soaked, tatty carpet was curling up at the edges. There were carpet tacks poking up through the floor; I stabbed my toe more than once doing private dances in that place. They turned a blind eye to a bit of touching, in fact the VIP rooms were fairly loose. The whole place had such a tawdry, down-at-heel vibe that it was almost charming.

Kings didn't deal with hiring dancers directly; they relied on a woman running an 'agency' called Susanne. She charged us an 'agency fee' of £100 per month just to be offered shifts. When we arrived at Kings we still had to pay the £45 house fee at the beginning of every shift. The club also took £5 from every £20 private dance we performed, and they would keep track of our dances by having a member of staff watching us to count how many dances we were doing. Financially I did OK there. Once I made enough to pay my dentist bill I got the hell out. It was kind of an opportunity for personal growth to examine the limits of my own personal boundaries, since by this point I was a much more experienced dancer with several years under my garter belt. But for me working there was unsustainable. I realise I was in an incredibly privileged position to be able to walk away when I'd had enough. I knew there were plenty others working there who were far less financially stable than I was, whose proximity to poverty created the kind of instability that made exploitation easier. I remember one dancer who was incredibly vulnerable. She told me after coming out of a private dance with a client who had been pretty hands on, how confused she was about her boundaries, thinking to herself, 'Wait, did I consent to that?'

I took May's letter from the council and showed it to a lawyer friend who specialised in licensing and tenancy law. He explained that if the dancer who signed it wished to retract it she could, or if she wanted to change her statement from a positive description of the club to a negative one she could, so long as she acted within the required period of consultation. He also said that if she wanted to attend the licensing hearing she could. The letter contained all the information regarding the deadlines for responses and when the licensing hearing would take place. I went back to her and we discussed her options. With my activist brain in gear I hit upon the idea of using the licensing procedure as leverage to improve working conditions within the club. What if we approached the owners and said, 'Hey guys, you want your licence to be renewed, don't you? Well, how about you drop your outrageous house fees, sort out your club and treat us with some damn respect, then we won't dish the dirt on the way you run your club to the council.' But we didn't – May's income was too crucial, she couldn't risk losing her job, as per usual. The licence was renewed, and it was business as usual.

The City of Westminster Council licensing sub-committee finally sat to decide whether to renew PL's SEV licence on 28 February 2019. It had been over seven months since Laura's mystery shopper and at no point during that time was she approached to give her interpretation of events. During the hearing she had no legal locus to speak, address the claims and represent herself. Laura sat in the public gallery like a chastised infant, feeling more subjugated than she had ever felt stripping, furiously scribbling notes for her legal studies as she gained remarkable insight into the patriarchal workings of licensing law. 'Not one voice heard at that council meeting was from a dancer,' she explained. 'There were literally no dancers' voices throughout the entire thing. We have absolutely no right-to-reply. We are looked at, spoken about, referred to in written descriptions, our only presence is as seen through the eyes of other people.' It seems clear that sexual objectification is not the only way that strippers are dehumanised. The annual strip club licence renewals, which are held each year by licensing authorities throughout the UK, perfectly exemplify the intricate and established legal and social structures that silence and condemn sex workers. It is a well-practised routine at these legal hearings, with licensing officials (predominantly male), clubs owners (also usually male), objectors and anyone else with tuppence worth to give or an axe to grind, all prevaricating over the actions and deportment of dancers without ever once hearing their testimony.

It seems clear from the licensing procedure that council officials do not understand the uniquely difficult position that dancers are in. Dancers do not have a forum for whistle-blowing or raising complaints about a club's business; they have only two options. First, make a statement in support of a club in which case the licence is renewed and it's business as usual. Or secondly, make a statement calling out the club for exploitation but put their own jobs at risk while doing so. Neither of these feels like a genuine option to most dancers, so it makes sense that they don't normally want to get involved in licensing hearings. The fact there is no mechanism within state policy for dancers to raise a complaint and effect change, without making themselves more precarious in the process, once again reflects how their lack of employment security *creates* the likelihood of exploitation. Some more unlucky dancers like Laura, however, are dragged into the procedure whether they like it or not.

'It was disturbing how much detail he gave about me in the report,' says Laura. 'He included my age, where I'm from, where I live now, he described how I look, he talked about how I'm an activist for sex workers' rights and fighting with the collective and the union for better working conditions for dancers. I told him all that in a private setting but it didn't matter. I'm just glad I didn't tell him *too* much about myself.' On a more serious note, though, she lamented, 'I've spent so much time in my life fighting for dancers to be acknowledged and advocating against stigma . . . but as well as that the amount of time and effort I spend on my hustle, crafting my stripper persona, choosing what I wear, creating the perfect back story, building the performance, all the little details even down to what perfume I wear – so much hard work all for nothing because of a lap dance.'

The hearing took over three hours in total. Most licence committee meetings take a fraction of the time. The two licence applications heard earlier that morning, both for new premises licences in the West End, took 30–45 minutes each. In their summing up, the council gave PL an ominous warning. Laura wrote in her notes how City of Westminster licensing officials stated in no uncertain terms that the evidence disclosed represented a serious infringement:

> SEV licences are not open to interpretation. Conditions are set out clearly, no touching means no touching. A substantial number of breaches have occurred. We find the evidence from the police officers credible, although strange that it wasn't provided sooner so that CCTV could be obtained. These incidents should not be minimised . . . The council expects appropriate disciplinary action to be taken regarding the dancers concerned.[10]

The club was reprimanded, but ultimately the licence was renewed. PL were told they could expect to see more inspections going forward, and should consider themselves on notice until they 'adjust standards' accordingly. But the breaches were not considered serious enough, despite the enormous number of man-hours spent examining the 'female performers', to warrant a revocation of their SEV licence. One might be forgiven for feeling that the entire process had really only one rationale behind it: to shame the club and their dancers.

CLASS WARS

Ideas of respectability and class are explored in a study titled 'Respectability, Morality and Disgust in the Night-Time Economy: Exploring Reactions to Lap-dancing Clubs in England and Wales', published in 2015 by Phil Hubbard and Rachel Colosi, professors of sociology at the University of Kent. The researchers set out to gather public opinions about lap-dancing clubs and their findings were remarkably clear: local residents and passers-by generally view lap dancing as vulgar, with a strongly moralistic tone interwoven throughout the public discourse.

Often targeted by campaigners in England and Wales as a source of criminality and anti-sociality, in this paper we shift the focus from fear to disgust, and argue that Sexual Entertainment Venues (SEVs) are opposed on the basis of moral judgments that reflect distinctions of both class and gender . . . the opposition expressed to lap dance clubs is part of an attempt to police the boundaries of respectable masculinities and femininities, marginalizing the producers and consumers of sexual entertainment through 'speech acts' which identify such entertainment as unruly, vulgar and uncivilized.[11]

Despite the fact that licensing laws and public policy are written to protect businesses from moralistic and religious opposition (for example, a Muslim cannot object to an alcohol licence for a local convenience store on moral grounds because of their religious beliefs), it doesn't seem as though lap-dancing clubs are protected against moralism in the same way, leading to discrimination throughout the licensing procedure. The licensing regime of striptease clubs permits local residents to object to an SEV licence application or renewal on grounds of geographical location and proximity to local schools, historic monuments and religious buildings, which strongly indicates a moralistic approach to the venues.

Laura is well aware of the set of privileges that have likely kept her position at PL open. She is white, British, well educated and articulate; and, most importantly, friendly with the bosses. She was grateful that the club only suspended her instead of firing her, although being suspended for a fortnight pushed her back to the limits of her personal finances; no joke with a small child dependent on her. It was a small victory that she didn't lose her job, but had she been anyone less advantaged, a non-UK citizen or a woman of colour for example, she knows she would have been long gone. She is not the only single mum stripping at PL (or any of the UK's strip venues for that matter) and if she lost her job it would make her role as a parent even tougher. She would risk losing her place at university and likely fall into financial hardship. She doesn't like to consider how wide and acute the ramifications would be had the club lost their licence that day.

Left out of the summing up was any mention of the cost of the SEV licence, which on average costs up to ten times more than a regular premises licence. An application for a new SEV licence costs between £1,000 and £3,500,[12] while a new premises licence costs between £100 and £1,905.[13] It stands to reason that (like the 'nudity waiver' fees mentioned previously in Chapter 4) the council have a financial incentive to preserve the SEV licence rather than lose another stream of revenue. The investigatory work done by civil servants like John Oddi is not done on a voluntary basis, and the hourly legal fees of running a three-hour hearing doesn't come cheap. The term 'jobs for the boys' springs to mind. Nor was there any mention of dancers' welfare; throughout the entire seven-month process there was no consultation done with dancers into the amounts of money being charged by the club in house fees and commissions, or the number of dancers working in competition with each other at any given time. The report paid no heed to the financial pressures placed on dancers, or the circumstances of their work; not one licensing official approached any of the dancers independently to come forward, either at work or, say, at the council offices, to provide witness statements as a self-employed group. Instead of obsessing over the precise number of seconds a foot made contact with someone's crotch, no time was spent looking at dancers' worker status, or looking more closely at the structural and systemic violations dancers face in the sector generally. But then again, if the purpose of licensing clubs has little to do with seriously protecting women from exploitation, or understanding what makes them vulnerable in the first place, why bother?

———

Something has gone very wrong when a fully-grown woman is told off for sitting in someone's lap. In all my years of dancing I haven't found a single club that dealt with the issue of touching without falling back on shame and condemnation to implement the rules. I've never been taken aside by a rational and sympathetic manager to talk it through with care and consideration. There's really only two approaches. One is to turn a blind eye, in which case there is inevitably a failure to protect dancers from unwanted contact and an inability to support and respect the variations between each dancer's boundaries. There is no regard for nuance; take the rules away altogether and workers suddenly have to fend for themselves without any support from employed staff members. The other approach is a despotic management style in which paid staff are given too much authority to micromanage and intimidate dancers, which leaves us feeling humiliated and customers feeling disturbed and unlikely to return.

As I travelled to work in different clubs I saw enforcement of rules in some venues that was bordering on traumatic. Some time ago I was at Stringfellows, Paris, a strictly no-touching club. Private dances were performed in a communal VIP area decked out to look like a sumptuous Rococo salon with low divans for customers to lay back on. Every time I performed a private striptease in there I would struggle to keep my balance in my teetering heels, and since there were no arms of chairs or sides of booths to hold on to, my only option was to reach up to touch the ceiling giving me an anchor point. I probably looked like one of those giant Greek column sculptures of goddesses holding up a temple roof.

While I was performing for one client I turned round to show him my back and bum, lowering myself into the classic bump and grind move in his lap. It had been a busy night and I was exhausted, my thighs were straining so I allowed myself to partially sit in the guy's lap, closing my eyes to enjoy the momentary relief of transferring some of my body weight onto him while allowing myself a few seconds of human contact. I was wrenched out of the moment when one of the enormous security guards who was patrolling the dance area yelled at me. 'TOUCHE PAS, EH?' was his remonstration, towering over me with pure disdain and leaving me feeling like a fucking school kid. After he was gone, my customer could see how shaken I was. How could anything like that ever be good for the business? Hashtag not-all-bouncers of course; there were some good guys over the years and they were only doing their jobs as they had been taught. But it only adds insult to injury when the very security staff who are employed for our protection become dictators, especially when our house fees are going directly into their wage packets.

Many different factors and external forces fuck with my ability to consent. Once again, top of the list is money. When I initially started dancing one of my earliest observations was the range of personal boundaries between dancers. This range was very rarely appreciated by club staff, and certainly wasn't acknowledged within the list of rules that were always spelled out to us on arrival at a new workplace. I'd be lying if I didn't say it was a source of frustration, and still is within the stripper community – strippers on social media forums frequently decry and bemoan co-workers who are more willing to cross lines and 'bring down standards' in the club, since this apparently makes the playing field uneven. But on closer observation the playing field was never even in the first place. When you have a group of workers who, instead of being paid a basic wage, have to pay for the chance of competing for an undisclosed amount of money in a contest where people aren't necessarily playing the same game, it's not surprising to find an assortment of means and limitations within the room. As a stripper when you're having a shit night and you've paid a £100+ house fee, got rent to pay and you've made hardly any money while watching dancers all around you selling private shows all night, then of course you're willing to cross your own boundaries to secure the income you need. And then there's those nights when you're raking it in, you're doing more dances than you think you can physically perform and you find yourself examining your limits because you can, for your own entertainment or arousal. Alcohol is another variable in the experiment, as are hormones and sexual chemistry, which have frequently taken me by surprise. Like recreational drug use, stripping can take you to some truly altered states of mind, sometimes ghastly and other times healing. There are few other environments as messy and tumultuous as a strip club in full flow and it isn't news to anybody who has worked in one that trying to uphold personal boundaries within that kind of mix can be extremely challenging. And then on top of that if venue staff are on your case, breathing down your neck and looking for you to slip up so they can mete out some form of discipline or another – firing, fining, suspending, or good old-fashioned humiliation – no one is going to be on your side when you have a grabby client and need back up. How anyone can think that such a space can be successfully managed using punitive and dictatorial methods beats me.

After a few years of figuring stuff out I began avoiding clubs that had controlling management styles, which were usually the big name chain clubs who charged the highest house fees and had a brand to protect. I preferred the smaller, scuzzier, independent places, where I normally had the freedom to set my own boundaries (although I still rarely had any guarantee I would have club staff on my side when I needed it). Kings was a horror show of a club but at least they left us alone when it came to touching. I vividly remember one customer who was clearly deprived of touch and probably had very few options for seeking it. He had a nervous demeanour when he walked into the empty club; I was the first to approach him and selling a private dance was an easy invitation. He followed me into a private booth and paid his £20; as I began to slowly move closer to him I could sense his need for intimacy. It wasn't unpleasant, he wasn't being gross or pushing my boundaries, he barely said a word, nor was he trying to touch me. I could clearly see how bereft he was of touch, perhaps from women, perhaps in general, and it started to feel like an honour to be giving him something so essential and human.

About half way through the dance, once I'd established that he wasn't a groper, I climbed onto his lap, straddling him in a kind of embrace that he may have never had before. His body responded, not sexually but energetically, he went limp and his breath escaped with a gasp. It wasn't an orgasm, he was just grateful. I don't think he was looking for sexual release; in that moment he was merely allowed to exist, and I think that need had become critical for him. Energy healers work with this kind of reaction from their customers on a daily basis, and I'm not the only sex worker to have felt something akin to an energy exchange with clients. He thanked me with a rare sincerity before he left the dance room, and as I sat down to put my underwear back on I could have cried, while stuffing the £20 I'd just earned into my purse. I'll never know what was going on in his life to result in such yearning, and while I'll likely never see him again I often remember him as another casualty of toxic masculinity, and hope that he's doing OK.

When I hear mantras like 'Objectification! Sexual Exploitation!' repeated by campaigners who want to shut down my workplace, I feel objectified by them. I know how humanising it can feel to give someone the gift of touch, no matter how briefly. I wouldn't say I'm a sex-positive 'happy hooker' and always glad to be doing good in the world. I'm sick of the toxic conditions I work in. But doing sex work is hard enough without the bizarre and dictatorial attempts at intervention made by local government and concern groups, or the chauvinistic arm of club management. Frankly, no one has the right to decide what I do with my body and whom I do it with. That right has been gradually eroded year by year, to the point that the strippers' own bodily autonomy is almost wholly absent from strip clubs these days. It wasn't always this bad. When I first started stripping in 2006 many clubs had a relaxed approach to touching. It was widely understood that customers could not touch us, they had to sit on their hands or keep them by their sides. In return for this act of trust we could get close, lap dance, sit on them, use their knees for balance, rub their chests and grind in their laps. There was an implicit social contract that if a customer tried to touch us the club would back us up, no questions asked. Normally if dancers were flouting the rules it was dealt with quietly by management, but most of the time we didn't have to; generally there were enough customers and enough money to go round, and we could walk away from a customer if they misbehaved. It was a surprisingly self-regulating environment, because it was private, intimate, and simply allowed. But the massive stigma campaign led by Object in 2009 aiming to smear and shame the industry into the gutter has succeeded, and now my physical contact with customers, whether sexual or not, is as reviled as sex work ever has been.

6

OBJECTIFICATION

Women had come so far, I learned, we no longer needed to worry about objectification or misogyny. Instead, it was time for us to join the frat party of pop culture, where men had been enjoying themselves all along. If Male Chauvinist Pigs were men who regarded women as pieces of meat, we would outdo them and be Female Chauvinist Pigs: women who would make sex objects out of other women

—Ariel Levy[1]

Closing down strip clubs is not a win for feminism, but try telling Sasha Rakoff that. Dr Sasha Rakoff is a feminist campaigner who has dedicated more than fifteen years of her life to one very particular aim: getting UK strip clubs shut down. She began her career in medicine and describes one singular experience as her moment of awakening. Working in a hospital one day she noticed a young girl pick up a copy of *The Sun*, the notorious British tabloid newspaper that made an institution out of printing an image of a different topless female model on Page 3 every day. Upon seeing the picture of a bare breasted woman, the child turned to her parents to ask, 'Why is that lady naked?' Dr Rakoff declares this instant as the final straw – seeing a young child exposed to a photograph of a topless glamour model was, for her, too much to bear. From that point on, Dr Rakoff has been campaigning whole-heartedly to shut down lap-dancing clubs and rid the world of what she sees as the scourge of sexual objectification of women.

It wouldn't be too much of a stretch to claim that Dr Rakoff is obsessed with strippers. In 2004 she founded the group Object, a human rights organisation set up to reverse the culture of commercial sexual exploitation. By 2016 she had left Object and begun a new group, Not Buying It. On their website, Not Buying It purport to 'challenge the exploita-tion of the porn and sex trade. We work side-by-side with survivors and the many others it harms.'[2] Since the website doesn't go on to qualify exactly who is meant by the 'many others' harmed by the sex trade, we are left with a gap for interpretation, into which any prejudice, stereotype or classic mainstream narrative about the harms of the sex industry may fit. Although, Object often work with local residents who disapprove of lap dancing on their high streets, so perhaps they might consider themselves to be harmed by the industry.

Object and Not Buying It have been the two most vociferous opponents of the strip club industry in the UK. Alongside an alliance of organisations, including the Fawcett Society, the Women's Support Project, Eaves Housing, and many individuals all united against the alleged harms being wreaked upon the British public, Dr Rakoff had her day during the public debate in the lead up to the Policing and Crime Act 2009. The reclassification of strip clubs that followed, which tightened up licensing laws and made running a lap-dancing club a whole lot harder, has had a noticeable impact on the prevalence and nature of sexual entertainment businesses in the UK. It ought to have been a win for Dr Rakoff and her team, but it would seem that she won't rest until she has eradicated the industry entirely.

Notable claims about her achievements abound. The One Hundred Women foundation website described her as having 'raised awareness of the realities of lap dancing and prostitution, changed the law so that local people now have a say as to whether a lap-dancing club can open, and made it a crime to pay for sex with someone who has been trafficked or pimped'.[3] The Policing and Crime Act 2009 did indeed include a list of new sexual offences alongside restricting the licensing regime around lap-dancing clubs, including paying for the sexual services of a prostitute subjected to force. It is a far cry, however, to claim that the entire bill of law can be credited to the work of one woman. Labour MP Harriet Harman who was Home Secretary at the time can shoulder a large part of the responsibility as well.

On paper it would appear that Dr Rakoff works hard fighting for female empowerment. It is true that the concepts of sexual objectification and exploitation are much higher up the list of things to worry about in mainstream culture now. The term 'objectification' itself is used routinely in a way it wasn't ten years ago. But on closer inspection it is unclear whether Not Buying It truly are having a positive wider social impact for all women or if Dr Rakoff's own version of empowerment actually comes at a price, the cost of which is borne by a smaller group of more vulnerable women. It is questionable the extent to which Not Buying It do indeed work 'side-by-side' with those who are harmed by the sex industry, or if Dr Rakoff is in fact creating counterproductive and incendiary narratives about women doing sex work (and about men who pay for sexual services), which are in turn harmful to sex workers.

In 2018 Not Buying It spearheaded a successful crowd-funding campaign in Sheffield, supported by an alliance of organisations including the Fawcett Society, Southall Black Sisters and Glasgow Women's Aid. Over £10,000 was raised to pay legal fees for a judicial review, a court hearing that requests a judge to re-examine a legal decision made elsewhere in a different court. When strip club licences are renewed a licensing committee passes them at a legal hearing, which is effectively a court of law. Sheffield City Council licensing committee had renewed the SEV licence of the only strip club in the city, Spearmint Rhino, for another year, despite nearly a hundred objections from local residents during the period of public consultation. To Not Buying It and their supporters, this decision was unacceptable. They were demanding a judicial review of the licence renewal, and this time they wanted the judge to look at the decision from the point of view of the Equalities Act 2010, a law that sets out to protect individuals against discrimination.*

Mounting a judicial review is no mean feat, and takes a tremendous amount of effort. It begs the question, what was it about this particular club that was deserving of such a targeted legal attack? A bit of digging around on the Not Buying It website reveals an eighteen-page pdf document titled 'Objec-

---

* Under the Equalities Act 2010, there are nine key characteristics to be protected against discrimination: age, disability, gender reassignment, marriage and civil partnership, pregnancy and maternity, race, religion or belief, sex, and sexual orientation. Those who were campaigning for the judicial review made the argument that Sheffield City Council were in breach of the Equalities Act by allowing a strip club to stay open. A council is a public body with a duty of care to their citizens, and so are legally bound to follow the Equalities Act to protect individuals – known as the Public Sector Equality Duty (PSED). If strip clubs are places where women may be subjected to gender-based violence and discrimination then renewing the licence would mean Sheffield City Council had fallen foul of their duty of care.

tion to Sheffield Spearmint Rhino Licensing Renewal by Dr S Rakoff, Not Buying It'.[4] The document is loaded with statements, demands, statistics, unreferenced quotes from strippers identified by first name only, all put together as Rakoff's own research. On the first page of the document Rakoff explains that when she comes to Sheffield for meetings, she most often meets people at the Showroom cinema café, which is directly opposite Spearmint Rhino. This may partly explain why Rakoff has decided to make Spearmint Rhino, Sheffield, the primary target for her ceaseless attacks on strip clubs. Its visibility in such a public space has become a symbol for the sex industry's existence and perhaps the regular reminder has become the motivation for her impressive workload. She doesn't clarify, however, why her meetings in a cinema café during the day would be disrupted by a venue that only opens at night.

The judicial review took place in June 2018. A local resident, known only as Irene, brought the claim to the court. Irene was a local grandmother who said she had 'serious concerns about the impact of establishments like these on the objectification of women. When the council consulted on the issue, various women came forward to say they had experienced harassment by men visiting the club.'[5] Irene was one of many local women who objected to the renewal of Spearmint Rhino's licence in 2017, stating there was a problem with harassment and public nuisance. During the hearing several witnesses came forward to give evidence. Many who had objected to the licence renewal

were there, as well as representatives from the various organisations. Local residents, including the claimant Irene, were given
a legal locus to speak at the hearing. A spokesperson from a
local disability charity took the stand to give testimony, claiming
that strip clubs could be compared to 'using dwarves as human
cannon-balls'. Statistics of gender-based violence at global and
national levels were proffered, and the dominant narrative in
the courtroom was a damning indictment against all strip clubs
in general. Many dancers showed up on the day of the hearing,
protesting outside the courtroom with placards and calling for
their workplace to stay open, defending their right to choose
how they make a living. Of course, in facsimile with so many
other legal hearings, none of the dancers actually working in
the club gave their testimony. They had to sit in the public
gallery in silence, listening to the court proceedings and shaking
their heads in dismay.

The outcome of the judicial review found in favour of Not
Buying It, confirming that Sheffield City Council were indeed
in breach of their Public Sector Equality Duty. The campaigners had cause to celebrate, and the press got their attention-
grabbing headlines. However, the war was not yet fully won.
The results of the judicial review did not mean that the doors
of Spearmint Rhino closed that night. A judicial review may be
a re-assessment of a legal decision but the council were still the
elected officials and were not legally compelled to change their
position. The counter-narrative about dancers being put out of

work and driven further underground into even more precarious forms of sex work hadn't gone unnoticed. The judicial review did not succeed in shutting down the club and Spearmint Rhino was allowed to go on trading. But Dr Rakoff was not ready to give up yet. She simply moved onto a new strategy.

Since the East London Strippers Collective was founded in 2014, getting involved with activism more seriously has led to all sorts of challenges. Media appearances were particularly demanding. In June 2018 I was invited to take part in a live debate on BBC Radio 4's World at One, *a prime-time national radio programme covering UK politics and current affairs. I was debating Charlotte Mead from the Women's Equality Party (WEP) via live link about the judicial review in Sheffield. Radio 4 felt like the epitome of middle-class politics; presenter Sarah Montague toggled deftly between topics, from discussions about Parliament, to Brexit, to global economics. But when she moved on to strip clubs, I could hear that unmistakable tension in her voice; a tone somewhere between curiosity and incredulity, the raised inflection at the end of her sentences, which seemed to say, 'Believe it or not, this is news.' I felt very welcome in the BBC Broadcasting House studios and Montague put me at ease. She didn't appear whorephobic in the slightest, and clearly understood the human side of the story; that attempts to shut down strip clubs would risk putting women out of work and into more precarious conditions, and actually seemed to be taking my side in the debate. But the tension around sex work was there nonetheless, this time so subtle that it was almost imperceptible.*

I'd already done several media interviews by then, but the pressure of live broadcasting is never diminished with practice. Charlotte Mead was live-streamed to the programme from Sheffield, a disembodied voice at the end of the line that was fed into my headphones. The campaign to get the one singular strip club in Sheffield shut down was clearly under way. The judicial review was set to happen later that week. I listened to Mead state all the usual arguments, that in a democratic society the public had a right to decide whether they wanted a strip club in their city, the reference to dubious statistics on violence and the well-rehearsed statement that places which encourage men to objectify women are bad for society.

When it was my turn I gave a stark warning. I pointed out that shutting down strip clubs was pushing the industry underground into unregulated spaces, where the real violence and coercion take place. I spoke about parties I've worked at myself, private events in flats and hotels where there is no security to speak of and strippers are booked to entertain clients who have none of the same restrictions on their behaviour in private as they do in publicly regulated premises. I mentioned striptease agencies who care nothing about welfare and safety, who send performers to any old address without properly screening clients. I explained how shutting down strip clubs is not a win for feminism, that driving women into ever more precarious work, seeking other, riskier, forms of sex work to survive, undermined the aims of the feminist movement.

Mead reacted with a familiar mix of resistance and disapproval. My perspective on the industry was a challenge to her entrenched views on strip clubs; I felt she barely registered what I was saying. Even though Sarah Montague seemed genuinely sympathetic and supportive, Mead was given the final word in the debate. To me this revealed the systemic structure of keeping control of a narrative and preventing it from straying too far from the status quo. In the interest of providing 'balance', giving Mead the final say reinforced the received narrative that mainstream feminists have been in control of for decades, that if we are to become a truly equal society then strip clubs must go. Yet again I was unimpressed with the media machine that sought to use me as a character in their tightly constrained news item. Of course the member of the WEP had to have the last word, not the sex worker. The last voice in the argument has the greatest opportunity to make a significant impact on the audience, leaving the last words ringing in their ears.

I needn't have been annoyed as Mead was soon to make a surprising final statement. For her closing argument she appeared to dismiss everything I'd said, despite having spoken from personal experience about private parties I've worked at myself. She said, 'Well, there's no evidence that shutting down clubs pushes women into doing less safe work, and when we close them all down then men will just go and do something less sexist.' At that point the interview ended. I felt quite disoriented. I was always ready to be challenged and scrutinised, I've always known there are people who disagree with me and it's been my great privilege to be invited to speak to audiences willing to even listen. But I wasn't ready for such a preposterous comment. It was slightly funny even. As far as I was concerned it contained within it the precise tone of reductionism and basic misunderstanding of what sex work even is, never mind the complicated truths that lie within the sex industry, which radical feminists have been ignoring for decades.

I left Broadcasting House feeling a bit like Charlotte Mead had done my work for me. I had to trust that enough people could see through the limitations of the debate and the unsuitability of its formula to actually glean something useful from it. Like all media appearances, I had to hope that I'd managed to articulate enough information to disturb the thoroughly ingrained core beliefs held by the public about sex workers, just a little. It wasn't possible to completely dismantle them in a forum that simply does not allow for it. The media machine literally relies on objectifying people and their stories, distilling them down into digestible sound bites that are inoffensive enough for middle-class people to have on the radio in the background as they are making their lunch. Perhaps the most challenging task as an activist is learning how to humanise and recontextualise the facts of the sex industry without pushing so hard against the widely accepted versions, alienating those who may otherwise listen. As if sex workers' rights and safety weren't critical enough without having to tiptoe around the bourgeois sensibilities of Radio 4 listeners. Which is why it was such a blessing when Charlotte Mead shot herself in the foot; if I ever meet her I owe her a Porn Star Martini.

Men visiting lap-dancing clubs seems to be a problem for Dr Rakoff. Narratives are woven throughout the Not Buying It website that portray patrons of sexual entertainment venues as mere punters; nameless, faceless, 'drunk, highly sexually aroused men' who have barely any recognisable qualities as human beings, besides their libidinous nature. It is a testament to Dr Rakoff's hard work for the last fifteen years that the currently universally understood idea of strip clubs, at least within mainstream cultural accounts, is of places where only one singular activity takes place: the gratification of male sexual desire. There is no talking, no complexity or nuance, no kindness or compassion, no power play, no humanity whatso-ever, no possibility for any non-sexualised behaviour or inti-macy, only sleazy, grabby, monstrous men, preying upon the flesh of tender young innocents. They are certainly not thought of as places of work. The portrait of men as abusive actors within the sex industry is thoroughly ingrained through-out Not Buying It's rhetoric. Male behaviours in lap-dancing clubs are so much of a concern to Rakoff that in 2019 she went to extraordinary lengths to take action.

In late 2018 rumours started up among the UK stripper community that a women's rights organisation were secretly filming strippers at work. In May 2019 a news story broke in Sheffield that confirmed everyone's suspicions. It didn't gain much traction in the national press, but the ripple effects were felt immediately throughout dancer networks. Private chat forums were flooded with stories that dancers were being tar-geted at work by private investigators, focusing on one club chain in particular – Spearmint Rhino. The investigators had been hired to secretly film strippers at work, without their consent, with the aim of catching them in the act of breaking the no-touching condition of the club's licence. Stories began leaking into the press accusing clubs of 'forcing lap dancers into sex acts'.[6] Dancers' voices were predictably absent from the media coverage as a familiar set of tropes about women in the sex industry were routinely paraded through the public imagination.

Rumours soon turned to fact, as dancers around the UK began to piece together what had happened. It eventually emerged that strippers had been targeted at branches of Spearmint Rhino in Sheffield, Manchester and Camden, North London. At first it looked like the Women's Equality Party were the organisation behind the sting. Footage gathered from the club in Sheffield was presented at a meeting with Sheffield City Council as evidence of the club's breach of their licensing conditions, in a bid to get the venue (the singular remaining club in the city) shut down. In attendance at the meeting was Charlotte Mead, Women's Equality Party member for Sheffield, who used her WEP credentials for extra gravitas when presenting the dossier of evidence to the council. Her strident support of the campaign to close down strip clubs might have given the impression that the WEP was involved with the investigation. In a speech given at the Sheffield City Council's investigatory hearing, Mead allegedly referred to the private investigators as 'our investigators'.[7] But within a matter of days the WEP put out a statement distancing themselves from the covert operation, claiming no responsibility for the underhand activity.[8]

Importantly, in their statement the WEP refrained from apologising to the women affected, and surprisingly trotted out some of the statistics linking strip clubs to increased levels of violence (which have long been debunked, as explained in Chapter 7, The Victimhood Industry) to justify their policy on campaigning against strip clubs. The statement sent out an unclear message: they didn't condone the methods used and didn't defend Charlotte Mead, yet they supported the campaign to close down strip clubs, citing that doing so will end violence against women and girls. Later that month WEP member Megan Senior, who was standing as a candidate in the local elections for nearby Ecclesall, was asked during her campaign to address concerns about the WEP's stance on SEVs. Her answer skimmed over the issue, without properly acknowledging any of the harm done:

> We fully respect and accept that women may choose to work in those places and that's their choice, but we will campaign on the licensing side of things, because we don't think that organisations encouraging men to objectify women are positive to society.[9]

Once again the term 'objectification' crops up as a patronising platitude without any discussion of how the word is being used. SEVs are simply referred to as places where men are encouraged to objectify women, reinforcing the by now widely received narrative that strip clubs are merely arenas where barbaric men abuse defenceless women who have been stripped of any agency or human characteristics along with their clothes. The word perfectly fulfils the need for a sound bite; a buzzword loaded with tension used cleverly by politicians and careerists to trigger an emotional response from their desired audience. But therein lies the rub. The term is used widely but without a wider public dialogue about what it actually means, leaving the door wide open for prejudice and stereotyping. Often those in a position of power with a public platform fail to perceive how their own words and actions tend to demean the very same women they would like to protect. By ignoring the highly nuanced and complicated set of circumstances found in the sex industry, and then creating a limited narrative that turns women into characters who cannot consent – *objects* of pity and/or derision – they are *still being* objectified, this time as a group of victims. The WEP cannot have it both ways. Acknowledging the agency of women who choose to work in strip clubs, but then immediately following this up in the same sentence with a disdainful dichotomy that places men in the active role of aggressor and women in the passive role of victim does little to progress women's rights. Campaigns seeking an end to the objectification of women cannot objectify women further by using reductive and frequently condescending language in public discourse. It is a sticking point.

Eventually it was revealed that Not Buying It were the group behind the undercover filming. Dr Rakoff apparently finds men visiting strip clubs so appalling that she hired two of them (both ex-policemen turned private investigators), paying them to visit several venues and party with the strippers they found there. Dr Rakoff no doubt had to look past many examples of chauvinism and maltreatment of sex workers within the police force generally to utilise the services of a couple of ex-cops to set up a sting that literally targeted sex workers themselves. Even the fact that hiring PIs was a tactic used by *strip club bosses* to investigate their rivals must have passed her by. Dr Rakoff's actions mirror the exact same strategies and behaviours of actual strip club bosses (as per Peter Stringfellow, who sent PIs into Spearmint Rhino to catch them out), the arch-enemies in her paradigm of gender-based violence. But using a method that technically falls under the very definition of violence against the women working in the clubs is a perfect example of the end failing to justify the means. In a BBC article, Dr Rakoff was quoted as saying, 'We were never going to, and never will make this evidence public in any shape or form', and that Not Buying It had 'already destroyed all footage that we have been able to'.[10] Which begs the question, were the women caught on camera just devices for her strategy? Does she know their names? Is she interested in their lives, feelings, in their *humanity*?

It's not so difficult to explain why the act of filming strippers at work without their knowledge or consent is a bad thing. Even someone with little to no insight or experience of strip clubs or the lives of the women who work in them can comprehend that making a video of women privately performing sexual labour against their knowledge and without their permission is a serious breach of privacy. When dancers in Sheffield learned that the footage existed many of them were understandably distressed. In April a dancer called Heather who was working at Spearmint Rhino, Sheffield, at the time, reached out to the East London Strippers Collective for support. In her message she wrote:

> None of us know if our names or video footage of us will be online and whether the club is going to be shut . . . I think I'm most concerned about what Not Buying It will put in their report as they have no problem objectifying us.[11]

Heather pointed to a page on the Not Buying It website titled 'Mythbusters' containing a description of women who are 'empowered by taking off their clothes and wrapping their implants around the nearest pole'.[12] The language used is surprisingly derogatory for an organisation founded upon the principle that women should not be objectified, given how easily it conjures up a degrading female stereotype: women with no identity beyond their breast augmentation and choice of self-expression. The misalignment between the aims outlined by Not Buying It and their subsequent content and behaviour is jarring. It seems to have escaped Dr Rakoff's awareness that actually filming strippers is an act of objectification in itself. In choosing a strategy that literally turns the bodies of strippers into two-dimensional media, divorcing them of all other humanising characteristics, it is the definition of objectification. Failing to make that connection and going ahead with the covert filming all in the pursuit of putting an end to the objectification of women was a far cry from achieving that goal.

Not Buying It set out to be an authority on strip clubs. The website is a well-curated and comprehensive resource with an extensive catalogue of press articles about clubs and their poor conduct. There is plenty to read and watch with links to studies, reports, videos, documentaries and endless press articles. There can be no doubt that Not Buying It oppose the existence of strip clubs. As well as the thorough collection of 'evidence', there is also a page dedicated to shedding light on the 'realities' of stripping, titled 'Background to Stripping'. When navigating to the page, the first image to appear is a photo of a stripper's naked buttocks, capturing her in the act of giving someone a lap dance. The image is a grainy, low-resolution, black-and-white video still, and the angle is shot from the eye-line of someone seated nearby. It can be assumed that the image is taken from footage captured by a hidden camera, filmed without the dancer's permission. It also seems unlikely that the dancer gave permission for the image of her buttocks to appear on the Not Buying It website. Her face is not seen on camera; in fact most of her body is obscured. She has been reduced literally to a bare arse, which contravenes one of the most common demands of radical feminism – that women deserve to be seen as more than just their body parts.

Not Buying It didn't just stray into an ethically questionable area by secretly filming strippers, they crossed a line into murky legal territory as well. The sting operation is highly reminiscent of revenge porn, which is a criminal offence. In the UK, revenge porn has been defined under the Criminal Justice and Courts Bill as 'the sharing of private, sexual materials, either photos or videos, of another person, without their consent and with the purpose of causing embarrassment or distress. The offence applies both online and offline, and to images which are shared electronically or in a more traditional way so it includes the uploading of images on the internet, sharing by text and email, or showing someone a physical or electronic image.'[13]

The gathering and sharing of the footage in the clubs could only have two possible outcomes: first, the dancers in question would likely be sacked for breaching the clubs licensing conditions, and second, the club could lose their licence and close down, thus putting all the dancers and staff out of work. There can be no doubt that the sharing of the sexually explicit video footage between the private investigators, Dr Rakoff,

Charlotte Mead and members of Sheffield City Council, presumably without the dancers' consent, can be compared to revenge porn. One can only imagine the scenario in which these various individuals watched the video. Did they view it alone? Together? Did they watch it all the way to the end or have to stop half way in disgust? Did the video include the male investigators' voices and features or were the actions of the women edited out of context? More importantly, did Dr Rakoff register the women appearing on her screen, being 'forced to perform' degrading acts by her investigators, as occupying any other role besides victim?

When details of the Spearmint Rhino sting leaked into the press via the meeting with Sheffield City Council, news outlets responded in a number of predictable ways. Stories were quickly published containing the sordid details, but little other information about context, regulations, working conditions or any of the nuances in the situation. Reports stated that dancers had been caught on camera touching men's legs, sitting in their laps and grinding their crotches while performing lap dances. There was also a claim that one dancer offered to 'prostitute herself' after her shift. The identities, stories and voices of the dancers are completely absent, leaving behind a limited version of events. The dancers had no right of reply, in most cases the news stories broke before dancers even knew what had happened to them, and the facts of the video were not interrogated thoroughly by journalists, who were in all probability more interested in a quick turnaround and a head-line to meet their click-bait quota.

Whether journalists saw the footage or not (it widens the revenge porn circle of implication if they did), it is not the job of the press to police the private activities that go on between consenting adults in adult entertainment venues – that is, for now, the job of licensing authorities. No matter the regulatory process, the language used to talk about strippers in the press is a perfect example of objectification, removing all subtlety and individuality from the dancers who find themselves caught up in a process they have no control over. Journalists have a free pass to describe sex workers with a level of objectification unlikely to be accepted when applied to any other female group in today's media environment. Much of the media reporting around the Sheffield club sting reduces the complicated, intri-cate and tangled realities of being a stripper in the twenty-first century down to a series of descriptions of grubby, forbidden acts; the act of touching male customers, or even worse, much to the titillation and moral outrage (possibly both) of the read-ership, the degradation of offering sex for money.

Practically every time a news article is published about strip clubs or sex work an attention-grabbing stock image of a face-less female is used alongside it. In the case of a sex worker, a photo of a woman in a short skirt and heels with bare legs or fishnets leaning into a car window or standing against a wall on a dark street at night. The image is almost always cropped or blurred to remove the woman's identity, removing the head and shoulders, leaving only a body. When it comes to strippers the typical stock image used is a photo of strippers' feet or legs, wearing plastic high heels on a stage with a pole. These are simply more body parts to be viewed and scrutinised by the gaze of the public (presumably half of whom are male). Maybe shoes and feet have become the least objectionable and most non-sexualised part of a woman's body to use as stock photos, since perhaps editors have started to wake up to the fact that using women's actual bodies to sell news stories about how women's bodies shouldn't be used is no longer going to fly with a more politically correct and discerning population. It's good news for foot fetishists, though.

These images only serve to further ingrain and entrench the received narrative about sex work, turning them into characters on a page, and limiting them only to what they wear and do for a living. By feeding the public a continuously dehumanised version of a sex worker as a victim, media coverage turns their readership into unwitting consumers of verbal and visual language that relentlessly objectifies women who do sex work. While there may be a semblance of progress in terms of editorial decisions to use images of less sexually suggestive body parts, it doesn't change the nature of the machine. Women are still *used* by the press as images, as stories, as objects of desire and titillation, or objects of shame and contempt. Using and objectifying women doesn't end just by shutting down strip clubs. It therefore stands to reason that by focusing in on strip clubs and targeting strippers in a way that whips up a media frenzy guaranteed to attract the attention of a news-reading citizenry, Not Buying It are contributing to an ongoing media culture of objectifying sex workers. If Not Buying It are so concerned with the sexual objectification of women in the sex industry, why aren't they disturbed by other forms of objectification as well?

—— ◆◆ ——

In 2017 I saw an email land in the East London Strippers Collective inbox that caught our attention. A solicitor working for a London borough council was reaching out to the ELSC hoping to find dancers willing to talk to her about a club called Blue Door. The venue was known among the dancer community as a club to be avoided and I'd heard many stories of wage theft, coercion, mismanagement and generally poor working conditions. The council were embroiled in a legal dispute with the club about their private VIP area – Blue Door had applied for a variation on their licence requesting permission to have a segregated area in the club for lap dances and VIP sessions, despite strict licensing conditions imposed by the council forbidding them from doing this. The council wanted to gather witness statements from dancers to provide testimony to the court about their working conditions.

One of the objectives of the ELSC is for dancers to have a voice and a say at a legal and political level about how clubs are run, so it felt like progress to be contacted directly by a licensing authority. I had done an audition at Blue Door several years prior, and fellow dancers and members of the ELSC had worked there also, so I could speak a little to the conditions encountered there. However, once I got past the initial introductory emails and was presented with the argument about the private booths, I was dismayed by what I heard. It became evident that within the council's SEV policy was a deeply established, paternalistic and misguided assumption that the existence of private booths made women fundamentally vulnerable. Many councils make it a licensing condition of all SEVs that they cannot build or create any sort of private area within the club, even just with a transparent gossamer curtain, because doing so would place women at risk. It seemed pretty ingrained that the reason the licensing authority did not allow private dancing to happen actually in private was for the safety of the women working there — to protect them from the wandering hands and manipulative intentions of the grotesque men who were only in the club for one reason, to assault women.

It was a clear opportunity to unpick this logic with someone who actually works for the council. I pointed out that what left dancers vulnerable was a business model that created competition among workers, house fees and commissions that turn us into gamblers and risk takers, and a disempowering ratio of dancers to customers that left us unable to walk away from disagreeable behaviour if it meant lost earnings. I took aim at their SEV policy, pointing out that by failing to acknowledge our employment rights it wasn't protecting workers from being financially exploited, which happens regardless of whether a club had private booths or not. I tried to explain that the problem of dancers being exploited ran a lot deeper than whether or not a club built in some MDF partitioning or hung up some net curtains. Taking this approach was at best simplistic, and at worst neglectful. It seemed insidious to me that the council had drawn such facile and superficial conclusions about violence and exploitation, and that as long as they could be seen to be doing their jobs and ensuring clubs adhere to their licensing conditions then women's safety can be dispensed as a sort of box-ticking exercise.

I also explained that, from a dancer's viewpoint, we needed those private rooms. The way we make our money is by selling private performances, physical and verbal intimacy, and emotional labour – all of which rely on privacy. We don't get paid otherwise, so we require a separate space from the rest of the club, and taking that away from us was removing a tool for us to close a deal, making it even harder for us to eke out a living in an environment where the economics were already stacked against us.

It wasn't what the solicitor wanted to hear. While she didn't have a hard time getting her head around what I was telling her, she didn't hide her exasperation about the fact that this particular court hearing was neither the time nor the place for dancers' workplace grievances to be heard. I asked her what was the right time and place; she told me I needed to talk to the Head Licensing Officer about their SEV policy. I asked for an email address, and much to my surprise she passed it on.

The dialogue about the court case continued, however, and once I was satisfied that the club's licence was not at risk, and my continued involvement would not jeopardise the jobs of the women working there, I decided to follow through purely out of curiosity and to better understand the regulatory process. I provided a statement for the council about my experience of doing an audition there.

After a few weeks of correspondence I was invited to come into the council offices to sign my witness statement, and was told me that one of the other witnesses would be coming in that day as well so it would be a good opportunity to meet in person. I arrived at the council building and was met in the lobby by the solicitor who introduced me to a lady named Sasha. I was immediately curious, wondering who this fellow witness was – my instinct told me she wasn't a dancer. As we got into the lift and went up to a glass-walled office that felt like a fish tank, I listened quietly observing the company I was in. It wasn't long at all before Sasha started to declare a very low opinion of strip clubs, talking about managers and bosses, and the lawyers who represent them, like sexist characters from Carry On *films*.

After we sat down the solicitor went off to make tea and print out our witness statements for us to sign. Once we were alone I turned to Sasha and asked, 'So, what's your connection to all of this then?' Her answer floored me. She said, 'Oh, I used to do a lot of campaigning around this about ten years ago . . .' While she was talking she reached down into her bag and pulled out a flyer for Object, which she handed to me without the slightest hesitation. I was staggered; disbelief caught up with me and I actually felt my jaw slacken slightly. I was alone in the same room as Sasha Rakoff, the founder of two organisations who had spent over a decade doing a stand-up job of stigmatising and destroying my industry, and she was trying to recruit me.

I almost choked out a laugh, followed by a quickening heartbeat and a curdling in my stomach, as I realised this wasn't actually a joke. I asked her if she'd heard of the ELSC, and she told me she hadn't. I said something like, 'Well, we started a collective because the Policing and Crime Act has done nothing for our employment rights and because we got sick of being misrepresented by people speaking for us so we decided to speak for ourselves.'

The conversation didn't progress much further. When the solicitor came back into the room she seemed confused and a bit taken aback by the change of atmosphere in the room. It seemed Sasha no longer wanted to talk openly about her witness statement. I walked out in disgust. She had an opportunity to talk to an activist in the field, a stripper fighting to end exploitation of workers. We could have spoken about how to join forces, where to focus our efforts, which clubs are the worst offenders and how to apply pressure to improve conditions for the women working in them. But it appeared she didn't want to engage in any sort of dialogue with me.

Some time after this meeting I visited the Not Buying It website for reference. There were loads of low resolution images of photos of women that looked like screen grabs from other parts of the internet, alongside quotes written in big fonts that were designed to shock, like 'I Was Drugged And Raped By Security On CCTV', without reference, context or background. I navigated to the Background page where I was confronted with an upsetting detail. In the paragraph titled Harm For Women In Clubs, I read:

> Every woman who has left the industry has told us that the overwhelming majority of dancers had come from abusive backgrounds. Many of the leading advocates of the industry are quite open about being victims of sexual abuse and even child sexual abuse.[14]

224 | *The Ethical Stripper*

But she doesn't qualify who she means. It's just a statement of fact. She shoots from the hip and doesn't care who she harms in the process.

Having our own histories rewritten is practically the definition of oppression. Along comes an organisation that claims to be fighting for women, and yet we continue to be oppressed by campaigners who are upheld as heroes of feminism, who win awards for their work. Campaigners who refuse to engage in dialogue with us, and invalidate our stories. As long as we are voiceless we continue to be objectified. Anger isn't even the right word for what I feel about it. When I think of the women I've worked alongside, and the strength and resilience I have witnessed in my stripper colleagues, they are my heroes of feminism. I'll never stop telling our stories, humanising our work and defending our right to exist on our own terms.

∽

When the word 'objectification' is hurled around, little to no attention is paid to the most common and classic forms of objectification – photography and video. Everywhere women's bodies are used to create content; two-dimensional imagery that is devoid of personality, nameless, immoveable, and in some cases faceless. Video footage turns action into fixed repetition, creating a person who cannot converse or answer back. There are few things more depersonalising than turning a human being into an image, a permanent depiction without agency.

The feminist academic Jean Kilbourne has throughout her career provided a rigorous and exhaustive critique of female objectification in mass media advertising and marketing. She outlined her thesis in a series of filmed lectures, called 'Killing Us Softly', that women's bodies were increasingly being objectified throughout the explosion of global consumerism to devastating effect. She argues:

> Turning a human being into a thing is almost always the first step towards justifying violence against that person.[15]

We see that logic apply to political violence and genocide; the objectification of marginalised groups paves a way to the systemic violence that is perpetrated against minorities. Kilbourne's analysis helps us place the sexual objectification of women within a cultural system in which women are silenced and victimised. Pictures of women being sexualised, infantalised, cropped down to body parts, packaged into uniform identikit versions, in some cases literally blended with actual products and turned into a commodity rendered entirely dehumanised, are indeed likely to have an impact on how gender is viewed by society. Importantly, though, Kilbourne is referring specifically to images of women in magazines, adverts, on billboards, TV, film, and all forms of two-dimensional media. Images are not people, and never can be.

When the Policing and Crime Act 2009 was passed into statute and strip clubs found themselves with a set of licensing conditions, one of the new limitations was a restriction on public advertising. Strip venues could no longer use signage to indicate the nature of the premises, no posters or images of women's bodies, no more LIVE NUDE GIRLS signs. Nor could they pay for public advertising in newspapers or magazines, on sides of taxis or billboards. The logic behind this decision is in line with Kilbourne's assertions; the new constraint placed on clubs is believed to decrease the negative wider social impact that clubs might be having. It's the same logic that lies behind the public call that demanded an end to Page 3. In 2015 *The Sun* finally bowed to public opinion and responded by instead printing a new image every day of a sexualised female in a bikini rather than topless.

Strip clubs in their current form occupy an unusual position within the cultural landscape of female sexual objectification. The imagery used to signify a strip club fits in with Kilbourne's logic as part of a violent process, but the actual reality of a strip club is subtly different, almost so subtle that it may seem imperceptible. Up until the arrival of table dancing and lap dancing in the late 1990s, strip clubs used to be places where audiences of mainly men went to watch strippers on stage, at a distance. The male gaze, a trope that has become synonymous with male power and misogynistic abuse, was palpable in that the only activity available was the simple act of looking. Men may have used such imagery for their own private, masturbatory pleasure, but the power relationship between audience and performer was fixed by the physical layout of a stage, curtain, and theatre or cabaret seating.

Lap dancing changed all that. A lap dancer steps off the stage and onto the club floor, hustling tables to earn her wage; she approaches clients, speaking to them, looking to strike up a conversation. The stripper is now not only seen, she is heard as well. No longer merely a vision, an image on a poster or an object on stage from the days of the Windmill, she walks and talks, she engages in dialogue, she moves freely within her workplace. She is as human as any of the male customers who enter the space. She may be limited by her job in the same ways any other workers are restricted by their work. Yet she drinks, she swears, her facial expressions, thoughts and reactions are her own, she speaks her mind, laughs at a joke or feigns interest, she performs a work persona or reveals her true nature. And, since she is not paid a fixed wage to fulfil a theatrical role for eight hours straight, she is therefore technically free to sit in the changing room for her entire shift if she so pleases.

The split between different factions of feminism is still being felt when campaigns to abolish Page 3, call time on Formula 1 grid girls, or shut down strip clubs result in a public backlash. Women who are most obviously affected, i.e. women who find themselves without a job, are seldom heard in the mainstream. Those who have made a career from glamour modelling or lap dancing find themselves caught in a trap, unable to break out of their roles and articulate their realities, least of all in a media machine that reiterates their objectification. A vast contingent of strippers, sex workers, topless glamour models, or any women who trade on their 'erotic capital'[16] do not identify with the role of victim assigned to them by Kilbourne's logic and the theory of rape culture. Even the models who posed for the advertising campaigns didn't feel dehumanised; when they were doing a job, interacting with stylists, makeup artists and photographers on set, it wasn't an act of violence to them when they were getting paid to simply look attractive.

Kilbourne's analysis falls short of helping us understand whether all acts of objectification are an act of violence; she states that we cannot have violence without objectification, but she doesn't interrogate the idea that we may be able to have objectification without violence. Is it possible to have *non-violent objectification*? We objectify the people who drive our buses, make our coffees and serve our food in restaurants as objects of service. Men as a group are frequently objectified as providers, objects of protection, or, at the other end of the scale, abusers. Many marginalised groups are objectified negatively to fit a received political narrative about them, whereas people who work in TV, film, theatre, cabaret and the arts thrive on being objectified. If people are going around objectifying each other all the time anyway, isn't at least some of it non-violent? For those who have found themselves consenting to the business of being objectified for a living, perhaps the reality is that if objectification isn't going away any time soon, maybe it's negotiable. If objectification has everything to do with power, maybe we need to pay very close attention to the power relationships, before we try and censor or outlaw types of objectification that cause some women to feel discomfort.

Pubic opinion is divided over whether women in the sex industry are 'empowered or exploited', presumably because some people can identify with their position of power and others can't. Some sex workers may be objectified at work without feeling like they were being exploited, or even if there was exploitation it wasn't experienced as an utter loss of agency or self-will, comparable to actual slavery. There are countless examples of radical feminism framing sex work as slavery, or of all sex workers as trafficked victims. Comparing an exploitative job with slavery, however, is disgracefully offensive to the descendants of slaves and to civil rights activists. But no matter how supportive the public may be of a woman's right to choose how to make her own living, it does little to hold back the juggernaut of mainstream ideology that seeks to stamp out all examples of female objectification, no matter the cost to anyone's income and/or safety.

At least some of the dissonance between opposing narratives can be apportioned to one thing – media representations of sex workers. If members of the public are spoon-fed a diet of stigma, conditioned by whorephobia, and everything they understand about the sex industry comes from the imagery they have been raised on instead of the lived reality of human beings doing a job, then it's easy to deliver them a narrative of victimhood. Every article with a photo of strippers' feet, every sex worker character in a dramatisation who was murdered, assaulted or used as a plot device, every lack of nuance and humanity leaves sex workers vulnerable as a group in more ways than one. It has made the re-humanising of sex workers a mammoth job for sex workers themselves, since they have to overcome multiple forms of objectification in order to reclaim their narratives.

At the time of writing this book, Spearmint Rhino, Sheffield, was still trading, but its days were numbered. The sting carried out by Dr Rakoff was successful in as much as the licensing committee's hands were tied. Licensing conditions applied to SEVs in England and Wales clearly state that physical contact is not permitted between strippers and clients. If a club is in breach of their licensing conditions the licensing authority has the power to revoke their licence. Even if the council is supportive of the club, Not Buying It's campaigns and the consistent drip feed of press coverage means that local residents become more righteously involved, and customers tend to back off for fear of being shamed within their community. Spearmint Rhino may continue trading, but with a dwindling clientele it looks like the strippers of Sheffield may not have a club to work in for much longer.

Sheffield is one of the ten largest cities in the UK, with a population of just over half a million people. A cursory Google search using the term 'book a stripper Sheffield' turns up a predictable set of results. Here is a list of the first ten agencies providing striptease entertainment in the city: Party Strip, Eye Candy UK, Entertain-ment, Stripper Online, Hayley B Entertainments, Bufflers, Andy King Entertainment, Event Sense, UK-strippers, Celebrate Just Right. Just taking the first website in the list, Party Strip, as an example, has the following written on their landing page:

Do you want to hire totally fit and smoking hot female strippers in Sheffield, available right now for hire. Our female strippers are professional entertainers and they like nothing better than showing bare flesh (of course!). You will definately [*sic*] have a fantastic night out in Sheffield. We provide female strippers in many areas of the country for Birthdays, Hen Night Partys [*sic*], Stag Night Partys or just to spice up your night out or party at home. With one of our totally hot experienced entertainers getting the proceedings into gear, the party in Sheffield is really going to explode! Read the serious stuff below if you must, I've already scrolled down to view the pictures! Your female stripper will come to almost any location you like from pubs to clubs or even to your home. The price you pay, which we negotiate with you at time of booking, covers all expenses including travel and costume (if required).

Our entertainers are happy for pictures to be taken and to sign
or kiss most body parts. Please note however that touching/
kissing is by invitation only! Our female strippers in Sheffield
are very popular so we recommend that you have a few alternatives in mind when you phone up in case your number 1
choice is unavailable. Now it's time to feast your eyes on our
selection!![17]

The website looks like it was thrown together in a day, the
poor grammar and spelling mistakes have been overlooked,
maybe since the images on display are clearly the main attrac-
tion. Not a lot of attention or effort seems to have been spent
on the graphics and layout, and the photos of strippers are
low-resolution screen grabs. The branding is reminiscent of
the 1990s lads' mags era, women's bodies are highly sexualised, objectified and laid out like products on Ebay to choose
from. The website offers a Roly Poly stripper service. Hayley
B Entertainment offers Corporate Dwarf Hire.

Online agencies can operate without an SEV licence.
There is no regulatory process to protect women who work for
striptease agencies; the company owners are not accountable
to any local authorities (besides the police). As stated on the
Party Strip website, strippers will come to 'almost any location' to work alone in a hotel, private function room, flat or
premises, which is extremely commonplace among striptease
agencies. Private addresses have none of the conditions and

restrictions that publicly licensed premises do. There is no security staff to safeguard and monitor anyone's behaviour, clients can be as drunk or intoxicated as they like, there are no health and safety standards in place. Clients can solicit for sex without a second thought. Coercion and violations of consent are a lot easier to perpetrate and harder to prove. Agency work is the precise definition of precarious work in the gig economy, even without the obvious issues around personal safety and gender discrimination added into the mix.

Despite the inconsistencies and inadequacies of SEV licensing policy, there are at least some checks and balances in place to safeguard workers in a strip club – CCTV is in use at all times as a requirement, for example (although far too often it is weaponised against dancers themselves). Closing down a strip club means erasing a regulatory environment that has been evolving since the Windmill opened in the 1930s, leaving strippers as vulnerable as they ever have been. These unsafe conditions of working underground in unsafe places are by no means new or unique. These are the exact same conditions in which full-service sex workers have always been operating; without legalised, licensed and regulated workplaces, strippers will be pushed further into the margins where violence and coercion are the norm.

Dr Rakoff's feminist accolades are contentious to say the least. She may well get to see the single strip club in Sheffield city disappear, and finally have her coffee meetings without seeing the Spearmint Rhino sign. However, if the true cost of her efforts have driven women into circumstances that are more precarious, behind closed doors and out of sight, where they are even more vulnerable than they were in the club, then her victory starts to look very stark indeed. One wonders if she succeeds in shutting down every strip club in the UK, will she then take aim at agencies? How will she even find them? Will she hire private investigators and crowdfund for judicial reviews against a transient business that can simply shut down their website and build a new one the next day? How can she apply pressure using the Public Sector Equality Duty if striptease agencies are not even regulated by the public sector? Is she really pointing all her efforts in the right direction?

In August 2019 a tiny number of news stories appeared on just a couple of news sites. Nine strippers in Sheffield who were secretly filmed launched a legal battle to sue Not Buying It for a major breach of their human right to privacy. In July they won a High Court injunction to prevent the video footage of them dancing naked being shared any further. A story about sex workers fighting for their rights, demanding justice and making a stand against a form objectification, which they did not consent to, should have received more media coverage than it did. But a story that humanises strippers by detailing their right to autonomy and self-determination doesn't fit the typical narrative of sex workers as silent victims. It's not so easy to tack on a stock photo of a stripper's legs when the story is about strippers demanding to be seen on their own terms. Strippers bringing a legal claim, however, is a significant step forward.* Private dancer forums on social media are awash with new kinds of rumours – that we have the right to work in safety, and that there is now help available in the form of trade union activism. Strippers can demand safer work environments, improved regulations, and appropriate policies designed by workers themselves. Dr Rakoff can back off, and let strippers demand an end to their own harassment and exploitation. If only she will listen to them.

---

* Sadly, the claim has since been dropped, but not before the nine women named in the law suit were named, revealing their identities on the public record. The story of how the dancers at Spearmint Rhino, Sheffield, have been let down repeatedly, by Not Buying It, by the legal justice system, by their club, by the press, by the wider community, could fill an entire chapter.

7

THE VICTIMHOOD INDUSTRY

Perhaps the single most effective strategy they've hit
upon so far is to pump out the myth contained in
the term 'sex work': the myth that is is possible to
commodify consent

—Kat Banyard[1]

The most insidious narrative laid out by the radical feminist
left is the straw-man argument that decriminalising sex work
will empower and embolden perpetrators of exploitation and
violence. The radical feminist analysis of decriminalisation
claims that abusers, pimps, rapists and traffickers will be given
state authorisation to carry out acts of violence and coercion
with impunity; therefore any sex worker fighting for harm-
reduction via labour rights is in fact part of a front for a powerful 'pimp lobby'.

In 2017 journalist Frankie Mullin attended the Amnesty

International UK Annual General Meeting to report on their recent policy change in support of decriminalisation. While she was there she witnessed the ugly extent to which the abolitionists could go. A number of sex workers including ECP members had gathered to speak about the decriminalisation policy and while waiting to be heard the group were verbally attacked by a spokesperson calling them the 'English Collective of Pimps'. In Mullin's article published by Verso, she sums up the meaning laced within the insult:

> What's really being claimed, when abolitionists sound the pimp lobby klaxon, is that they don't believe sex workers. They don't believe sex workers could be this organised, don't believe they could be this united, don't believe anyone in the industry could be clear-headed enough to understand misogyny, or racism, or the complexity of how these inequalities play out within the industry.[2]

Within this interpretation, the very phrase 'sex worker' (used by activists to connote the shared struggle of workers *against* the harms inflicted upon them by abusive managers and exploiters) has come to signify a vanguard for a dangerous, Machiavellian movement, driving a project that is founded on the degradation of women. According to this logic, behind the street protests and placards demanding greater welfare and protections are seedy characters and monstrous whoremongers, pulling the strings of their hapless puppets. Sex workers are seen as victims in favour of their own exploitation; turkeys voting for Christmas.

Doubling down on this straw-man feud will achieve nothing: it simply inflames a myth that undermines the aims of the sex workers' rights movement. But at the same time it's essential to the progress of the movement for sex workers and allies to understand how the position of abolitionism came about, and why it dominates mainstream commentary. And also why proponents of radical feminist rhetoric are so invested in the abolitionist viewpoint that even major policy decisions of global human rights organisations cannot be accepted. Julie Bindel, a prominent writer and researcher, and co-founder of the Justice for Women law-reform group, is known for asserting this argument *ad nauseam*:

> Thanks to organisations such as Human Rights Watch (HRW), World Health Organisation (WHO), UNAIDS and Amnesty International giving support to exploiters as opposed to the exploited, the 'sex workers' rights' movement can present itself to the world as one based on the liberation of an oppressed group rather than the unpalatable truth: that such a policy only helps pimps and punters, rather than the prostituted.[3]

Similar arguments have been made about strip club activism, and efforts made in the UK to unionise strippers and establish employment rights in clubs. In the aftermath of the targeted sting carried out by Not Buying It, several strippers at Spearmint Rhino, Sheffield, joined the trade union United Voices of the World and began collectively campaigning to protect the licence of their club and preserve their only available regulated workplace in the city, while at the same time beginning to outline demands for improved working conditions. The UK press reacted with a variety of responses, some sympathetic to the dancers, some more circumspect, but the inevitable reply from the radical feminist cabal was unequivocally derisive. Janice Turner, columnist for *The Sunday Times*, referred to strippers organising for improved working conditions as 'Spearmint Rhino's useful idiots' in her article 'Feminists have fallen for the strip club myth'.[4] The idea of strippers unionising to begin a process of self-determination and demand power in the workplace is continually maligned and reinterpreted by radical feminism as something that can only ever benefit club bosses, thus portraying the organising efforts of workers themselves as meaningless. An article in the *Morning Star* by Joan Hardwicke, 'Sex work organising – a lot of hot air?', does exactly this:

> Considering many strip clubs are under threat of having their licences revoked for often being hotspots for sleaze and sometimes organised crime, far from being hostile to a token union deal, many owners are happy to give a partnership recognition deal as it makes them look better in the eyes of the council,

and more generally rehabilitates their image as liberal human-itarians as so many 'ethical capitalists' and 'good bosses' are eager to do nowadays.[5]

Referencing every example of SWERF voices undermining sex workers' demands for harm-reduction, recognition and rights would fill up the rest of this book, and it's important not to get bogged down in a dispute that's built on a fallacy. A straw-man argument is one that ignores an opposing position and substitutes a distorted, exaggerated or misrepresented version of that position. Sex workers are not in favour of their own exploitation, and every effort to establish labour rights and empower workers to protect themselves from abuse is a step closer to ending exploitative business practices. But with every article published about pimps and abusers, SWERFs continually respond to a distorted argument that has never been put forth by the sex workers' rights movement, riding roughshod over the voices of people actually doing the job. This disregard for the lived experience of sex workers could be seen as a form of narcissistic gaslighting; a means of psychological manipulation in which doubt is introduced in order to undermine self-confidence. An article that aims to place uncertainty in the minds of any would-be trade union supporters, including strippers themselves, by ridiculing and belittling their efforts is an example of gaslighting at its finest. The sex workers' rights movement cannot be a continual battle for recognition from a group who will not bestow on them the basic courtesy of recognising their genuine ideological position. Once again sex worker activists have to perform the extra labour of trying to disprove an argument they have been falsely attributed with making; that they are in fact supplicants for their own suppression.

THE LILITH REPORT

In 2003 a report was published that was to have a lasting effect on public perceptions of lap-dancing clubs, the effects of which are still being felt today. 'The Lilith Report on Lap Dancing and Striptease in the Borough of Camden' (also referred to here as the Lilith Report) was commissioned by Eaves Housing For Women, a charitable company founded in 1977 originally as a homelessness charity offering supported housing for women at risk of domestic violence. According to the Charity Commission, Eaves' aims were to provide 'supported accommodation for women trafficked into the UK and a drop in centre for women affected by the criminal justice system. The life skills service is an advice and advocacy service for women who are affected by violence or are at risk of homelessness. Eaves also conducts research, lobbies and responds to government papers on violence against women issues.'[6]

In the early 2000s, Eaves Housing For Women received several million pounds of government funding and became a leading authority on gender violence. Several subsidiary groups were set up under Eaves, which in turn became an umbrella organisation; these groups included the Poppy Project, the London Exiting Advocacy Project, the Alice Project and the Lilith Project. The Poppy Project was founded in 2003, and became the only UK government-funded dedicated service for trafficked women; the project was committed to ending prostitution on the grounds that it 'helps to construct and maintain gender inequality'.[7] The Lilith Project was set up as a research agency, intending to address the 'lack of services available to combat violence against women. In conjunction with Hackney Women's Aid and the Women's Resource Centre, Eaves intends to research the services already available in London to victims of a range of violence, including rape, sexual assault, FGM, stalking, harassment and bullying in the workplace.'[8]

Very early on the Lilith Project quickly homed in on lap-dancing clubs as a site of research into violence against women. The outcome of this was the Lilith Report, 2003, which laid out claims that, when taken at face value, had dreadful implications; that the arrival of lap-dancing clubs had a devastating impact on women and, specifically, that they were responsible for increased levels of violence against women and sexual assault. Focusing on the London Borough of Camden, the report compared police crime rates between 1999 and 2002, and based on these findings made two disturbing assertions:

1. Since 1999 rape of women in Camden has increased by 50 per cent

2. Since 1999 indecent assault of women in Camden has increased by 57 per cent[9]

The importance of this particular period of time is clear: between 1999 and 2002 Camden became host to four new licensed strip venues, including the international brand Spearmint Rhino. The report sought to establish a clear cause-and-effect relationship between lap-dancing clubs and sexual violence.

When the Lilith Report was published a slew of headlines followed, leading to a wave of moral panic that swept across the country. While the lap-dancing industry entered into a boom period, which was boosted by the Licensing Act 2003, alongside it there was a growing parallel movement of horrified feminists and disgruntled local residents, whose objections to the appearance of lap-dancing clubs in their towns were backed up by this piece of government research. The Lilith Report suggested that their worst fears were correct; that strip clubs were a blight on an area and were demonstrably leading to increased levels of violence. The claims laid out in the Lilith Report were assimilated and regurgitated by local and national press reports, readily feeding into existing stereotypes and core beliefs about the sex industry in the public imagination, and serving to stigmatise lap dancers.

The effects of the Lilith Report can still be seen today. A recent national prime-time TV news debate illustrated perfectly how deeply ingrained the narratives purported by the Lilith Report have become. In August 2019 Channel 4 News broadcast a section about strippers in Sheffield unionising and fighting back against Not Buying It's campaign to shut down their club. Following the report the news channel hosted a live debate between Eleanor Mills, editorial director of *The Sunday Times*, and Penny, a student and fellow unionised stripper. Eleanor Mills, vocalising the radical feminist position, immediately drew on the statistics published within the Lilith Report to bolster her arguments for the abolition of stripping and lap dancing:

> There's actually rather a lot of evidence that strip clubs have a really bad effect on the women who live around them, so there was some interesting figures in Camden Town in London, which is actually where I live, which showed that, erm, instances of sexual assault had gone up 57 per cent and instances of rape 50 per cent since . . . in the time, um from . . . um, during which the . . . er, strip clubs . . . and the lap-dancing clubs were there . . .[10]

During the debate Mills appeared to be reading the statistics aloud from a sheet, and her slight hesitancy as she stumbled through her words disclosed a lack of certainty, almost as if she had quickly scraped together some facts to back up her stance, rather than having a honed, academic knowledge of the subject. The subtle insecurity of Mills' delivery does indeed reflect the unreliability of the figures quoted. Since its publication, the Lilith Report has been discredited several times. In 2009 an article was printed in the *Guardian*'s corrections and clarifications column, after fact checking a previous article titled 'I was seen as an object, not a person' containing the following amendments:

> The article below cited statistics from a 2003 study which said that the number of rapes increased by 50 per cent and indecent assaults by 57 per cent in the London borough of Camden after four lap dancing venues opened. According to the Lilith Report on Lap Dancing and Striptease in the Borough of Camden the statistics were based on information published by the Metropolitan police relating to the financial years 1998-99 and 2001-02. The Metropolitan police have provided us with the following figures: 72 rapes and 162 indecent assaults in the borough in 1998-99, and 96 rapes and 251 indecent assaults in 2001-02, which corresponds to a 33 per cent increase in rape and a 55 per cent increase in indecent assault.[11]

A 33 per cent increase in rape statistics may still be atrocious, but it's not even close to the 50 per cent number given in the report. It seems an unlikely mistake to make in such an important, government-funded research report.

246 | *The Ethical Stripper*

There was also a news article published in 2010 in the *Newquay Voice*, which indicated that using the same methodology of comparing police crime records from different years produced quite different results when applied to a different part of the UK.

> Police figures show that the number of recorded sexual assaults has fallen by more than 50 per cent since the town's first lap-dancing club opened . . . The figures, gained by using the Freedom of Information Act, appear to contradict claims that lap dancing venues put nearby females at risk from sexual assault due to aroused male customers.[12]

The article perfectly demonstrates how befuddled and almost farcical the narratives around lap dancing and sexual violence have become since the publication of the Lilith Report. When speaking of licensing conditions imposed on lap-dancing clubs, including the no-touching rule, local Police Inspector Dave Meredith is quoted as saying, 'A three foot rule . . . is a practical and realistic method of minimising sexual arousal and therefore reducing the risk of sexual assault to vulnerable women in the nearby area.' The logic of this statement is not just shaky; it unveils worryingly misogynistic views about rape and assault.

The suggestion that sexually frustrated men go looking for women to attack, and therefore the solution to rape is to prevent arousal, is an age-old and deeply fraught belief that is harmful to both men and women alike. It would seem within the field of clinical psychology there is a consensus that sexual assault is more linked to issues with control and unchecked mental health than it is about actual arousal. The notion that male sexual desire is inherently dangerous, and that men are not accountable for their violent behaviour if their arousal has been stimulated, because erections equal assault, is one of the social attitudes about gender that really does deserve to be consigned to history. This is another one of the ways that men can be objectified, as abusers and potential perpetrators of rape and sexual assault. Merely reducing the male population into a category of latent aggressors does nothing to address the underlying social and psycho-emotional circumstances of trauma in which sexual violence occurs.

THE LILITH REPORT DEBUNKED

In 2011 Dr Brooke Magnanti published a research paper that demolished the statistics contained within the Lilith Report. Magnanti earned a PhD in Forensic Pathology, as well as working extensively in her research field of forensic science, population trends and biostatistics. In her study 'The Impact of Adult Entertainment on Rape Statistics in Camden: A Re-Analysis' she makes easy work of dismantling the problematic claims. By comparing sets of data she points out some glaring oversights in the Lilith Report, showing the numbers to be at best flimsy, and at worst entirely misleading. According to Magnanti, the research:

> suffers from numerous statistical problems in its analysis. The first is that the use of raw numbers rather than rate of occurrence does not accurately reflect the risk per head of population in Camden. The second is that the paper failed to show a trend long enough from which to draw meaningful conclusions. The third is that the study did not accurately put the results in context with trends elsewhere in London and in the UK as a whole, in order to test the theory that any change in crime rates was an effect specifically of the existence of lap-dancing clubs.[13]

A graph in Magnanti's paper tells a very different story to the one publicised. The figures in the Lilith Report are placed in context by widening the sample size to a period of ten years instead of two, and by comparing sets of data available from other London boroughs with similar demographics, as well as England and Wales as a whole. Statistics accessed from police records over a decade showed that Camden in fact had consistently lower levels of sexual assault than Islington and Lambeth, despite the fact that Camden had the highest number of strip clubs while Lambeth had none. It also showed a consistent decline of sexual assault in Camden over ten years between 1999 to 2008.

If a cause-and-effect relationship between the number of lap-dancing clubs and the occurrence of rape existed, we would expect Lambeth to be lowest of the three because it has no clubs. By the same assumption we would expect Islington to be higher because it has a couple, and Camden highest because it has more than those other boroughs. The analysis however shows that Camden is consistently the lowest of the three. The results do not support a causal link between the number of lap-dancing clubs in a borough and the risk of rape . . . Apart from the early 2000s peak, Camden's numbers are similar to the overall rate for England and Wales, and are sometimes below it. In the original report it was claimed that Camden's rapes were 'three times the national average,' and this has been reported elsewhere. This new analysis shows that statement is not true at any point within the studied time period.[14]

The Lilith Report drew together various isolated bits of research, such as street noise level readings taken by the local environmental health agency. It also included statistics on rape and sexual assault committed by unlicensed mini-cab drivers across London (taken from the now disbanded Met Police Sapphire sex crimes unit). The implication here is that lap-dancing clubs have led to an increase in levels of women being raped by mini-cab drivers, but the logic of this is confusing to anyone who has worked in a strip club. Are the female victims women who work in clubs? Are mini-cab drivers going to strip clubs as customers and then leaving to go and look for drunken women to assault? As Magnanti points out, the Lilith Report strongly implies an increase of stranger rape, yet wider long-term analysis of sexual assault shows that stranger rape only accounts for 17 per cent of all cases reported. A quote from the Report of Director, Environmental Health Department, Camden suggested 'the area around the University Street and Tottenham Court has now been denigrated into a "no go" area for female shoppers and male passers-by who are often accosted by pimps and other strip clubs offering sexual services and favours.'[15] This quote was not supported by any quantifiable research data, but stated as fact in the report. The Lilith Project's Research and Good Practice Officer, Isabel Eden, wrote in her final statement for the Lilith Report, 'Of course it would be wonderful if strip clubs could be eradicated tomorrow.'[16] There is no effort to hide the contempt and inherent confirmation bias held by the researchers; the Lilith Report is a perfect example of how problematic research can be when it is carried out by organisations that have a biased position on the subject.

A report by Julie Bindel, commissioned by Glasgow City Council in 2004, titled 'Profitable Exploits: Lap Dancing in the UK' also raises some questions around research methodology. Interviews were conducted with dancers, managers, customers, journalists, staff and passers-by outside clubs. According to Bindel, 'Information from interviews [inside the clubs] was recorded contemporaneously using brief notations and then transferred onto pro formas as soon as possible afterwards.'[17] It is not clear whether dancers knew they were being interviewed or if the researchers paid the dancers for their time or not; if we think about how a club is run, and consider that dancers are giving a performance even if they are off stage, researchers are going to glean a very skewed perspective from interviewing dancers in the workplace while they are actually on shift. If dancers were not provided with a formal opportunity to give an interview, outside of work hours, it seems questionable how valuable the information gathered by Bindel would be. Yet Bindel's paper became a determining piece of research, influencing public and political perceptions of lap-dancing clubs in the lead up to the Policing and Crime Act 2009, and contributing to the wider call to ban strip clubs altogether.

As summed up by Magnanti in her concluding statements, the direct consequences of misreporting or misrepresenting ideas or beliefs as facts are clearly detrimental to wider progress on the subject of gender violence:

The causes of rape and violent crime are not well understood, and there is much research and discussion devoted to understanding the causes of this crime so that it may be better controlled. It is possible that repeating limited and erroneous numbers can derail efforts to control violence and deflect attention and funding from alternative causal theories. It is because rape is such a serious crime that researchers must be at least as rigorous in their analysis as they would with other serious life events, and apply the same careful methodology as would be used in other areas of research. Other research supports the conclusion of no demonstrable causal link between adult entertainment and rape. A meta-analysis of 110 studies looking at the impact of strip clubs and other adult businesses found that the studies in favour of abolishing exotic dancing suffer from flaws in research methodology. Of the papers that did not contain fatal flaws, there was no correlation between any adult-oriented business and any negative effect.[18]

Bizarrely, Maganti's paper has never been given anywhere near the massive media attention that the Lilith Report has received. There may be a clear reason for this; as well as being a highly qualified scientist and academic, she is also the author of the international bestseller *The Intimate Adventures of a London Call Girl*. Maganti worked as a full-service sex worker while studying for her PhD, and used the experience to write a successful blog under the pseudonym 'Belle de Jour'. Magnanti worked as an escort for all of fourteen months, yet she will for ever more be known for her sex worker identity, regardless of her many other accolades. While on the one hand her personal insight into the sex industry could account for her excellent research credentials on the subject, in the eyes of a radical feminist this presumably makes her a write-off since an ex-sex worker turned scientist is a dangerous proponent in favour of the abuse of women, no matter how many qualifications she has to her name.

This ongoing conflict demonstrates how easily important research gets drowned out by an ongoing political battle between two opposing sides. Radical feminists are less willing to drill down into the actual numbers, preferring instead to look for reasons why their opponents are either controlled for gain, personally profiting from the sex industry, or mentally ill. Sex workers in turn look for evidence that their detractors are equally supported by and invested in their own ideological viewpoint, whether in the form of government or media funding, or a personal vendetta. Ultimately policy and legislation should never be shaped by these political battles, but rather led by what the evidence tells us. While there is an abundance of research about the sex industry, there is a scarcity of non-partisan, methodologically sound data upon which to base legislation. The way the Lilith Report was eaten up by the press is a case in point of what happens when a fallacy becomes so entrenched that it now seems almost impossible to reverse.

FOSTA/SESTA

In 2017 an American documentary aired on Netflix titled *I Am Jane Doe*, which chronicled the stories of several mothers of teenage sex trafficking victims, and their battle for justice. It revealed how, for many years, traffickers had been using personal ads on major US online platforms such as Backpage.com and Craigslist.com to exploit the underage girls under their control. The grim story of systemic child protection failures implied within the documentary became the backdrop to a new legal regime in the US ratified in April 2018 known as FOSTA/SESTA, shorthand for the Fight Online Sex Trafficking Act and the Stop Enabling Sex Trafficking Act, a package of legislation designed to curb sex trafficking on the internet. The laws make online platforms criminally liable for the content that appears on their websites, effectively outlawing all forms of digital soliciting. When the US government fast tracked the ratification of FOSTA/SESTA, they didn't consider that alongside the underage victims on Backpage.com, a generation of sex workers had been utilising the internet to create their own safety procedures by screening clients and sharing safety advice.

Advances in technology and telecommunication devices actually make it easier to identify criminal activity; accountability, traceability and digital trails all lead to greater levels of policing. Academic research in New Zealand has shown that 95 per cent of sex workers interviewed by the University of Otago after sex work was decriminalised felt safer and more in control, thanks to their newfound abilities to screen clients properly and work in open safety. This research had to have been ignored; if indeed the research ever made it onto the tables of any policy makers. It is unclear if law enforcement were using the advancements in technology to actually track and pursue suspected perpetrators of trafficking. Once more, we see how evidence-based harm-reduction policies are thrown out in favour of narrative-led strategies that pull at the heart strings of the consuming public, hungry for real life stories upon which their imaginations can feast. Under criminalisation there can be no differentiation anyway between independent escorts working safely and victims of coercion and violence, which means there can be only one approach: tighter restrictions for all.

In the weeks following the law change, the very traffickers that the law was aimed at saw an opportunity. Knowing full well how to use fear and insecurity as tools for exploitation, pimps started circling sex workers' social media accounts like sharks. Lawmakers didn't foresee that actual traffickers may be empowered by the law to offer 'protection' to sex workers, aware that without access to the advertising platforms and the relative safety it afforded them they may be more likely to turn to pimps and 'agents' to find their clients for them. They also didn't know that the sex worker community quickly started suggesting among themselves that SESTA should really stand for 'Start Enabling Sex Trafficking Act'. They didn't properly assess the potential outcomes of the Act, that by criminalising online advertising for sex workers they have been pushed further underground; in many cases back into street work or illegal brothels, and more dependent on the exploitative practices that are so completely predicated on a black-market economy. But then, without consulting with the sex working community, how could they?

The term 'trafficking' has become another buzzword like 'terrorism' or 'objectification'. High-profile cases like that of Jeffrey Epstein have made trafficking a hotly discussed topic. Like the word 'objectification', every time it is used but not explained it leaves an invisible meaning hanging in the air, a gap of understanding to be filled by the horrors found within the public imagination. Human trafficking connotes images of kidnap, rape, violence, being bundled into the back of a van, badly decomposed bodies found in shipping containers. It is by no means the intention of this book to deny evidence of trafficking or claim it doesn't exist, nor to play down the lived realities of victims; there can be no doubt that people endure untold suffering when exploited by predatory players. But since trafficking is a term that has become linked so integrally to the sex industry, it is essential to investigate the meanings and intentions that lie behind its use.

According to the United Nations Office on Drugs and Crime protocol, trafficking is defined as:

> recruitment, transportation, transfer, harbouring or receipt of persons, by means of the threat or use of force or other forms of coercion, of abduction, of fraud, of deception, of the abuse

of power or of a position of vulnerability or of the giving or
receiving of payments or benefits to achieve the consent of a
person having control over another person, for the purpose of
exploitation. Exploitation shall include, at a minimum, the
exploitation of the prostitution of others or other forms of
sexual exploitation, forced labour or services, slavery or practices similar to slavery, servitude or the removal of organs.[19]

If a strip club boss is abusing their power, taking advantage of
workers' vulnerability (lack of workers' rights) for the purposes
of exploitation (wage theft), does this mean strippers are in
fact trafficking victims? By the same definition, if workers in
other industries, such as fruit picking or construction, who
don't have access to their employment rights and find themselves victims of wage theft, does this mean they are trafficked? If someone living in poverty consents to cleaning toilets, emptying bins, wiping arses, washing cars, or any of the
countless other disgusting and menial jobs there are to do in
the world, because their need for money makes them vulnerable, is their consent being bought? Once more we see how
the lines between work, exploitative work and trafficking can
be blurred once the definitions are tested to their limits.

The frustration among the sex working community is palpable. Under late capitalism, vast numbers of people can
receive payments or benefits to achieve their consent while
their bosses have control over them by virtue of their need for

money, and can be exploited, underpaid, sacked, and just generally treated as disposable. For sex workers it isn't somehow inherently different because it involves taking off their clothes. Laws like FOSTA/SESTA do nothing to address the *material conditions* that push people towards sex work. It is also difficult to see how the laws make underage girls less vulnerable to sexual exploitation. If a generation of children trafficked and exploited through the use of social media were failed by their social infrastructure, *despite the visibility of their abuse*, how can we suppose they are made safer by simply banning internet adverts?

In July 2018 I attended a protest right outside the Houses of Parliament. The call to action had come from several sex worker-led organisations including the English Collective of Prostitutes, X-Talk and the Sex Worker Advocacy and Resistance Movement (SWARM). It was amazing to see how quickly everyone had mobilised; hundreds of protesters had gathered with about two days' notice. I was working with the Sex Workers' Opera at the time and we were in the middle of rehearsals for our first international run. We took an afternoon off and went along to add our voices to the throng of colourful protesters.

The rally was in direct response to a Parliamentary debate, which was actually happening live in the House of Commons while we were shouting outside, clattering our pots and pans to make ourselves heard. It was kind of amazing to know that we were on the other side of the wall while politicians were talking about us, while also infuriating to know we weren't being invited to join the debate. It had been called by Sarah Champion, Labour MP for Rotherham, to discuss the possibility of introducing a new law in the UK styled on the FOSTA/SESTA legislation over in the US. There had only been two days' notice for us to mobilise and there was a real sense of urgency on the day. I didn't fully understand at the time, but in hindsight and after more investigation I realised how significant that afternoon was, and how the intersection between sex workers' rights and many other complex and seemingly disparate factors were touched upon by that protest.

The debate was chaired by Ian Paisley, an eighty-eight-year-old ecumenical Protestant minister and founder of the Democratic Unionist Party (DUP), well known for their anti-abortionist and homophobic policies, which gave some idea of the attitudes towards sex work harboured in the room. Also present was Jess Phillips MP, a strident abolitionist who sits on the Parliamentary group for 'Prostitution and the Global Sex Trade', regularly speaking in favour of the Nordic model and higher levels of criminalisation in the sex industry. Despite the fact there were hundreds of sex workers outside the building while the debate was going ahead not a single sex worker or representative from any sex worker-led organisations was present at the actual debate. Our chant 'Nothing About Us, Without Us' was playing out before our very eyes.

When I heard that Sarah Champion had called the debate I realised that her constituency of Rotherham had an awful history. For decades in Rotherham, organised gangs of abusers had been sexually exploiting children. When five men were eventually convicted in 2010 for rape and sexual assault on girls between the ages of twelve and sixteen it was described as the biggest child protection scandal in modern UK history. The story of vulnerable underage girls being groomed and sexually abused by British Asian men was immortalised by the 2017 BBC series Three Girls.

To properly understand the story of the Rotherham abuse scandal you need to look at the backdrop of poverty and social neglect, Islamophobia, and the unwillingness of local welfare authorities to act on the repeated referrals, red flags and warnings from health workers that children were being seriously exploited by a gang of local men for years. The build up of years of unchecked abuse not only wreaked havoc on the lives of the victims; it also had wider repercussions in terms of a rising anti-immigration nationalist movement in the UK. On 19 June 2017, almost one year to the day after the Brexit referendum (which for many in the UK became a national debate on immigration), a Welsh man with psychiatric disorders and a history of aggravated crime hired a van and travelled to London where he drove it into a crowd of British Muslims gathered outside Finsbury Park Mosque for Friday prayers, killing one person and injuring at least nine others. During the investigation that followed, the attacker's ex-partner stated that he had been angered by the BBC drama Three Girls, *which had aired a month earlier.*

Rotherham is about a half-hour drive from Sheffield, seven miles as the crow flies, the battleground for radical feminism with Not Buying It and the WEP mounting their attack on Spearmint Rhino. One person who has become inextricably linked with both the Rotherham child abuse and the Not Buying It campaign is Sammy Woodhouse. She was one of the *victims who was groomed and abused as a child; later on as an adult she went on to work as a stripper in Spearmint Rhino, Sheffield. The club says they have no record of her ever working there. I know when I joined the industry in 2006 many clubs wanted proof of age and identification from new dancers, but some were more laid back than others. It seems unlikely to me that a club would keep records of every dancer that passes through their doors, which means Woodhouse could have very easily worked there, even for a short time. Plenty of women did.*

For radical feminists trying to shut down clubs, someone like Sammy Woodhouse is a godsend. That might sound cynical, but her story plots a clear path connecting childhood sexual abuse with exploitation in the adult industry. For feminists everywhere convinced of the relationship between sexual abuse and sex work, Woodhouse is a poster child for abolition. I've seen her appear in the media speaking out against clubs and in favour of Not Buying It's campaign alongside Sasha Rakoff and Charlotte Mead. It's hard to not be compelled by her story; there's no doubt she was a victim of abuse.

With such an appalling history on her turf, it makes sense that Sarah Champion may need to be seen to be doing something to protect and defend vulnerable women and girls. In the eyes of an average member of the public, calling a Parliamentary debate to discuss policy on trafficking would be a good thing; any call to arms on behalf of women and girls, especially in today's post #metoo era, can only be a good thing, right? But people who don't have insight into the sex industry and how it functions don't see what we see. The general public have no awareness of how the FOSTA/SESTA laws in the US have only added to the problem of sex trafficking, not reduced it. They aren't able to share in our dismay every time we see another news story or political crusade that fires up more anti-trafficking rhetoric, helping to confuse and conflate the issue even further. They aren't aware that every time a victim is upheld in the press, triggering collective guilt, the misunderstandings and misrepresentations around human trafficking are driven even deeper.

Since I started stripping in 2006, I've worked in ten cities across two continents, and networked with strippers from all over the world. In almost every club in the UK since the 2009 law I've had to provide a copy of my passport, and club bosses have been hypervigilant around checking identities of dancers for immigration purposes (the last thing they want to do is put their licence on the line). I've never seen evidence of kidnap, women being held against their will or ensconced in venues. I have, however, seen wage theft, workers being coerced and threatened with fines and sacked unfairly, and club bosses abusing their power, treating dancers as employees when they are actually self-employed. I have met women in abusive relationships, and I have encountered women with personal histories of abuse. I've met dancers who were totally on top of their game, making bank and setting up their own business empires and exit strategies. And I've met dancers carrying trauma, addiction and impossible levels of vulnerability. I've met women who operate at every level along the spectrum of consent, but I don't believe I've ever met a slave. Every dancer I met, no matter how limited their choices were, always had some choice.

There seems to be a special kind of hysteria reserved for the possibility that women doing sex work may have limited ability to consent, but a total blind spot around other workers of any gender whose consent is also limited for similar reasons. When it comes to sex work there is no nuance allowed, it's entirely black and white: sex workers are either totally 'empowered' Belle de Jour types, studying for their PhD and using sex work as a stepping-stone to get wherever they're going; or they are slaves. Nothing in between. No one who's freewill is undermined by economics and free-market Neoliberalism. No one who consents to appalling working conditions in the sex industry, because it is still a better economic choice than wiping up puke from a hotel bathroom floor for minimum wage. There are some who will go far enough to describe all sex work as trafficking, based on the belief that no one in their right mind would consent to such degradation, no matter how much freedom or power they have to consent. But then there are those on the other side who say that all work is prostitution under capitalism, since for the greater majority of people their options in life are limited.

Grouping victims together is harmful. When society can't tell the difference between an underage victim, who has been groomed, exploited and is unable to consent, and an adult worker in the sex industry who is denied their employment rights and is unable to stand up to exploitation because they themselves are at risk of being criminalised, then we have a continuous problem. If we can't tell the difference between who needs help and who needs to help themselves, we'll never be able to work out what kind of help anyone needs. We won't be able to make distinctions between different types of exploitation, and how to effectively tackle the causes. If we widen the definition of victimhood, put everyone touched by exploitation in the same group and just say 'shut it down', we create mass *numbers of victim groups but never properly address the reasons anyone became vulnerable in the first place. We never address the causes of poverty, why women continue to have such little value in the job market, how austerity makes people desperate, and how cutbacks to public education and health budgets lead to impossible levels of vulnerability.*

So when Sarah Champion mooted a similar law on this side of the pond, we weren't going to take it on the chin. Of course hundreds of protesters showed up on the streets of Westminster demanding to be heard. The press turned up and some of them actually made a decent job of explaining our collective demand, for a change. Mercifully, the debate didn't amount to much but the threat of increased criminalisation always rumbles along. Radical feminism has a foothold in politics, and trafficking is still the go-to buzzword for whipping up moralistic two-sided debates instead of calm, considered evidence-based discussion.

During moments of the protest outside Parliament, while the portable sound system started blaring Missy Elliott and bikini-clad strippers started twerking in earnest in the hot summer sun, it felt more like a carnival. But beneath the surface it had a deadly serious point to it – that by continuing to ignore sex workers' voices, failing to look at the evidence and continuing to drive us deeper underground into criminalised markets, politicians place us directly in harm's way. The divide between those in a position of authority, whose decisions can have direct consequences on the levels of danger or safety we can work in, and those of us who know our industry inside out, has to narrow if we are to make any progress.

HARM-REDUCTION AND THE 'RISE OF THE SOCIAL'

Demanding harm-reduction for sex workers is not so different from demanding harm-reduction for any other marginalised group. Any potential allies involved in similar struggles will be able to make the link between sexual exploitation and exploitation of other kinds. Homelessness, addiction, gender violence, immigration, poverty and mental health are all social justice movements that recognise a basic vulnerability that occurs when people cannot access their rights. What unites sex workers with migrant workers, for example, is the stigma of coerced or undermined consent; that is to say, labour performed under duress. Writer and professor of Women's Studies, Catherine M. Roach, explored these ideas in her book *Stripping, Sex, and Popular Culture*:

> In terms of prostitution, stripping, and sex work generally, what is most morally problematic and exploitative are the societal conditions of poverty that push women unwillingly into this industry ... if a woman decides to work as a prostitute or a stripper simply out of the desperation of poverty because she sees no other feasible choice open to herself or because her society offers her none, then her 'consent' is severely compromised.[20]

Rather than thinking of consent as a dichotomy between freely given or fully denied, it is more helpful to conceptualise it as a spectrum. Workers may be on a sliding scale of consent, which can change depending on personal circumstances, by the week, day or even hour-by-hour. A person's consent may be undermined by a host of elements, not least the need for money and the risk of poverty, but also by their criminal or immigration status, race, gender orientation, addiction or health status, level of education and general access to privilege. In this way we see how sex work is deeply intersectional; it is not the stand-alone issue that radical feminism treats it as. In her book, Roach quotes Carol Leigh once again: 'The problems of prostitution don't get solved until the problems of poverty get solved.'[21]

Mac and Smith also make excellent work of illuminating the socio-political context in which trafficking occurs in their book *Revolting Prostitutes*. When discussing the problem of sexual exploitation in the sense of a global sex trade, looking specifically at Thai sex workers trafficked into German brothels, they outline clearly how current immigration policy increases the likelihood of exploitation:

To locate the problem in the existence of prostitution . . . renders invisible the material things that made them vulnerable to harm. Europe's border regime meant they had to pay exploitative people huge sums of money in order to be smuggled in, and that once in, they had zero access to labour rights as their discovery by the state risked them being prosecuted. These two factors combined to produce a situation wherein they could be horribly exploited by their employers.[22]

Framing trafficked people as victims of systemic political failures, rather than focusing in on the endless stories of appalling abuse, may be a first step towards the complete shift in perspective needed to begin tackling commercial sexual exploitation. This is not to say appalling accounts of abuse are not important or undeserving; victimhood is real for all who have suffered it. It is not the intention of this book to downplay any lived experience of victims and survivors. But it is clear that sex workers and radical feminists are not aligned when it comes to working out the solutions. To quote Mac and Smith again:

> We disagree not only on the solution but on the *problem*: for carceral feminists, the problem is commercial sex, which produces trafficking; for us, the problem is borders, which produces people who have few to no rights as they travel and work. The solutions we propose are equally divergent. Carceral feminists want to tackle commercial sex through criminal law, giving more power to the police. For sex workers, the solution includes dismantling immigration enforcement and the militarised border regimes that push undocumented people into the shadows and shut off their access to safety or justice – in other words, taking power *away* from the police and giving it to migrants and to workers.[23]

The term 'carceral feminism', coined by Elizabeth Bernstein in her 2007 paper, 'The Sexual Politics of the "New Abolitionism"',[24] may be substituted for radical feminism, in as much as both ideologies involve a favourable approach to police power within the sex industry.* The anthropologist researcher Laura Agustín asserts the historical genesis for radical or carceral feminism in her book *Sex at the Margins: Migration, Labour and the Rescue Industry.* Her research into postcolonialism, undocumented migration, informal labour markets and sex work, reveals how early trends in social reform created a blueprint of government and social programming to this day. When looking at early philanthropist movements during the period of European colonialism, she says:

They position themselves as benevolent helpers, in what seems to be a natural move. Through historical research, I found that this self-positioning began at a time in European history when interest was awakened in the art of government and the welfare of the governed. Those who were concerned, the growing middle class, saw themselves as peculiarly suited to help,

---

* While there may be some differences when it comes to deciding who is criminalised – i.e. radical feminism often advocates for the Nordic model, which looks at ending demand by criminalising buyers of sexual services, while other feminists view the criminalisation of sex workers themselves as a deterrent – all are in support of incarceration as a solution. Few, however, are willing to draw comparisons between the loss of agency that comes from trafficking with the loss of agency that results from incarceration and criminal prosecution.

control, advise and discipline the unruly poor, including their sexual conduct. I speculated that examination of this impulse to control during the period when the modern sense of 'prostitution' was produced would help explain what goes on today, and my historical research did prove that early proto-feminist concepts relied on notions of helping and saving that go some way to explain social programming today.[25]

Agustín's work offers a chronicled account of humanitarianism from the period she calls the 'Rise of the Social', and how it came about that charitable causes and concern for the needy was taken on as middle-class women's work. As colonisation and imperialism brought in rapid economic growth for European countries, new demographics emerged including educated and financially secure women with time on their hands, for whom idleness was a sin. 'A newly empowered bourgeoisie set out to define how society ought to be constituted and how citizens should live; in the process, our contemporary understanding of "prostitution" was fashioned and philanthropy was carved out as a women's sphere of work.'[26] Beginning around the time of the French and US revolutions, the social as a concept, according to Agustín, plays a huge part in modern government; it relates to the ways social problems are identified and social reform is implemented.

There is much historical evidence to show that during pre-enlightenment periods, sex work was accepted as a necessary evil, linked to sin and vice but nonetheless, in some cases, ordained by the church. During the Rise of the Social new philosophers, social experts and philanthropists began reclaiming power from the church and rewriting narratives about social ills to justify their newfound authority. In this way we can see how the term 'prostitute' changed in definition from someone with a role in society, albeit derisory, to a victim in the true sense, deserving of being rescued. There can be no doubt that modern efforts to aid and assist sex workers, migrant or otherwise, come from a period of colonialist rule. By mapping current trends onto historical ones, we see how so much of present day radical feminism mirrors the words and deeds of bourgeois female philanthropists, which helps place the Lilith Report in context.

This is not to suggest, however, that the sex industry doesn't contain trauma. To reiterate, this book is not intended to obscure the continuing sexual exploitation of victims and survivors; nor does it suppose that returning to a pre-enlightenment era of church-licensed brothels, viewed by the rest of society as spiritual sewage systems, would be a sensible direction. It is, though, an effort to point out the problem of attempting social control and reform when those with the authority to write narratives are not members of the affected population they are offering to help. Throughout history various interest groups, whether they be churches, charities, police officers, journalists, government officials, NGOs, website engineers, social services, local licensing authorities, have had a hand in shaping cultural impressions of sex work. As long as sex workers themselves are left out of shaping the culture around them, we can expect exploitation to continue for a very long time.

THE POPPY PROJECT

In 2011 an article ran in the *Guardian*, titled 'Sex-trafficked women's charity Poppy Project in danger after Funding withdrawn', with a photo of seventeen smiling female support workers, whose jobs were all under threat if the charity didn't find £450,000 in funding. Like the Lilith Project, the Poppy Project was one of the subsidiary organisations set up under Eaves, founded in 2003, to provide services and support to trafficked women in the UK. Companies House financial records show that between the years of 2003 and 2008, Eaves received at least £11 million in public funding. At any given time the charity had more than £200,000 in reserves in a high interest account managed by Close Brothers Asset Management. However, records also show that income began to dwindle around the time of the 2008 economic crisis, and their accounts have not been filed since 2014.[27]

The Poppy Project can be credited with a number of activities. By 2006 Poppy were able to offer twenty-five crisis bed spaces to women who had been trafficked into prostitution in the UK at any one time, with an additional ten bed spaces to accommodate women who required less intensive support. Right from the start, they were part of a multidisciplinary Advisory Group, which included the Poppy Project, Immigration Services, and the Metropolitan Police Clubs and Vice Unit. An appraisal of the first year of the scheme, published by the Home Office, goes some way to explain the often opposing agendas between different parties within the Advisory Group. According to the 'Evaluation of the Victims of Trafficking Pilot Project – POPPY Summary Findings':

> The POPPY project was introduced as a Home Office funded pilot scheme in March 2003 to provide accommodation and a support service for women who had been victims of trafficking for sexual exploitation in the UK. Provision of the service was either temporary (for up to four weeks while the victim decided whether she wished to assist authorities) or conditional upon the recipient's agreement to co-operate with the police and immigration authorities to provide intelligence that might lead to the arrest and conviction of traffickers. Original eligibility criteria that excluded women who made claims for asylum were changed at quite an early stage of the project's implementation.[28]

In other words, the Home Office were initially not keen to include women seeking asylum in the project. This isn't the only example of conflict in the report, which is loaded with points of tension. The fact that material support was highly conditional, only available to women willing to engage in the prosecution of their abusers, is highly contentious. Out of 169 referrals only forty-three victims were placed in safety. There were no arrests or prosecutions as a result of the information provided by the women. Immigration Services expressed disappointment, 'whilst acknowledging the victim status of the trafficked women, the IS also has a statutory duty to remove those persons present in the country illegally'. There were 'mixed expectations about the main outcomes of the scheme' which were prevalent right from the inception of the Poppy Project. These mixed expectations never went away.

By the time the Poppy Project lost their funding it was clear their anti-deportation approach was at odds with Home Office procedure. As stated in the 2011 *Guardian* article, 'Since the charity joined an oversight board two years ago, assessing the government's compliance on tackling trafficking, it has successfully appealed 17 UK Border Agency decisions on identification of trafficking victims and forced countless re-assessments.' It appeared that much of the work done by Poppy had shifted from placing women referred to them in safety, to in fact intervening in the deportations of women who had been trafficked and were about to be sent back (presumably to the places they had been trafficked from, or had at least tried to migrate from initially). By 2011 it was revealed that the Ministry of Justice had awarded the public sector contract to the Salvation Army. This was followed by a public outcry that the mantle of responsibility to support trafficked people was being passed to the Christian organisation. The inference from a number of critics was that the government's decision to redirect funding to the Salvation Army was due to their likelihood to cooperate with border enforcement; a claim that appears to have been substantiated.*

From the point of view that the Poppy Project took a critical stance on government immigration policy and prevented the deportation of a number of trafficking victims, there is no doubt they did some good work. However, their track record on sex workers' rights was more dubious. Taking up an abolitionist position, they dedicated themselves to 'ending the sex trade' and aligned themselves with the radical feminist narrative that all sex work equates to violence, despite their close proximity to migrant sex workers and the intersectional

---

* A 2019 article ran with the headline 'Home Office "infiltrating" safe havens to deport rough sleepers'. Journalist Diane Taylor found the Salvation Army to be one of a number of charities allowing Immigration Services access to their homeless shelters by offering service users 'immigration surgeries' in spaces that are normally reserved for safety and support. Service users were being reassured that the 'surgeries' would not be part of an 'enforcement approach' and instead would help them receive financial support. But closer investigation found the surgeries were being run by border officials, and 'if officials conclude that attendees have no right to be in the country, they may be asked to agree to their voluntary removal. If they refuse they risk being subjected to the Home Office's "case-by-case" discretion and deported.' https://www.theguardian.com/uk-news/2019/oct/15/home-office-infiltrating-safe-havens-to-deport-rough-sleepers

nature of their strategy. In 2009 investigative journalist Nick Davies named Poppy as one of a long line of charities, NGOs and government bodies responsible for the incremental rise in estimated numbers of trafficked women in the UK. In his article 'Prostitution and trafficking – the anatomy of a moral panic'[29] Davies plots a chronology of the evolution of trafficking statistics.

It begins when the Home Office published a paper in 2000 titled 'Stopping Traffic: Exploring the extent of, and responses to, trafficking in women for sexual exploitation in the UK'. The paper was a research analysis of police statistics by Dr Liz Kelly and Linda Regan from the Child and Woman Abuse Studies Unit, University of North London. The two academics attempted to put an estimate on the number of trafficking victims in the UK. They looked at multiple sources and applied various different methodologies, and the academics themselves cautioned that their estimate was an unreliable statistic given the lack of reliable data. In their own words, 'Finding accurate estimates of the scale of trafficking in women has proven problematic.'[30] Police data revealed there were seventy-one victims of human trafficking in 1998. Using various other data, Kelly and Regan estimated that there may have been anything between 142 and 1,420 women trafficked in the UK during the same period.

However, when the data became public the upper end of

the estimate of 1,420 was printed as fact. Over time the research was reinterpreted, recycled and regurgitated by various organisations, including the Salvation Army, Christian charity Care, Anti-Slavery International, several cabinet ministers and MPs, and the *Daily Mirror*, and by 2009 the statistic had reached 25,000. Each time it was reported the estimate became massively inflated, despite there being no verifiable data to support the increase in figures.

In 2008 the Poppy Project published a paper titled 'Big Brothel: a survey of the off-street sex industry in London', by Julie Bindel and Helen Atkins, claiming to be the most comprehensive study into brothels in the UK. Research methodology involved recruiting male friends and colleagues to pose as punters to call London brothels and conduct quick over-the-phone interviews with whoever answered to ask about services.[31] As stated in the report, 'Whilst the statistics in this report represent exactly what researchers were told over the telephone, it is presumed that the source data contains some misleading information.'[32] Despite acknowledging the methodological limitations within the paper, Bindel used it to imply evidence of trafficking, saying 'Brothels offered women of 77 different nationalities and ethnicities, including many from known-source countries for trafficking'. Like the Lilith Report, the Big Brothel paper was later accused of being seriously inadequate. As explained by Davies:

That report was subsequently condemned in a joint statement from 27 specialist academics who complained that it was 'framed by a pre-existing political view of prostitution'. The academics said there were 'serious flaws' in the way that data had been collected and analysed; that the reliability of the data was 'extremely doubtful'; and that the claims about trafficking 'cannot be substantiated.'[33]

Much can be inferred from taking a closer look at research papers such as the Lillith Report and Big Brothel. While it is true that the research is considerably out of date, and one has to hope that research methodology has improved over the last twenty years, there has to be some acknowledgement that present day attitudes about sex work and trafficking have almost certainly been shaped quite considerably by poorly researched and unreliable data. There can be no doubt that human trafficking is very real and devastatingly harmful. But exploitation cannot be understood by pulling together a set of narratives and calling it research. Not only is this misleading for all who are genuinely concerned and wish to support vulnerable people, it also does a serious disservice to victims themselves.

Eaves Housing For Women is no longer a functioning charity. In October 2015 they ceased operations after the last of their essential government funding ran out. Records for 2020 show the appointment of a liquidation manager. After providing shelter services for vulnerable women since 1977, they published a heartfelt statement announcing their decision to close. In their statement they wrote the following comments, lamenting the new Tory Government austerity budgets, which by then had devastated the non-profit sector:

> Cuts, reductions and closures have of course hit a whole range of non-governmental organisations. However, there is much evidence to suggest that women are bearing the brunt. Fair Deal for Women found that it is women who have paid off 79 per cent of the deficit to date. It is more likely to be women in low-paid, insecure, part-time and public sector work, it is more likely to be women with caring responsibilities who may have to top up their incomes or rely exclusively on benefits and it is more likely to be women who need to rely on public, voluntary sector and specialist services. Yet these are precisely the areas being cut.[34]

These sentiments not only ring out a stark warning for tough times ahead for women, they also resonate loud and clear with a critical detail pointed out by sex worker-led organisations. The English Collective of Prostitutes have consistently argued that since 2010 austerity budgets have hit women hardest, putting them at greater at risk. They frequently point to a report published in 2016 by the Women's Budget Group, an independent network of leading academic researchers, policy experts and campaigners who scrutinise government policy from a gender perspective, that between 2010 and 2020 an estimated 86 per cent of austerity cuts in the UK will have fallen on women.[35] In their submission to the United Nations Special Rapporteur on Extreme Poverty and Human Rights they made the following statement:

> As poverty increases, more women, particularly single mothers, turn to sex work to survive and feed their families. In some cities massive rises in prostitution are being directly attributed to benefit sanctions.[36]

Considering how at odds sex workers and radical feminists have been in their approaches to sex work and harm-reduction, it's staggering to see how aligned they were in perceiving the *underlying conditions* that put women at risk in general. One can only imagine how, if this alignment were the basic commonality for a partnership, a group of well-resourced middle-class women with a knack for funding applications, and a collective of plucky, politically outspoken and dedicated sex workers with years of lived experience from working in the industry, could band together to launch a searing attack on the government's poverty and immigration policies.

If radical feminists and sex workers were to ever collaborate, there would be a better chance of effecting change for all women everywhere. But that would require monumental shifts in perspectives and an abandonment of long-held social identities that are centuries old. Thankfully, there are signs that a new generation of feminism is emerging that includes sex working feminists, and which recognises that harm-reduction policies must be centred around survivors' voices and experiences. And there are now more sex workers willing to fight for their rights than ever before.

8

HUSTLERS

> *Hustlers* is an intersectional Marxist feminist film about
> workers subverting the means of production in the face
> of 2008 financial collapse and posits queer feminist the-
> ories of chosen family and matriarchal lineage to survive
> the violence of cisheterosexist patriarchy.
>
> —Jean Chen Ho[1]

On 13 September 2019, a hotly anticipated movie was released
in cinemas worldwide to critical acclaim. Based on a true
story, *Hustlers* is about a group of strippers working in New
York City during the 2008 global economic crisis. Lauded as a
film focusing on female empowerment, the media hype surrounding the film promised an electrifying and inspirational,
never-before-seen production that subverts gender roles. The
impressive roll call of A-list celebrities and big budget publicity campaign meant the press junkets went into overdrive,

working up a frenzy before the film's release. Every promotional video or interview given by the all-female cast and production team made some kind of statement about female empowerment. Feminist themes about women working together, supporting each other and becoming a family were woven throughout the promotional campaign, promising a storyline that championed women like never before.

The message about female empowerment feels less clear, however, from the point of view of sex workers themselves. Strippers based in the US who were aware of the film going into production seemed uneasy from the outset. Even before the movie was released, there were red flags. Strippers whose lives had been touched personally by the film started internal discussions in private sex worker chat forums; to them the movie was a betrayal. Rumours began flying about where the storyline officially came from, and there were misgivings about the content of the film right from the get go.

Jordan Kensley is a semi-retired stripper turned fitness entrepreneur based in California. Kensley runs her own company, Head to Heel, supporting people into health through physical movement, spinal alignment and structural integration. She is also well known for teaching pole dance workshops in LA and around the world, specialising in stripper-style pole, which also until recently was euphemistically called *exotic* style. Efforts are now being made within the pole dance and fitness community to phase out the term 'exotic pole' because of its connotations with colonialisation, nineteenth-century World Fairs and cultural appropriation. Kensley has become an advocate for sex workers in the pole fitness community, where she fiercely defends strippers and strip clubs as the genesis of pole dancing. She staunchly challenges stigma and whorephobia wherever she encounters it, whether at pole tournaments, conventions, expos, or in the dance studios where she teaches. She began stripping in 2012, working in some of the most prominent strip clubs in Los Angeles including Jumbo's Clown Room and Cheetah's, which was one of the locations used for *Hustlers*. Kensley had misgivings about the film well before it was released. She says, 'My partner works in the film industry, so he kind of knew about it well before the public did. Through his contacts I was able to go to a screening of an early version of the trailer. We both watched it and thought, "Uh oh, this isn't going to be good for strippers at all."'[2]

Her first impressions of the film were coloured by what she already knew of the real life story that the film is based on, which at the time attracted serious media coverage. 'I knew about the story before the movie was written. I heard about the strippers' arrests when they happened; it was all over the news here in the US. Their court case got a lot of attention, and then there was the long article in *New York* magazine that went viral. I just knew that making a film about strippers who scammed their clients was not going to help us. The messages that the public get from the film are not conducive to sex workers' rights.'

The storyline of the film is indeed borrowed from a real life criminal case that garnered several years of press coverage in the US. Samantha Barbash and Roselyn Keo ran a gang of strippers in New York City who were arrested in 2014 and charged variously with forgery, conspiracy, grand larceny (theft) and assault. Clients being lured to a strip club, drugged with a homemade cocktail of ketamine and MDMA before being financially defrauded was a hot news item. Every time one of the defendants appeared in court to hear charges or receive a sentence, details of the case were relentlessly publicised. Legal proceedings continued up until 2017, when Barbash was sentenced to five years' probation. An image of her leaving court flipping both her middle fingers at a press photographer went viral.

In 2015 *New York* magazine published an article that also went viral thanks to its racy, cutthroat angle. Journalist Jessica Pressler developed something of a friendship with Keo, initially meeting her in person for interviews, which turned into longer phone conversations at night and even attending court appearances together. Pressler admittedly found Keo to be not entirely trustworthy as a source of information since, as she readily admitted in person, 'I am out for myself.'[3]

The article tells a grim tale of women working in the sex industry who exact a type of indiscriminate revenge on men;

all men everywhere, or at least the ones they come into contact with. The trigger for their vengeance is the 2008 financial crash that saw strip clubs change overnight from glittering goldmines to empty shells devoid of life. The implied logic is that they are sticking it to the man by taking back what is rightfully theirs, or somehow owed to them, by an economy that exploited them and left them high and dry. They did this by drugging clients, rinsing their credit cards and relying on the men's internalised shame and fear of losing social status to not file police reports.

These fears were exploited particularly well when Keo and Barbash also drafted full-service sex workers into the scheme, laid on as a kind of party-package for the wealthy Wall Street bankers they were fleecing. The ringleaders were in the habit of booking escorts via online listings sites and then cutting them a percentage of the takings – effectively incriminating themselves as pimps in the process, although these charges were never filed against them. Links to organised crime seemed par for the course as Keo and Barbash came into contact with drug-dealers and hustlers as part of their regular routine. Rather than working in strip clubs themselves, the gang would approach wealthy men in upscale Manhattan bars, lure them back to the clubs and render them unconscious by slipping illicit substances into their drinks, plundering their bank accounts and making off with as much as they could – often cutting the club a percentage of the haul as well. No strip clubs have ever been legally implicated, although Scores, Manhattan, the club where Keo and Barbash befriended each other while working together, was named as one of their preferred locations.

The tale, as told by Pressler, is a distressing account of people engaging in nefarious and criminal behaviours, treating their list of affluent customers as prey, without a great deal of context. If there is any lesson to be learned from the film it's that strip clubs are bad places, and exploitation turns people into amoral operators. Pressler quotes Keo, who goes by the name Rosie in the article:

> In the beginning, after work, Rosie would pick fights with her boyfriend, accusing him of cheating. 'It fucked me up in the head a little,' she said of the window her job gave her into the male psyche. 'The girls develop a terrible contempt,' one former Scores manager told me. 'They stop believing men are real. They think: *They are there for me to manipulate and take money from.*' And when it came to that, they all preferred the assholes. There's something extra-satisfying about persuading a man who thinks you're trash to spend his time and money on you. Preferably so much that in the end, *they* hate *themselves*. It's like, *Who doesn't have any self-respect now, motherfucker?*[4]

The implication, which is then replicated in the film, is that the women who had come to rely on their clients' spending habits decided to take matters into their own hands once the cash flow dried up post-2008 crash. Quite whom they were taking their revenge on, however, remains unclear. Was it the men who had patronised the clubs pre-2008, whose gratuitous displays of wealth had put Keo through college and helped her financially support her grandmother? Was it the men who ran the clubs, exploiting the dancers' lack of employment rights by imposing made-up rules, fees and fines on them? In either case, the logic doesn't stack up. The women weren't drugging and ripping off their old clients or bosses; instead they targeted any wealthy guys they could find. In fact, if any clubs did benefit from the racket then it's hard to understand how the women were getting their own back.

As for their wealthy customers, once again it doesn't seem that obvious exactly what they were seeking revenge for. Revenge that they weren't spending like they used to? Were they too wealthy for their own good? In Keo's words, 'What's an extra $20,000 to them?' Did she feel entitled to the money after years of earning it more easily prior to the financial crisis? Or was she working from a quasi-socialist ideology of wealth redistribution? If the bankers of Wall Street were responsible for the global economic crisis then was she assuming the role of a modern day, feminist Robin Hood with her band of merry women? In this case, the details of her own conspicuous consumption of caviar and iPads, Louboutin and Gucci undermine her radical credentials. Had she been redistributing even some of her illicit earnings back to women's shelters or sex worker charities the scam may have had more integrity. Survival sex work is no joke, but the stereotypical version of sex workers as told in this story, with their triviality and lavish expenditure, makes a mockery of the movement for sex workers' self-determination. In an article published on the blog Autostraddle.com, sex worker Janis Luna made the following observation: 'Rather than being a savvy indictment of capitalism, Ramona and Destiny (and Samantha and Roselyn) become the same type of entitled and violent abusers the movie shows them rebelling against.'[5]

Keo self-identifies as a hyperorganised businesswoman destined for greatness. She speaks of herself as the smart one, the girl with future prospects thanks to her refined perceptive abilities and opportunistic streak. She was the one trying to professionalise the scam by drawing up a rota and trying to maintain a sense of decorum amid the scene of hookers, drug-pushers and thieves she was working in. Her book, published the same month as the *Hustlers* movie was released, is titled *The Sophisticated Hustler*, implying a self-image of 'being above' all the emotional violence and carnage around her. A regrettable detail of Keo's story, according to Pressler's article, is her attitude towards the women she and Barbash cut in to the process:

> Running a team of hookers, strippers, and thieves was complicated. The prostitutes were unreliable. 'They wouldn't show up for work, they would be intoxicated, they would get beat up by

their boyfriends and had to be in the hospital or had asthma,'
Rosie said. And her attempts at being a den mother had been
met with indifference. 'You have *opportunities*,' she'd told one girl
in frustration. 'You just don't take advantage of them.'[6]

Keo has fallen into a classic pattern of whorephobia, attempting to distance herself from the full-service sex workers she
hired. The whole article is laced with slut-shaming language
– 'I have my dignity,' says Barbash. Their hypocrisy wasn't lost
on their arresting officers, who, according to the article, said,
'I liked the part when one girl I was interviewing had a
derogatory comment about the prostitutes they called in . . .
You think that drugging people without their consent is okay,
but a prostitute is derogatory?' By the end of the article, and
according to most of the news coverage that subsequently followed, Keo and Barbash had no higher opinion of each other
than the sex workers they hired. What started out as a friendship, at the very least of convenience, soured soon enough
once law enforcement was on their trail. One final detail of
the story seems to sum up the state of their relationship at the
point of their demise; when they found themselves under
arrest and incarcerated together in a cell at Rikers Island
awaiting charges, a correction officer asked them:

'Which one of you is the ring leader?'

'Samantha pointed to me,' Rosie said. 'I pointed to her.'[7]

Keo took a plea deal to avoid jail time. If we have learned

anything from our cultural obsession with dramatisations of organised criminal gangs, it's that nothing smacks more of betrayal and disloyalty than capitulating to the authorities. Throughout the story, if there was ever a feminist narrative of women working together, supporting each other and reclaiming their power, it seems to have dissolved by this point. Any commitment to each other as collaborators appear to have been built on shaky ground since Keo was, as she originally asserted to Pressler, 'out for myself.' As Jordan Kensley had feared, the messages about strippers signalled to the public are mainly negative, age-old tropes about sex workers as bad women – self-interested aggressors, whores who disrupt the moral fabric of society, threaten the family unit and fuck men up by leading them astray. Which is why, when the movie *Hustlers* was released, its declarations of female empowerment were so incongruous to the sex working community, who have long been waiting for something better.

─── ❧ ───

A few weeks before the movie Hustlers *was released in the UK, the ELSC got an email from a high-profile media PR company. I Googled their website and was impressed by the list of global productions they had previously worked on. They were asking if they could book us for a bespoke corporate event for a private list of special guests. They had found our life-drawing classes online and were reaching out to include us in their publicity campaign. I followed up the email with a phone call and the girl from the company I spoke to was courteous and friendly, and seemed excited to be working with us. I asked her what the purpose of the event was, and after swearing me to secrecy she revealed they were programming a series of events to publicise the release of* Hustlers. *They wanted to include one of our life-drawing classes as part of the hype and excitement building around the film.*

We have been running life-drawing classes with strippers as models for over five years, and we have built up a regular following. Our online event page explains the ethos of the collective:

> *ELSC are a bunch of feisty, feminist, fiercely independent women, who also happen to be strippers. They aim to shatter stereotypes and challenge stigma, whilst improving their own working conditions. They are bored of working in badly run strip clubs, being financially exploited and having very little say in how venues are actually operated. To counter this they have begun organising their own pop-up events, to create their own working conditions.[8]*

The life-drawing class set out to create an alternative workplace and business model to a strip club, and now provides a regular income to organisers, who are all strippers and share the responsibility of managing bookings and running classes. All models are from the stripping community and no previous life modelling experience is necessary; the only prerequisite is that they must have worked as a stripper, regardless of whether they engage in any other forms of sex work or not – their sex working status is not important to us. We set out to acknowledge the skill and proficiency of sexual entertainment. We've had some of the most talented pole dancers in the country model for us, and what they can do on the pole is breathtaking.

The thing I'm most proud of is that ever since we began the profit from the class has gone to strippers themselves. Everyone who has been involved in running or modelling for the class has been a stripper or ex-stripper. The public pay £15 per head to attend. We pay a nominal hire fee to the venues we use, and the rest we divide between the models and the organisers. We call the shots and control the money – no strip club bosses or managers have any say in how the class is run, nor do they have their fingers in the pie. We've consciously chosen venues with a history of sexual entertainment, but always remained in control of the finances. We started the class at the White Horse, one of the last remaining old school strip pubs in the East End of London, where we ran the class for two and a half years. After it shut down we moved to another striptease venue, 23 Paul Street, before finally moving to the Crown and Shuttle, a pub that used to be a strip venue back in the day when any pub could book strippers, before licensing laws put a stop to it.

The class is more than an opportunity to draw; it's a defiant celebration of our culture. We don't need an SEV licence to get naked for a life-drawing class, but we perform some of the same sexual labour for the artists who attend as we do for customers in the club. We're updating the relationship between artist and muse by reasserting the reputation that sex workers have always held in the art world. From Manet, Picasso, Schiele, Lautrec – male artists have been consuming sex workers' labour throughout art history. This time we are no longer just the muse, we are also the protagonists in the arrangement, and the beauty of it is that we've found a way of breaking down stigma. Men looking at naked women in strip clubs is gross says society, but middle-class people looking at naked women while drawing them is art, right? Sure. As long as we get paid we don't mind. But we don't see the people who attend our classes as punters, we don't treat them like walking ATMs. We treat them with respect, since that's how we expect to be treated in return. We've created a space where men, women and non-binary folk can appreciate the sensuality, strength, discipline and effort they see when strippers perform. The visual artistry of striptease is met with the visual artistry of drawing and illustration, and the results are often magnificent.

People who attend our classes come from all walks of life – men, women, queer, all ages. Professional artists sit next to first-timers, and people travel into London especially. One of my favourite artists is Helen, a lady in her fifties or sixties (I've never had the balls to ask) whose enthusiasm and artistic practice has been a gift to us. She so loved the class that she brought her eldest daughter along when she was in her final year of art school. We had another mum accompany her teenage daughter, who had apparently been pestering her mother for months for permission to attend the class. Initially her mum had been horrified by the idea of her daughter having any contact with the sex industry, but eventually relented on the condition that she would sit at the bar while her daughter partici- pated in the class. She did indeed spend the entire session sitting at the bar, closely monitoring proceedings. At the end of the session she approached us to say, 'You've really changed my mind about all this. I thought strip clubs were dangerous places, but this is not what I thought. You've really opened *my eyes.' We know how much difference our life-drawing class makes and the potential it has for changing the powerful narratives about sex workers.*

━━◦◦━━

The publicity campaign that ushered in the release of *Hustlers* was impossible to avoid. The bright pink neon font used for the film title was splayed across billboards, on the sides of buses, it filled up half-page ads in newspapers and magazines, and online coverage was relentless. The movie trailer promised audiences the sexiest flick of the year, if not the decade – flashes of Jennifer Lopez's unbelievable body (unbelievable by any standards, but all the more impressive at her age of fifty), carrying off athletic pole tricks with all the vivacity of a professional, were guaranteed to command attention. Alongside J-Lo, the roll call of actors and celebrities is impressive enough at the outset to ensure box office success. Constance Wu, Lili Reinhart, Keke Palmer, Trace Lysette and Julia Stiles perform alongside R'n'B superstars Usher and Lizzo; award-winning rapper Cardi B, an ex-stripper herself, exalted by an adoring fan base for her honesty and openness about her past occupation, was an obvious fit for the movie. The soundtrack also packs a punch with a list of heavyweight pop and rap legends, including Janet Jackson, 50 Cent, Big Sean, Rihanna, Fiona Apple, Fat Joe and Lil Wayne. The film's production budget of $20.7 million was by no means modest; it grossed $33 million in its opening weekend, and within thirty days of its release hit $100 million in box office sales, placing it high up the ranks of top selling movies of the year.

A good deal of its success can be owed to the amount of media coverage the film got. A sex industry plotline was always likely to get airtime, but in the post #metoo age a film written, directed and produced by an all-female team, in which all the lead characters were women, sent the news outlets into overdrive. *Hustlers* wasn't just light entertainment, it was a statement; a powerful call to arms for all women and female identifying people, it represented a zeitgeist. Every major news outlet ran a story, whether focusing on the real life court case behind the film or simply using it as an excuse to publish pictures of Cardi B's breasts; plenty of independent media channels ran with it too. *Good Morning America*, a prime-time morning TV show that regularly attracts average ratings of 3.5 to 4.5 million viewers per day, ran a piece on *Hustlers* featuring a joint interview with the stars of the film, Lopez, Wu, Reinhart, Palmer, Cardi B, and the director, Lorene Scafaria. The presenter narrated the movie's sales pitch: 'A star-studded female lead drama where the women flipped the script. Inspired by true events, *Hustlers* is about a group of strippers taking back their power from the men who run the club and their wealthy clients.' Sounds great. Everyone knows strippers are abused and exploited, right? Who wouldn't want to see them come out on top? In the interview, J-Lo makes an impassioned speech in support of strippers:

For me, the women in the story are very strong, you know, they're very powerful. You realise there's a baring of soul, vulnerability, but also a power and a strength they have that is really impressive. It takes a lot of bravery, a lot of courage . . . We gotta be there for each other and we gotta take care of each other, and we gotta have a good time, and I mean we spent hours and hours on the set . . . We're all hustling, that's the point. That's why the movie in a sense is very universal and people can relate to it.[9]

The problem with J-Lo's statement was that, in reality, strippers in New York had suffered the indignity of being booted out of their club, Show Palace, for a week while the film shoot took place. Luna's Autostraddle article explored the facts behind the making of the movie in more detail; co-workers told her that club management gave dancers little more than two weeks' notice that the club would be closed. They were given the opportunity to audition for work as extras but not all were chosen, and they were offered less than Screen Actors Guild industry standard rates; the film jobs were not guaranteed, nor did they account for anyone who for personal or family reasons couldn't be 'out' as a stripper in a major blockbuster and risk being forever identified with the sex industry. This meant that while the club was used as a film set, and paid a lucrative location fee for the hire contract, workers lost out on a week's earnings. Workers with no employment rights or protections, no contracts of services with their workplace, no salaries or actual employment status ultimately have no power to claim indemnity for loss of earnings.

Pressler's original magazine article makes a light reference to the working conditions of strip clubs and the after-effects of the 2008 financial crisis on the New York club economy that the women had built their livelihoods upon. If Pressler had concentrated on writing about an industry that doesn't recognise the employment rights of its workers she would have drafted a very different article, but explaining the impact of a sudden economic downturn on a relatively unregulated marketplace with virtually no protections against exploitation is less sexy than seductresses spiking drinks. The flavour of the story remains centred on the women and their choices (or lack of them) in a world where their actions seem clouded and confused by several different, often competing, narratives.

Voices from inside the sex industry were, of course, mainly absent from the mainstream discourse about *Hustlers.* The Internet Movie Database (IMDB) published the following synopsis:

Inspired by the viral New York Magazine article, *Hustlers* follows a crew of savvy former strip club employees who band together to turn the tables on their Wall Street clients.[10]

Strippers are not employees; had they been granted employee status Barbash and Keo may have been able to access some rights and protections that could have mitigated some of the devastating effects of the economic crash, without the need to go rogue. Much of what the film is actually about is what went on when a group of women who had discovered an atypical method of earning a living (stripping) then found themselves deprived of income in a context of precarious work. A sudden shift from abundance to scarcity causes suffering for everybody, but it can be particularly acute for marginalised, vulnerable workers, who have little to no social support or infrastructure to safeguard them.

Of course, J-Lo can't personally be held to blame for the alleged treatment of strippers at Show Palace, or any workers in a powerfully exploitative system; nor can Cardi B, director Scafaria or any of the *Hustlers* cast and production crew. The private business dealings of Show Palace and how they treat their workers is more of an issue for the Labor Commissioner's Office, not a film location scout. But the real indignity for strippers comes when the film includes scenes that appear to be some kind of attempt at unpacking and exploring the exploitative conditions in which dancers work. Constance Wu's character Destiny (based on Roselyn Keo) is the victim of wage theft and coercion, when she has to pay the club manager more than the agreed percentage, and tip his colleague, with no choice but to suck it up or lose her job. If it is no secret that clubs exploit dancers, then couldn't the film production team have demonstrated some awareness around the subject? Were Show Palace contractually compelled to distribute a percentage of the corporate hire fee among workers, as a goodwill gesture? Did they offer any kind of structural support to the dancers who lost work? A week of no house fees, or at least a discount? According to dancers who worked there, they got nothing whatsoever.[11]

The PR company offered us a decent corporate fee to put on a special one off life-drawing class for a specially chosen guest list of 'social media influencers', which we accepted. As the date approached, however, we started to have second thoughts. I'd heard from fellow stripper colleagues in the States and picked up from disgruntled social media posts among the online stripper community that the film wasn't going to have a positive impact, and we shouldn't be supporting it. I kept an open mind and asked around – Jordan Kensley put me in touch with strippers and pole performers who had been directly involved in the making of the film. I asked them what the beef was and a picture began to emerge about strippers being let down and put out of work when the other club used as a location, Show Palace in New York City, was closed for a week for the film shoot. No workers' rights, contracts or salaries make us precarious, so of course the New York strippers were left out of pocket when the film was being made. I knew Jacq the Stripper, a kind of celebrity of our community, had been brought in as a consultant and some actual strippers were hired as extras. And Cardi B can do no wrong in our eyes. But either way it started to look like another worrying piece of cultural appropriation – we had a dilemma on our hands.

I don't like to jump to conclusions based on what I hear from others, and always reserve the right to judge things for myself. The night before our life-drawing class we were invited to a premiere screening of the movie at Leicester Square, so I was glad of the opportunity to scrutinise the film before our event. By coincidence the cinema complex used for the screening was near a strip club, and the PR company were savvy enough to organise a special pre-party there before the screening, which we were also invited along to. It all felt quite exciting – we gathered together a small crew of ELSC members and arranged to meet each other at the party. I dressed up in a slinky red cocktail dress and strappy black heels, I even did my nails which I hardly ever do, wondering who else was on the guest list.

I arrived at the party and found Jade, a fellow ELSC organiser. She was wearing thigh-high iridescent stripper boots and drinking a mocktail through a straw. I looked around at everyone else and asked her, 'Why is this club full of teenagers?' Scanning the crowd I instantly recognised a particular demographic – young social media influencers, for whom attending high-profile events was a business strategy. The average age of the audience seemed to be about nineteen. The company had put together a guest list of image conscious party kids with huge Instagram followings, dressed up to the nines with the latest iPhone fused to one hand. They were taking selfies everywhere, standing in front of the stage with the pole in the background, tweeting 'OMFG! GUESS WHERE WE ARE???? IN A STRIP CLUB!!! #tweetyourhustle'. Party-goers could get their nails done at the pop-up nail bar, and branded photo booths ensured the Hustlers *logo had maximum impact on the combined social media reach within the room. There was a twerking competition and fake money being thrown around like a jamboree. Party bags were filled with packets of fake nails and eyelashes, free cocktails were being served at the bar with names like 'Karma's a Bitch'. As I took it all in I observed with dismay that we were the only actual strippers at the party. This event wasn't for us. This was for our culture to be consumed.*

The venue weren't prepared for the number of people at the party; the bar was mobbed and there was a twenty-minute wait for a drink. One of the managers appeared behind the bar, not to jump in and help serve drinks, of course not. Instead he strutted around with the intimidating physical arrogance of someone who was displeased, like strip club managers do. I knew he wasn't seeing the potential of this situation to generate new custom and increase their client base, only the nuisance of having more people to serve than the usual handful of male clients propping up the bar throughout the evening. I got sick of waiting so when the staff had their backs turned I grabbed one of the bottles of champagne from the display on the bar and found some empty glasses on a nearby tray. My fellow stripper colleagues were entertained by how brazen I was. 'Well, we're supposed to be hustlers, aren't we?' I felt no hesitation about stealing a bottle from the venue, given how much money I knew they would be making from dancers' fees later. I felt my frustration quickly rising – and it was focused on mainly one thing. Where were the actual strippers? Why weren't any girls from No. 14 on the floor working the crowd? The club wasn't officially open until 9 p.m. and the party started at 6 p.m. So the club was packed full of people but no lap dances in the private rooms, no strippers on the stage.

There was one performance, an incredible pole show performed by a highly accomplished aerial pole dancer, but we couldn't tell if she was a stripper. She didn't tease the crowd or remove any of her dazzling costume; none of us recognised her from any clubs we'd worked in. There was a very good chance she was a member of the pole fitness community who has perfected the art of pole dancing but never worked in a strip club. A horrible realisation was sneaking up on me, and everything I observed began to confirm it. There was clearly a lot of money changing hands to make this party happen – the free cocktails, the gift bags, the nail bar. There was a budget for this party, and a serious portion of it was going into the pockets of the club owners for hiring out the venue. And was a single penny of it going into any strippers' purses? A massive event celebrating strip club culture was happening, and the strippers hadn't been invited.

The film was scheduled to start at 9 p.m. so we all started moving next door to watch the film. As we were leaving a handful of dancers started turning up on the club floor, early birds eager to catch the first customers of the night. They looked conspicuous in their lingerie and heels, wondering what the party was for, and as I walked past them I knew they would still have to pay their house fee to the club that night – despite the corporate hire fee the club had just made. The familiarity of strip club economics left me feeling sick. As I walked up the stairs to leave I heard some of the Instagram kids screaming excitedly, 'Oh my GOD, did you see those girls? They were real strippers!' I mean, would it have done any harm to invite the dancers to the party before starting work? Or offered them a small cash fee to perform, a discount on their house fee for the night even? Would it have sullied the mood of the party if the crowd had been confronted by their own feelings in the presence of real life sex workers?

We grabbed some popcorn and settled into the VIP theatre seats at the front, the massive leather reclining ones. Watching it was slow motion carnage. Once we saw what direction the plot was going in whatever sense of pride and elation I had left began to plummet. Everyone else in the movie theatre behaved like they were at a panto, shouting out words like 'Liar!' and 'No, Sis! Don't trust her!' at the screen. One of the other ELSC members was going mental, yelling at people in the audience to have some respect, 'We're real strippers, for fuck's sake! Shut the fuck up!' We were seeing live in action the direct consequence of turning strippers into characters in a film, and sex work culture into something to be consumed. The audience weren't relating to us; strippers hadn't been humanised one bit. Our stories, struggles and realities had been commodified and packaged into pretty pink bow-tie bags, packets of fake nails, paper money and a beautiful pole dancer with an amazing body but no voice.

Just before the film was announced some young women representing the production company, STX Films, made a proud announcement that the film was written, directed and produced entirely by women. The declaration was met with rapturous applause. I was staggered. I felt such a disconnect between their enthusiasm for the film and my own trepidation. What difference did it make to have an all-female team produce a movie, if the actual women at the centre of the whole concept – strippers – had been sidelined? I'd just witnessed a real life edit of a strip club in which the women being celebrated on screen had been erased from their own workplace. What the actual fuck?

By the end of the film I was appalled. All my fears had been substantiated. We went for a late dinner together and there were mixed feelings among us. As an Asian-Canadian, Jade wasn't as hurt as I was; she could identify with Constance Wu's character, based on Rosie Keo. 'I felt like I was watching myself!' she yelled, happily. 'I used to sit and study at the bar with my college coursework like that. The old house mom backstage? That was basically Susanne!!!' There had been moments in the film that were entirely accurate portrayals of our world, that had felt so completely true and validating. The strip club scenes, J-Lo's pole dance, the soundtrack – it was all so beautifully shot and perfectly produced. If anything that made it a particularly bitter pill to swallow – seeing Jacq the Stripper and Cardi B, real strippers killing it in a Hollywood blockbuster, was everything. The joy and camaraderie backstage, the sisterhood and friendship, it was all in there attached to a storyline that none of us could relate to. The thought of being represented as criminals, drugging people, stealing their money and leaving them unconscious made us shudder. We've been collectively fighting to overcome stigma for years, and it felt like we'd just had a whole new fresh, steaming pile of stigma dumped on us from a great height. I felt cornered. And I knew the film wasn't something I could condone.

As much as I felt disappointed by the plotline, I also felt there had been positive intentions poured into the film. From talking to Jordan Kensley and the strippers she had put me in touch with, I got the impression that loads of people had got involved in something that looked and sounded amazing from the outset, but they hadn't foreseen the longer-term outcomes. But that didn't matter to the hundreds of enraged voices coming from within the sex industry, screaming blue murder that the film was a misrepresentation of their reality. The director of the film, Lorene Scafaria, eventually posted an apology to the New York strippers who lost work and pledged to donate money to the sex worker-led organisation SWOP Behind Bars. I wondered if three years ago, right back at the start of the project, Scafaria had just stumbled across a storyline that looked like a great film plot, not realising what a can of worms she was about to open.

Next day I decided to use our life-drawing class as an opportunity to move forward. I didn't want to pull out and lose the nice juicy corporate fee that was being shared between ELSC members. And I didn't want to miss the chance to share a message among a room of people with a massive combined online following. The ladies from the PR company turned up looking nervous; by then they had picked up on the tension among sex workers surrounding the film. It struck me that they were all so young, mid-twenties (prime stripper age), and that they were totally out of their depth, not very switched on to the issues coming to the surface. They'd organised food and brought some branded banners and posters; they had some cute cupcakes especially made with tiny edible dollar bills, champagne bottles and of course the Hustlers *logo on them. I had to hide a lot of eye-rolls.*

Once the guests were in their seats, we got their attention with a jaw-dropping pole dance routine given by ELSC member Sasha Diamond, arguably one of the best pole dancers in the country and a proud stripper. They did some drawing. Then we spoke. We talked about the threats of strip club closures and how that makes us more vulnerable, we explained the economics of a strip club and the exploitation we deal with on a nightly basis. We unpacked stigma and explained the definition of the term 'sex worker'. We opened up the room to questions and by holding space for dialogue this way we invited everyone to think and feel differently about the sex industry. If the PR company didn't know how to humanise us, we'd just do it ourselves. And if any good could come out of our involvement with the film it would be to use the publicity to draw attention to the really pressing issue – the lack of rights and protections that leave women who work in the industry vulnerable to exploitation.

The event was a success. We left with a restored sense of purpose, like our efforts had made a difference. Some of the people in the class became genuine allies, whose concerns for other marginalised communities aligned with ours. We felt the balance tipped back towards something that may look beneficial to sex workers. And we got so many kind words of support online, the extra boost really helped. A few days later I was scrolling through our ELSC feeds and stumbled across a post from the PR company. It turned out that there was a grand finale planned for their week of promotional events: a special private screening of the film at an intimate members-only cinema theatre in Soho, with a discussion panel afterwards.

I quickly Googled the chosen speakers for the panel. A former lap dancer who found fame as a Love Island *contestant, a pole fitness instructor and studio owner, a content creator and ambassador for the Young Women's Trust, a plus size model with a child psychology qualification, and trans rights activist and DJ. No working strippers then. No members of our trade union. No one to talk about efforts to establish workers' rights in strip clubs. No activists to share insight about the industry and explain the exploitative economics and nonsense regulations. No one to explain that when sex workers are constantly made invisible, powerless and vulnerable they turn to more risky and aggressive activities to survive. Even after we'd spent a couple of hours face to face with the PR company, unpacking and explaining the problems in our industry, the hypocrisy of being silenced on social media and misrepresented in mainstream culture, they didn't invite a working stripper to join their discussion panel. I felt my bile rise; there is still so much work to do.*

The problems in New York were not the only shortcomings of the film identified by the stripper community. Much of the public excitement fixated on J-Lo's pole dancing, which many members of the pole fitness community saw as a progressive milestone. Professional pole dancers have long been fighting to establish pole dancing as a serious vocational activity, and in 2017 their endeavours were fruitful when the Global Association of International Sports Federations officially recognised pole dancing as a sport. The trouble is that at least some of those efforts are spent on trying to distance pole dancing from stripping, exemplified when the hashtag #notastripper began trending in 2016. The hashtag prompted a rapid backlash from strippers and sex workers, who quickly pointed out the dire sanctimony of learning a skill invented and perfected by strippers while at the same time rejecting its originators.

Kitty Velour is a prominent British pole dancer and champion of stripper-style pole, who began her journey working in UK strip venues, including the White Horse, Shoreditch. 'I definitely felt that stripper style wasn't encouraged when I started, and people did turn their nose up at it. There were lots of competitions that restricted anything too sexy, using specific rules – like, the gluteal fold must be covered, no twerking, no removing any clothes on stage. It was as though it was something unnecessarily frivolous.'[12] Restrictions on 'sexiness' in the pole fitness world have only served to stigmatise the sex industry further, but thanks to those willing to resist and demand a reappraisal of this emerging culture, like Kitty Velour and Jordan Kensley, there has been a recent sea change within the pole community. More pole dancers do now seem willing to acknowledge and support sex work culture, from which pole dancing is derived, in order to avoid inflicting further harm on marginalised women. After all, stealing culture from a marginalised group, divorcing it from and/or practising it outside its original cultural context, while disrespecting or refusing to acknowledge its origins and giving nothing back in return is the very definition of cultural appropriation.*

---

* The concept of cultural appropriation emerged as recently as the 1980s 'in discussions of post-colonial critiques of Western expansionism' (*The Concise Oxford Companion to English Literature, 2012, Oxford University Press*). The theory continues to divide opinion, as some remain wedded to the belief that in a multi-cultural, globalised society there can be no such thing; rather that there is merely continuous exposure to and assimilation of different cultural norms between groups and nations. Marginalised or indigenous populations say otherwise; cultural appropriation of 'creative or artistic forms, themes, or practices' is more harmful when members of more dominant, powerful groups take from those who have less power. Put more simply, it is a culture of theft.

'One of the things that bugs me,' says Kensley, 'is that the pole artist who coached J-Lo, Johanna Sapakie, worked at Cirque du Soleil for ten years and was a pro-athlete before that – but she's never been a stripper.' Sex workers are no strangers to watching their work being appropriated in mainstream popular culture, by performers and artists who have little to no lived experience of the sex industry. The appropriation of sex work in pop culture has become such a ubiquitous feature that it's now practically impossible to imagine a world without it. Female artists who have championed the sexually suggestive imagery that was once denigrated and assigned to the sex industry have become household names: Nicki Minaj, Beyoncé, Rihanna, Lady Gaga, Cristina Aguilera, Britney Spears, Madonna, Janet Jackson and Lil' Kim are just some of the music industry legends who have borrowed heavily from the sex industry, strip clubs in particular. When Kate Moss pole danced her way through the music video for the White Stripes hit 'I Just Don't Know What To Do With Myself' in 2003, it was considered a ground-breaking piece of performance art. When compared to the stripper-style pole dancing and explicit choreography used in Rihanna's video for 'Pour It Up', released ten years later in 2013, it hardly raises an eyebrow these days. It therefore was no surprise, given the history of strip club facsimiles in pop culutre, that when real life former stripper Cardi B moved into the music industry she was propelled to fame over night. Cardi B certainly isn't the first mainstream celebrity to have a past as a stripper (Lady Gaga, Brad Pitt, Javier Bardem to name a few) but she is probably one of the first to make it a central aspect of her identity, using it proudly to capitalise on recently emerging anti slut-shaming, sex-positive and pro-women attitudes. Her arrival may herald a new era in which former sex workers may no longer have to conceal their past lives in favour of a sanitised version of themselves, although that remains to be seen.*

It's by no means just the music industry that deliberately appropriates sex work culture, nor is it a new phenomenon; Hollywood has been using sex workers as subject material almost as far back as the dawning of cinema itself. Narratives of 'fallen women', who are lured into forced prostitution often rescued just in the nick of time, date back to at least 1900 with the silent, black-and-white production *The Downward Path,*

---

* In May 2019, just a few months before the release of *Hustlers*, Cardi B came under fire when a video of her resurfaced on social media in which she speaks openly about drugging and robbing clients when she was a stripper working in New York. Mainstream public outrage immediately followed, comparing her actions to those of Bill Cosby and R. Kelly, men accused of having long histories as abusers of women and girls (in Cosby's case also of drugging women as well as sexually assaulting them). While the blowback has done little to harm her career, the video unfortunately served to contribute further to sex work stigma and whorephobia. The comparisons to known sexual predators, despite there being no suggestion or admission of her committing sexual assault against the men she robbed, demonstrates how, in the public imagination, a sex worker can be seen as equally as harmful as someone with a verifiable history of sexual predation.

directed by Arthur Marvin. Other titles of short silent films directed by Marvin included *The Slave Market, A Raid on a Women's Poolroom* and *Rescue of a White Girl from the Boxers*. The film industry's obsession with prostitution has only grown over time, with many high-profile actors nominated for and awarded with Academy Awards for their portrayal of sex workers, almost as a rite of passage. Who can forget Charlize Theron's indelible role as real life prostitute turned serial killer Aileen Wuornos in *Monster*, 2003? Or Kim Basinger in *L.A. Confidential*, 1997? Silver screen icons Jane Fonda, Susan Hayward and Elizabeth Taylor are among the many celebrities who have been awarded Oscars for their work playing sex working characters, while the inventory of nominees, too long to list, includes Julia Roberts, Anne Hathaway, Jon Voight, Marisa Tomei and Audrey Hepburn. In the 2019 documentary *Whores on Film*, director and sex worker Juliana Piccillo points out the double bind those in the sex working field find themselves in as a result:

It's really uncomfortable being a sex worker and on one hand being used as a source of entertainment and inspiration, and on the other hand being thrown in jail and having your children taken away for what you do for a living.[13]

When human rights organisation Amnesty International released their draft policy on sex work recommending full decriminalisation in 2015, it was quickly followed by a

312 | *The Ethical Stripper*

knee-jerk public outcry. A petition demanding that Amnesty International reverse their proposed policy, by adopting heavier punitive measures and criminalisation, immediately picked up momentum, catching the attention of celebrity advocates. Among the thousands of co-signatories were Meryl Streep, Kate Winslet, Emma Thompson, Lena Dunham and (perhaps most egregiously of all, due to her Oscar nomination for her role as the prostitute Fantine in *Les Misérables,* 2012) Anne Hathaway. Sex workers were quick to point out the hypocrisy of a petition calling for tougher criminalisation of the sex industry that was supported by a host of film stars and celebrities, many of whom literally 'get paid to have sex on television'. Is there a single Hollywood A-list actor who hasn't performed sex for the camera? A Canadian sex worker and writer, Fleur de Lit, subsequently published an article titled 'What's Lena Dunham got against sex work?' that deftly cut straight to the core issue:

It wasn't long ago that hookers and women actors enjoyed more or less the same questionable reputation . . . Because of our connected history (those of us who were known to do both were referred to as demireps), I often wonder what would have happened if sex workers had been the ones who ended up with the more respectable social profile. Would we be signing petitions that claim acting 'is predicated on dehumanization, degradation and gender violence that can cause life-long

physical and psychological harm' to those exploited by Hollywood executives, agents and unattainable beauty standards? Would we declare that acting, especially for women, 'is
a harmful practice steeped in gender and economic inequali-
ties that leaves a devastating impact on those sold and
exploited' in the acting trade? Would we want to make sure a
woman actor never again had to shave her head, spend
months practising crying while she sang to make sure she
could hold the tears and the note simultaneously, lose ten
pounds and then another fifteen on a near starvation diet that
consisted of two puny servings of oatmeal paste a day, as
Hathaway did to prepare for her role in *Les Misérables*? . . .
Would we be using Hathaway as a symbol of the suffering and
degradation faced by all actors, gravely and knowingly saying
things like 'And Anne is one of the lucky ones. There are so
many actors struggling in complete obscurity, forced to attend
parties with fondling executives and giving blow jobs to big-
wigs just for an opportunity to get an audition'?[14]

Given this article was written well before the Harvey Wein-
stein and Bill Cosby scandals demonstrated the extent to
which sexual coercion and sexual predation has been rife
within the film and TV industries for decades, it seems
remarkably insightful. If the #metoo movement has proven
anything it's that women everywhere are vulnerable to sexual
violence, including precariously employed women working in

the arts and entertainment. The glaring double standard embodied by the celebrity petition flagrantly disregards voices from within the sex industry, while being championed by women who have directly benefited from *playing the roles of prostitutes,* appropriating the lives and stories of the very people they wish to save.

There were rumours flying that Jennifer Lopez was tipped to receive an Oscar nomination for her role as Ramona in *Hustlers,* adding her to the illustrious register of stars prized for their ability to perform a role in the realm of fantasy that is so heavily reviled in real life. In the end she didn't, and one has to wonder if the Academy Awards just didn't want the associated furore that might follow if an Oscar nomination had been on the table. How would it go if sex workers turned up to protest outside the ceremony? She did, however, get a Golden Globe nomination for Best Supporting Actress. What is it that authenticates these roles according to the viewing public and awards ceremonies? Is it a performer's bravery for *degrading* themselves that is so deserving of the accolades and trophies that inevitably follow? Their *boldness?* Which begs the question – where are the prizes for the women with, in J-Lo's own words, 'a lot of bravery, a lot of courage' to perform sexual labour in clubs, flats, brothels, hotels, restaurants, on the streets and behind closed doors every day? There is a common in-joke between sex workers, when they successfully complete a challenging booking or endure a gruelling night with a difficult customer in VIP – 'I should've got an Oscar for that.'

Strippers by now are quite used to seeing their intellectual and artistic property being ransacked to sell records, lingerie, and boost ratings. But raids on strip clubs in New Orleans, restrictions on licensing in New York City, and feminist campaigns to shut strip clubs down in the UK, while Hollywood executives grow rich from a movie that depicts their private domain, is a stretch too far. These disparities reflect the precise transfer of power and economic growth that leaves sex workers forever on the back foot. One of the very real after-effects of FOSTA/SESTA in the US, restricting the use of internet advertising platforms by sex workers, was that strippers and sex workers were booted off the internet by social media giants like Facebook and Instagram. Social media accounts are regularly suspended and deleted for any suggestion or depiction of adult material, while on the other side of the hill *Hustlers* appeared to have no problem distributing sexually suggestive images of Cardi B's boobs or J-Lo's bikini-clad flesh writhing around in a pile of money, on any of the major social media platforms. Sex workers are compelled to become activists and start petitions, like UK-based alternative model, webcammer and content creator Rebecca Crow,[15] who started an awareness campaign to challenge the inconsistent and seemingly discriminatory practices of censoring, deleting and 'shadow-banning' on Instagram.

To the uninitiated, it may sound fair; social media wasn't created with the needs of sex workers in mind, and the average public member probably doesn't want to be confronted by sexually explicit content, particularly when children are involved. But by the same logic, the internet becomes a reflection of the high street and the arguments used to ban sex workers online mirror the same justifications for shutting down strip clubs – *It's harmful! It's objectification!* In fact for sex workers themselves, using the internet has become an essential tool for harm-reduction. It's not merely a matter of self-promotion; sex workers, like anyone trading on their image or profile such as actors, performers, personal fitness instructors, life coaches (or just about anyone selling themselves in the new Neoliberal era), use the internet to build their brand, grow followings and most importantly screen clients. It also enables members of the sex-working community to share info and red flags with each other, build community and safety networks. The awful truth is that the FOSTA/SESTA laws are more likely contributing to higher levels of violence and coercion for sex workers, not only in the US but around the world since social media platforms are global, by removing one of their best weapons for self-determination.

Whether inadvertently or intentionally, *Hustlers* as an entire production manages to touch upon some of the most fraught and fiercely debated issues in mainstream feminism, intersecting with, race, class, gender and sex workers' rights, albeit in some cases clumsily. As director Scafaria put it in her *Good Morning America* interview, 'I was excited to explore . . . the humanity of it, and I mean we've seen a scene in a strip club in every single TV show and movie ever, and so few have been told from their perspective, and that's what really interested me just from a human level.' It's clear, particularly from the scenes in *Hustlers* that were more accurate than most usual Hollywood depictions, that the production went to some lengths to avoid the usual pitfalls of cultural appropriation. Several strippers and former strippers were brought in as performers and consultants on the project, as a conscious endeavour to bring authenticity to the scenes. Much care and attention was spent on trying to get the depictions right. Casting Cardi B was a shrewd move in this respect, not least because of her embodied experience of working in Manhattan throughout her stripping career. As she says on *GMA*, 'I knew that scene very well, like, I have danced in the New York City Manhattan strip clubs, because there's different types of strip clubs, you know what I'm saying. And it's like, oh man, I'm having flashbacks.' Jacq the Stripper, a comedian, writer, artist and stripper was also given a role. Her inclusion as a consultant on the film, as well as a short cameo, helped define it as one of the most convincing representations of a contemporary strip club.

Another celebrity who had first hand knowledge of stripping in New York during the period the film was set was Trace

Lysette, a prominent transgender actor, who has since spoken candidly about previously working as a stripper at Scores, the club at the centre of the story. Her rise to fame as a transgender woman, landing mainstream roles on prime-time TV before being cast as a stripper in *Hustlers,* is heralded as a progressive development in the movement for greater trans visibility. Including Lizzo, a plus size woman of colour whose larger physical proportions have rarely been affirmed by mainstream acceptability, as one of the *Hustlers* strippers is another example of diversifying from the typical white-skinned dominant ratios of Hollywood productions, by centring on sex workers of colour. In fact, if *Hustlers* set out to be one of the most diversely represented films of the twenty-first century it has succeeded.

In preparation for playing the lead character, Destiny, Constance Wu worked in a strip club for real for three nights. She didn't have to audition, but she did have to pay her house fees and commissions to the club, and tip out to the DJ and security like everyone else. At the end of her three nights she donated her earnings back to the women who were working in the club as a gesture of thanks for showing her the ropes of the club, which is perhaps the only example of solidarity with strippers in the entire production. Wu's contribution to the *GMA* interview went a little deeper than her fellow co-stars as she attempted to critique societal norms:

I feel like in our society, once you hear that type of a profession, whether it's stripping or sex working or anything like that ... the judgement stops there, and they don't get to know people as humans and understand their stories ... In, like, the patriarchal society there's only, like, one position for a woman. But that's a comment on scarcity, not gender. I think our relationship in this movie really proved that because it was all run by women.[16]

Despite her best efforts, the confused messages conveyed in her statement reflect the confusion inherent within the film. Wu has been one of the only celebrities to use the term 'sex work' on her public platform, which may be deemed as progress. But the mixed messages about sex work, as rightly pointed out by Jordan Kensley, don't help move the conversation on if they include a storyline loaded up with stigma.

Throughout *Hustlers* the lines between victim/abuser are obfuscated, not least because everyone's motivations appear compromised by greed and self-interest. Between the male patrons looking for a good time, the strippers working the clubs, the scammers working their client lists, the hookers and dealers who were cut in on the scams – by the end it becomes impossible to figure out who is screwing whom (no pun intended). Once again we see the clubs get away scot-free; club bosses are virtually absent from the story. Of course, from a feminist angle that's a good thing – who wants to hear and see male characters in positions of power anymore? But by focusing on the personal stories, proclivities and rationales of individuals as players in a dangerous game, it is no longer necessary to explain or critique the working environments in which the story plays out. Understanding strip clubs as places of work, and understanding the complex power relationships within them, is such an integral part of the fight for sex workers' rights; but this seems to be a fact that mainstream media has not yet reconciled.

If the aim was to prioritise female voices and storytelling over male ones, *Hustlers* has been a triumph. Post #metoo, mainstream feminism seems to be working overtime on countering centuries of culturally dominant male voices and narratives. But is it simply enough to swap the presiding gender, subjugating men instead of women for a change? And in the case of *Hustlers,* is it feminist to prioritise women's stories if they actually help to perpetuate stigma, violence and regressive tropes about sex working women? Regrettably, the only male voices within the *Hustlers* narrative, besides one or two of the victims, are those of policemen; their contribution to the plot was to ridicule both the male victims and the female perpetrators. It is yet another serious oversight on behalf of the *Hustlers* production team to disregard historical abuse of police powers against sex workers, and allow the male voices of authority to be occupied by cops.

Antonia Crane is a stripper, adult entertainer, professor,

activist and writer based in the US, focusing on the labour rights movement and trade union activism in the sex industry. Following the release of *Hustlers* she wrote an article titled '*Hustlers* Is Ugliness Wrapped In J-Lo's Chinchilla Coat', providing the following analysis:

> *Hustlers* assumes we'll root for this brand of poetic justice and its 'hurt people hurt people' lazy logic, when in fact there is no settling of the score without addressing the systemic global market and the corruption within it . . . As beguiling as certain authentic moments were to watch, *Hustlers'* failure to interrogate its own logic was distracting. To drug and rob strip club clients (and assorted strangers) in order to even a score is supposed to be funny, but it's acutely sad.[17]

Hustlers has since proven to be a highly divisive piece of popular culture. Films that represent sex workers have a notable role to play in popular opinion, and with an audience reach as considerable as that of *Hustlers* they have the potential to influence vast numbers of people. Opportunities to move the conversation on only come along once in a while, and when they do they reveal just how far we have (or haven't) come. It's clear from the perpetual representation of sex workers as fallen, disgraced women who do bad things that more discussion is needed.

What is badly missing from the cultural narratives are sex working characters for whom their job is not the source of their demise. We are missing stories about sex workers who provide for their families, start their own businesses, raise kids, go to college, overcome poverty, or just happily exist on their income from sex work, without the need for virtuous self-improvement storylines to justify their choice of livelihood. We are lacking tales about sex workers who don't get arrested, killed, beaten up, raped, demoralised by their clients, partners, pimps or any other male abuse figure. We are starved of examples of sex workers building resilience, learning how to stay safe and establish their rights in the workplace. We are in need of storylines that illuminate how sex workers are contributing members of society with value and worth, and how criminalisation and workplace exploitation have deleterious effects not just on individuals but on the wider community as well. When we see J-Lo playing a character in full stripper get-up, demonstrating outside her local city hall with a placard proclaiming SEX WORK IS WORK and demanding employment rights, perhaps then we'll know the conversation has moved on.

9

SEIZE THE MEANS
OF TITILLATION

Together we're rewriting a story about strength and
grace. We're not an invisible revolution, we're forming a
powerful new visual language that demolishes shame.

—Rachel Lena Esterline[1]

What does the future hold for strippers in the UK? As we see
numbers of strip clubs dwindle in the UK, at least one thing
is clear – stigma works. Stigmatising strip clubs has proven
extremely effective for those wishing to see them disappear,
not least because of the internalised stigma carried by those in
the industry itself. By presenting themselves as legitimate business owners, club bosses like Peter Stringfellow and John Gray
have achieved little besides the further debasement of sex
work. One has to wonder how things may have turned out
had they accepted and embraced their role as sex industry

324 | *The Ethical Stripper*

operators, and spent their money, time and resources standing up for all vulnerable workers in the sex industry, rather than looking after their own business interests. However, it should be clear by now that strip club bosses and sex industry operators cannot be relied upon to uphold the rights and freedoms of workers or even women in general.

Hugh Hefner is probably one of the clearest historical examples of this. The founder of *Playboy* magazine, which went on to become a giant international media brand, died in 2017 at the age of ninety-one after building yet another global business empire from sexual labour. The Playboy bunny logo has become a ubiquitous symbol of the sex industry. Hefner is less commonly known, however, for having funded the legal fees for the pro-choice argument during Roe vs. Wade in 1973, the court case that set a legal precedent for abortion in the US. Roe vs. Wade was a monumental triumph for the feminist movement, and for a brief moment Hefner was a champion of women's rights. However, once the victory had been achieved Hefner walked away from the ongoing fight for equal pay and equal opportunities for women. His motivations for funding the pro-choice legal fees eventually became clear; access to abortion was as convenient for men as it was a relief to women. It allowed men the freedom to enjoy multiple partners and sexual encounters without the marital and economic responsibilities of raising infants conceived accidentally. Hefner's main concern was protecting the interests and rights of his male patrons, a commitment that never changed for the rest of his life.

Besides industry magnates, law makers can no more be expected to suddenly wake up and listen after demonstrating a long history of problematic and ill thought-out policies that have simply appeased disgruntled constituents and fanatical opponents. Harm-reduction is complex work and requires a dedication to investigating and understanding the often invisible realities of the sex industry. The last decade of licensing procedure, its obsession with 'no-touching' and enforcement, expensive licence renewal showdowns, and extremely poor relationship building with workers themselves, shows how far off the mark council officials have been with their approach.

The next logical step in the journey towards self-determination for sex workers is policy and law designed around harm-reduction, with their voices and lived experiences at the core. But if club bosses, radical feminists, licensing officials and media executives can't be depended on, that only leaves one group: sex workers themselves. In the UK, sex worker activism has been growing louder and more visible every month. For every club raid, there has been a push back from the stripper community, with help and support from the newly formed sex worker branch of the trade union United Voices of the World (UVW).

In June 2019 strippers in Sheffield, along with other sex workers and allies, took to the streets in brightly coloured clothes and wigs, with placards saying things like TWERKING

CLASS HEROES and WALK A MILE IN MY PLEASERS. With support from UVW, the Sheffield strippers fought back to reclaim the narrative, demanding that their choice and consent to work in a strip club be publicly recognised. Strippers are in a uniquely difficult and strange position, having to organise and protest to preserve licences and keep their clubs open, despite the fact *they know* they are being exploited at work. Just like the dancers of Hackney ten years ago, the Sheffield strippers' lack of employment status gives them very little power to organise from. If they try to demand change in the workplace their jobs are not safe, even if they make significant personal contributions by protesting to save the club's licence. Once again, we see how sex workers find themselves stuck between several hard places – public opinion and feminist outrage, misclassification and exploitation at work, risk of unemployment, media misrepresentation – and so the list goes on.

Despite this, the movement has well and truly begun. There is a tremendous amount of energy required to sustain it, but since establishing the trade union sex worker branch in 2018 momentum has been gathering pace. Voices can no longer be silenced, and what began with whispered murmurings in club changing rooms is turning into a roar. Strippers are on the move, and this time they are showing up alongside sex workers; perhaps the most important lesson to be learned from the last ten years and beyond is that solidarity between workers is needed now more than ever before, no matter their job. If strippers want fair working conditions, it cannot be at the expense of other less privileged groups. Whether they chose to or not (as in Hackney where dancers were forbidden from standing on a picket line alongside ECP), distancing themselves from sex workers has not helped dancers in the long run. Recent events in the UK can show how quickly and effectively action can be realised when collaborators from different intersections can come together.

This chapter is written with both sex workers and potential allies in mind, in the hope that discussing activist tactics can be of use and inspiration to those who are sick and tired of working in toxic workplaces and those who dream of meaningful change. The work of salvaging their rights, reclaiming their own narratives, and positioning themselves as powerful agents of their own destinies, might sound like an insurmountable workload for sex workers; which is precisely why the need for allyship is more crucial now than ever. If strippers want to reshape and transform the SEV industry from within, then the current obstacles can be grouped into four main categories, each requiring a complex set of strategies, sacrifices, personal effort and individual dedication from sex workers and allies if they are to be resolved.

I. EXPLOITATIVE BUSINESS PRACTICES IN THE WORKPLACE

Since the rise of Neoliberalism, Western governments have been busy deregulating markets and divorcing workers from their labour rights. Under Neoliberalism everything is for sale; there are no limits or boundaries to the marketplace and all labour can be monetised, since the belief systems underpinning Neoliberalism are the rights and freedoms of the individual to make a profit. However, the sex industry serves as a perfect example of what happens in a deregulated economy; there is no economy more deregulated than a criminalised one. Criminalised economies are controlled by coercion, violence, greed and exploitation, and sex workers have for the most part historically been labouring in unregulated marketplaces. This goes some way to explain the need for decriminalisation; the way to end the abuses in the sex industry is by recognising the labour rights of those working in it.

Strippers are the original zero hour contract workers; perpetually on the fringe between regulated and unregulated work, strip clubs are a kind of Neoliberal dream. Extraordinary wealth *is* generated, precisely because the clubs can operate freely and uphold their right to profit, at the cost of workers' conditions. But regulation should be deployed to protect those who are most vulnerable to being exploited. Strippers have been experiencing the kind of retrogressive labour standards that workers in other fields have begun to organise against, particularly in the gig economy; misclassification of worker status is the underlying indicator that has allowed business operators in many industries to abuse their power.

Under Neoliberalism, strip club bosses (along with Uber,

Deliveroo, and many other companies) have had it good. Without any serious monitoring of business standards these practices have been accepted as normal. There are historical reasons for how this situation arose, chiefly that club bosses have taken advantage and built their business model on wage theft *because they could*. Dancers have got so used to being told that they are self-employed that it is accepted as fact without closer inspection. Very few efforts have been made, besides abolition, to rectify things. Looking at historical attempts to intervene shows us how previous strategies were less than successful and what lessons can be learned.

In 2008 Nadine Quashie, a lap dancer at Stringfellows,[2] was sacked after falling out of favour with management, despite having worked there for many years without any problems. Rather than acquiescing, she decided to embark on a four-year legal battle in a bid to prove her labour rights. She took Stringfellow Restaurants Ltd to an employment tribunal for unfair dismissal, where she initially lost her case. However, the Employment Appeal Tribunal found in her favour; Stringfellows then appealed against her and this time the Court of Appeal ruled in their favour. Quashie then tried to test the ruling in the Supreme Court but her case was rejected. As the case went back and forth over several years, Quashie's employment status was scrutinised in extraordinary detail; ultimately she lost because she didn't legally meet the criteria of *employee*. Had she won her case, it might have had a wide impact on the industry, sending out a clear message to club owners that dancers had employment rights like anyone else. Losing her case, however, sent out a different message to dancers everywhere – not to bother.

Had Quashie brought her case today, she wouldn't be arguing for employee status; she would be bringing forth strategic litigation to prove *worker status*. This is exactly what a small but growing number of strippers in the UK, with the help of their trade union, are attempting to do now. Under EU directives, worker status is a relatively new employment category aimed at protecting workers in the informal gig economy, who often work without contracts or fixed salaries. Lap dancers fall into the same category of workers as the Uber drivers, Deliveroo workers and people in the gig economy, who have frequently been misclassified. In the case of Pimlico Plumbers Ltd vs. Smith 2018,[3] a Supreme Court ruling found that plumber Gary Smith met all the criteria for worker status, rather than being self-employed. Days after the ruling, Pimlico Plumbers boss Charlie Mullins appeared on Channel 4 News to discuss the ruling and defend his business. Wearing a snazzy three-piece suit and speaking with an unapologetic tone, Mullins repeatedly pointed out that the plumbers working for his firm were making substantial amounts of income, as though their lack of employment rights was perfectly justified. He had mannerisms and characteristics similar to a strip club boss, right down to his haircut, tone of voice and Rolls-Royce with personalised number plates, CH4 RLE.

While I was in the final stages of writing this book, a case was brought by a unionised lap dancer in East London against a club who sacked her. In January 2020, a judge ruling in the case of Sonia Nowak vs. Chandlers Bars[4] found in favour of the dancer, Ms Nowak. Sonia was working at one of the Shoreditch strip pubs, Browns, and after becoming a member of United Voices of the World she began talking to her stripper colleagues about unionisation, which, as someone with worker status, she had every right to do. The right to collective bargaining is one of the key employment rights of workers, protected under the Working Time Regulations 1998; a list of other rights include holiday pay, protection against unlawful discrimination (e.g. age or race), protection against unlawful deductions from wages, and the right to not be treated less favourably for working part-time. Workers are also entitled to National Minimum Wage for the hours they work. Many dancers baulk at the idea of minimum wage, however, since one of the key reasons anyone chooses sex work is to escape the demoralising drudgery of low-waged work. But one of the possible changes proposed by the UVW sex worker branch is for dancers to be paid minimum wage for the hours they work, plus tips and VIP/lap-dance earnings on top of this, ending the routine of charging dancers house fees.

In order to establish the employment rights listed for people with worker status, it must first be established that dancers do indeed have worker status. In Sonia's case, the judge found that she did meet the criteria of worker status, based on the particular business practices at Browns. She was told when to work, what to wear, how to behave, and (the most important test for determining whether someone is self-employed or a worker) she was not allowed to send someone else to do her job in her place.* The list of rules and compliance for dancers is what actually pushes them away from the self-employment category, into the category of worker. Sonia's case established legal precedent, opening the door for all dancers in the UK who meet the same criteria at work to claim their employment rights in the workplace.

Both Quashie and Nowak are pioneers, who have made huge personal sacrifices for a wider cause. Both are relatively privileged women; both are well educated, and able to engage with the legal justice system without fear of recrimination. Both relied on the aid of legal advocates to put forth an effective argument on their behalf. Fighting exploitation in clubs requires a remarkable level of commitment from individual dancers willing to go through court proceedings and take on the personal burden that comes with it, such as backbiting from opponents, negative press reporting and loss of earnings. Being identified as a claimant against one club means probably never finding work in the industry again. It is a monumental contribution from anyone willing to make a stand for a legal principle that goes beyond his or her own

---

* A key element of self-employment is the right to come and go freely, accepting work or turning it down and passing it to someone else in the same field. When strippers are disallowed from doing this, they meet the legal criteria of worker.

individual benefit. To continue momentum and finally establish workers' rights industry wide, more dancers and allies will need the courage, fortitude and support to come forward.

2. LACK OF REPRESENTATION AT A POLICY-MAKING LEVEL

Another important date passed during the writing of this book: November 2019 saw the tenth anniversary of the Policing and Crime Act 2009, a policy that was formulated without properly consulting the women most affected by it. Since then, considerable amounts of taxpayers' money has been spent on council and police inspections of strip clubs, annual (sometimes six monthly) licence renewals with lengthy licensing panel hearings, untold man-hours spent watching lap dancers on CCTV footage, enforcement of conditions on clubs like no-touching rules, and expensive and unnecessary provisions for dancers (showers, lockers etc.). They are no better off for it. The last decade of compliance and monitoring has not shown any improvements to dancers' welfare; they are no less vulnerable to unfair and exploitative working conditions than they were ten years ago. In fact the punitive and costly measures imposed on clubs have arguably contributed to further exploitation. Every year that a club gets more expensive to operate translates directly into higher house fees, more dancers on shift and more fines/commissions to find the extra cash to pay.

In 2018 the Scottish Parliament passed a new bill to introduce the same SEV licensing regime as England and Wales.[5] In 2019 Scottish councils held periods of public consultation to gather public opinion. When presented with the simple question 'Should strip clubs be licensed?' the public consultations all came back overwhelmingly in favour of licensing strip clubs. What the public didn't know was that strip clubs in Scotland already operate exactly the same as in England, with the same business model of charging dancers to work and misclassifying their employment status. The public weren't aware that councils in Scotland had already adopted a code of practice for sexual entertainment, as recommended by the Adult Entertainment Working Group*, mirroring all the same restrictions and licensing conditions on English clubs.

The public weren't told in the consultations how a strip

---

* In 2005 the Adult Entertainment Working Group (AEWG) was formed by the Scottish government to 'research, review and scope the impact of adult entertainment activity and make recommendations on a way forward for Scotland'. A subsequent report titled 'Adult Entertainment Working Group report and recommendations to Ministers on the adult entertainment industry in Scotland' was published in 2006, which included a series of recommendations not dissimilar to the paternalistic licensing conditions and restrictions placed on SEVs in England and Wales, focusing on the continued surveillance of dancers with CCTV and the existence of private booths. An AEWG public consultation consisted of interviews with 42 members of the public. The chair of the AEWG said in her foreword, 'Members arrived at the Group from different backgrounds and with differing views, yet we have all worked well together.' Unsurprisingly, the AEWG did not include anyone with a background of working in adult entertainment; the only representative from the night-time industry was Eddie Tobin, a middle-aged male executive from the Glasgow bar and leisure industry. Dancers' voices were once again conspicuously absent.

club operates, how the power relationships between club bosses, dancers, staff, customers and licensing officials vary wildly from club to club, regardless of the SEV licensing regime. Nor were they informed of the impact SEV licensing would have on women working in the industry, and how their continued misclassification and lack of employment rights is the primary cause of exploitative conditions. Instead they were asked questions like 'Do you think an SEV should be in close proximity to an historical monument?' If public consultation can only gauge people's opinions – in other words what people think they know about strip clubs – its value in terms of objective decision-making will always be limited And while licensing is a good idea in theory, without a comprehensive understanding of the industry, and of the impact licensing has directly on workers, it can fail miserably. What's missing, and has been absent all along, are the voices and perspectives of dancers themselves.

In February 2020, Edinburgh City Council took the unprecedented step of inviting dancers to a plenary session at the City Chambers for the purpose of providing testimony to licensing officials. As a result of the newly formed trade union branch, United Sex Workers, the council were compelled to respond to requests for dancers to be heard by the council as a group of independent workers, not as representatives of their clubs or accompanied by bosses. Club owners had already been given their session with the council earlier that day; one of the Edinburgh club owners had in fact threatened workers at their club with being fired if they attended the independent dancers' meeting. They had handpicked a preferred dancer to accompany them to the owners' meeting and speak favourably of the club. Unbeknownst to them, however, the union had informed the council of the threats to workers, and with the help of council staff a rather cloak and dagger affair ensued with dancers congregating in secret at an undisclosed location and sneaking in to the building, concealed along the private corridors of the City Chambers out of public view. In this way, dancers were able to quite literally take a seat at the table to discuss their working conditions frankly and openly, pointing out the failures of SEV policy in England and making it known to the council that their employment rights were their most urgent demand.

Thanks to new lines of communication opening up between dancers and council officials, these new opportunities to be heard by policy makers are becoming more frequent. Councils around the country are beginning to take more seriously the idea of treating dancers as an independent group of stakeholders, with their own vested interests separate from their clubs'. Similar meetings have taken place in Camden. A Senior Licensing Officer of Camden Council explained in a recent meeting with unionised dancers that they finally understood dancers' hostility and why doing years of spot checks and inspections had not helped build trust between dancers and council officials, nor had it led to more positive social outcomes. The dancers' silence was linked entirely to the threats to their jobs; every time a council inspection took place it was a reason for club bosses to threaten dancers with the sack if they 'got caught' trying to simply do their job. No wonder they didn't want to talk to the council.

The sea change has come about thanks to trade union activism; by involving themselves in trade union, dancers are being taken seriously at a policy level. Since unionising, dancers have been organising in earnest, submitting responses to public consultations, showing up at licensing renewal panels and providing testimony, remonstrating with councils that current licensing regimes are not working and need to change. Dancers are getting wise to the licensing procedure and beginning to engage in the democratic process to get their Pleasers in the door and find their voice in governmental settings. The amount of time and energy required to perform this kind of unpaid labour, not to mention the level of personal privilege which allows anyone to carry the social stigma of being out as a sex industry worker, especially in spaces which traditionally and historically disregard the lived experiences of marginalised under-classes, can't be underestimated.

Like dancers who bring legal claims to court, the dancers who take time to engage with the process of local government are pioneers. For working-class women, organising childcare, attending council meetings, wading through hours of online

consultation forms, reading notes and watching hours of footage from renewal hearings, scanning through policy drafts for
details that require further attention, responding to emails and
chasing civil servants for updates, and in some cases risking
their jobs to stand up for a principle, are all major burdens
that require adequate support and provisions. And, like the
legal claimants, more dancers and allies are needed to share
the work around and continue challenging the status quo.

3. POOR MEDIA REPRESENTATIONS

Louis Theroux, known for his kooky and disarming style, has
made a successful career from ingratiating himself among some
of society's most marginalised groups. From porn stars to pris-
oners, dementia patients and anorexics, Theroux has made an
art of documenting and revealing private and unusual worlds
that are normally hidden from view. When his research team
approached the sex worker community, there were cautionary
rumours as to the nature of Theroux's probing style. The individuals who eventually took part in a documentary with him
were not blind to the overt misrepresentations of sex workers
within popular culture. The final edit is every bit as disap-
pointing as other mainstream depictions of sex work, of which
there are countless examples – playing up to stereotypes of
victimhood, fixated on the *people who sell sex* rather than saying
anything particularly useful about the material circumstances

and labour markets that sex work happens in. Theroux's palpable discomfort, prying into the personal histories of the two contributors looking for evidence of trauma, added up to a typical set of narratives. There had been high hopes that someone as astute and perceptive as Louis Theroux might come up with something more progressive and useful to sex workers. The participants may have been motivated by the possibility of being seen differently, but unfortunately the final cut fell back on all the usual tropes.

Just like *Hustlers,* when a production is large-scale sex workers cannot retain full control of their own narratives. Decisions about representation are made at an executive level. While researchers, freelance writers, juniors and interns may have limited control over the messages put out by media organisations, it is the commissioning editors, scriptwriters and production chiefs who more or less control what the public think about sex workers. Changing the narratives about sex work within mainstream media, therefore, relies on the opinions and attitudes among those who *commission* films, articles and documentaries.

Constant stereotyping, whether as a victim, a plot device or the butt of a joke, all add to the everyday stigma experienced by sex workers. Overcoming this form of objectification takes a tremendous amount of intensely focused effort; sex workers who are willing to deal with the media need to be aware of the structure of decision making, and keep their eyes peeled for the risks of misrepresentation on a case-by-case basis. Privileged sex workers who can afford to make media appearances need to be on guard; not only are they under the intense scrutiny of trying to represent members of their own community as well as themselves, they also have to do the extra work of trying to ensure their words and image won't be edited out of all context.

Sex worker-led organisations are inundated with requests for interviews and comments from media outlets. Ideally, rather than giving interviews to journalists who often have very little working knowledge of the subject, sex workers need to move into media positions themselves. In 2010, Thierry Schaffauser, a sex worker, activist and president of the GMB-IUSW union branch,* had a column in the *Guardian* for all of four months. He published a number of articles with titles such as 'Let sex workers advertise', 'Sex workers need power not brothels' and 'Sex workers are not criminals'. This new platform within a major British broadsheet newspaper was short lived, but still serves to inspire more sex worker

---

* The GMB (General Municipal Boilermakers) Union is one of the largest unions in the UK, with over 600,000 members across many industries including health and social care, education, retail, distribution, security and public utilities. In 2002 members of the International Union of Sex Workers voted to affiliate with the GMB, as an early attempt to organise a 'sex workers' trade union branch. However, problems soon arose within the structuring of the branch, which served to undermine organising efforts. The GMB still have a sex worker branch today; however, no strategic litigation has been brought forward as yet.

journalism. Of course, there are countless sex workers who can write with authority on their own circumstances pitching articles to editors, fighting for a position within media organisations, and creating platforms and followings of their own. But, again, the decision over whose voices get to be heard in the mainstream comes down to the attitudes of commissioning editors.

It can also be argued that censorship of sex workers on social media is deeply harmful and another example of how mainstream narratives are controlled, and by whom. Some remarkable work has been done in the UK by campaigners like Rebecca Crow, the Suicide Girl and professional web-cammer, who has organised protests outside Instagram's UK headquarters in response to online censorship of sex workers, and Carolina Hades, the pole dancing PhD student behind BloggerOnPole and the EveryBodyVisible awareness campaign. Their endeavours highlighting the inconsistencies and hypocrisy of the community standards policies of social media giants has helped move the public dialogue forward, showing the link between sex worker safety and social visibility.

Of all places, the comedy scene wouldn't be the most obvious place to find sex worker solidarity, but in recent years very tiny inroads have been made there, perhaps a sign that the tide of mainstream culture is slowly turning. Comedians Fern Brady (an ex-lap dancer) and Desiree Burch (ex-professional domme) have openly used their public platforms to talk about their pasts. In 2019, successful comedian and TV presenter Sara Pascoe used the publication of her book *Sex, Power, Money* to release a podcast under the same title, featuring voices of sex workers and advocates, including members of ECP. Sex workers have a much higher chance of remaining in control of their own narratives when they are invited to participate in independent media productions such as podcasts; these are ideal opportunities for sex workers to contribute to public dialogues, since they are not beholden to mass media budgets and agendas or commissioners' attitudes.

Controlling the narratives is the all-important key here. As, previously outlined, losing control of one's own narratives is the ultimate form of objectification. As long as sex workers are represented by non-sex working voices they relinquish that power, or watch as it is removed (as it was by Louis Theroux). Once more, they have to do the additional labour of challenging media narratives, asking pertinent questions of journalists, saying no to researchers when required, and demanding to see inside the media machines they are being asked to perform labour in. Getting wise to the pitfalls and perils in the field of publicity is a job of work, another kind of activism alongside bringing legal claims and fighting a way into local government; those who can afford the extra time, effort and power to step up to the exhaustive trials of media are also pioneers.

4. RADICAL FEMINIST CAMPAIGNS

Out of all the battles faced by strippers, this is perhaps the most insidious and the least straightforward to overcome. When radical feminists refuse to meet with and listen to sex workers, there isn't an obvious route to lessening the harmful impact of abolitionist crusades. It seems unlikely that campaigners who are willing to utilise underhand methods like private investigations, secret filming and as part of targeted stings, are going to abandon their firmly held beliefs about the industry anytime soon; certainly not when there is government funding involved. Given the difficulty of trying to meet the onslaught of industry attacks head on, the strategies required for reversing some of the damage done by anti-strip club campaigners is a combination of all of the above.

When national mainstream media outlets bought into the myth that lap-dancing clubs caused sexual violence in Camden, SWERFs gained huge ground in terms of public opinion about sex work, and with that came significant power. A large portion of the work being done by sex workers to regain control over media narratives is about reclaiming that ground, and redistributing the power of storytelling. However, some of the more formal arenas in which two sides battle it out – combative prime-time media disputes, for example, or university debating societies where sex workers are pitched against SWERFs – have mixed results. It is unclear that having two opposing ideologies compete with each other serves to do anything besides inflame conflict. Real power comes from reducing the charge around the topic of sex work enough to have informed, evidence-based dialogue, not from inciting personal politics between adversaries, like a blood sport.

Radical feminists have long held a position of power in media and in local and national government. Since the formation of Object and the massive power grab that was made in the lead up to the Policing and Crime Act 2009, Not Buying It have become 'experts' in the field of strip club licensing and engaging in the democratic process of public consultation periods, mobilising local residents and community members to fill out template letters to councils. They have brought forth strategic litigation, such as the judicial review in Sheffield, and major media outlets have provided a robust media presence. Strippers need to follow suit. Identifying renewal cycles and consultation periods, submitting testimony and showing up to council plenary sessions which can go on for several hours, bringing forth legal claims against abusive business owners, and stepping into the harsh lights of the media circuit to help direct attention where it needs to go; all of these strategies are equally important and essential in order to meet radical feminists in the places of power they have long been residing. The whole movement requires many sex workers and allies in many different roles, all collaborating and working towards a collective aim – harm-reduction.

Jacqueline Frances aka Jacq the Stripper is a person whose work I find endlessly inspiring. I think I first became aware of it when we started up the East London Strippers Collective, and I think she's a genius. As a stripper, writer, stand-up comedian, artist and merchandise entrepreneur, she has figured out how to reappropriate sex work culture back from its mainstream appropriation, repackage it and sell it back to the wider public in the form of books, hats, badges, mugs, comedy, memes and clever cartoons. Her colourful merch is emblazoned with slogans like SOME-ONE YOU LOVE IS A SEX WORKER and OFF-DUTY STRIP-PER. She has cleverly tapped into new markets, capitalising on the public appetites for sex worker culture, reaching thousands more 'punters' than she ever could in a lap-dancing club. She has figured out how to maximise her own market potential of being a stripper beyond the confines of the sex industry.

Using her sex working identity she has built a platform for herself to safely challenge age-old stereotypes in wider society, while at the same time being in control of the narratives and celebrating her own community. 'The Inquisitive Stripper' is probably my favourite segment of her work; she drew a series of witty, satirical, utterly hilarious cartoons, which are acutely accurate and to the point. They demonstrate what it would look like 'if strippers showed up to other people's workplaces to ask the questions civilians can't seem to stop asking us'.[6] They all feature a stripper talking to people from different professions, plumber, therapist, office worker, construction labourer, coffee barista, and repeating the same lines that strippers hear on a regular basis: 'How could you denigrate your body like this?' 'Do you even like your job?' and 'Are you just doing this to pay for school?' For strippers everywhere having these observations of hypocrisy and stigma captured and preserved with such levels of wit and humour was a revelation. When I first started dancing there was no one like Jacq for me to look up to. There were no stripper icons or role models, there was no Instagram (social media had barely taken off) and there was no easy way for us to find each other and congregate as a global community. Jacq the Stripper's Instagram account eventually became like a meeting place to hang out with other women like myself.

For years it looked like Jacq the Stripper could do no wrong, until she was invited to participate as a consultant on the film Hustlers *as well as playing a tiny cameo role as a backstage stripper in one of the changing rooms scenes. Working alongside Hollywood film stars and being paid a consultancy fee by a major budget production while being out and proud as a stripper was a no-brainer for her. However, being a contributor on the movie took a massive toll, which she is still feeling to this day.*

Hustlers *was a let-down for sex workers in so many ways, but when I saw Jacq on the giant screen at the Leicester Square premiere I knew how much blowback she was going to get. I was aware of how much vitriol was flying around already, and that was just the opening weekend. I knew she couldn't have been blind to the problems of the movie; she was shrewd enough to see the stigma woven into the plot line and the wider repercussions that the film would have. I also knew it may have been one of the biggest opportunities of her career, although by taking part in a project so massive she was only a tiny cog in the machine, with no real power over production decisions. I felt let down by the film, but I didn't feel personally let down by her. However I knew there were thousands who would and when I checked in on her social media pages over the days of the film's release, I was staggered at the levels of abuse aimed at her. The outright emotional violence being expressed in the public comments was hard to read.*

I'd been in touch with Jacq previously, so the day after I saw the film I called her to ask how she was doing, knowing that so many strippers were feeling betrayed by her involvement in the project. I just wanted to reach out as a friend, even though we'd never met in person. She seemed pretty crushed when she replied, 'Yeah, I've been getting dragged pretty hard online. And people don't hold back on those channels, you know? It's like, I wanted to contribute to it, and also it was a great opportunity. There are so many problematic things about the film, but so much of that was outside of my control. I can't be held personally responsible for restorative justice.'[7] I agreed with her. I told her I didn't think all her years of incredible work could just be erased overnight. Nothing could be gained from apportioning blame.

We caught up again several months later, and she wasn't as bubbly and enthusiastic as I'd remembered her. 'Has the last year been tough for you?' I asked her. 'Heartbreaking,' was her answer. 'Social media used to be a fun place for me to play, but then it became my job. There had always been a handful of people hell-bent on breaking my spirit, and every community has its trolls. But since Hustlers *there's been a change of tune internally. You know energetically that it's happened.' Jacq told me how some online commentators were holding her personally responsible for the shortcomings of the film. 'I was like, guys, I mean I'm flattered anyone would think I had that level of authority, but when it came to strippers not getting hired or paid indemnity [at Show Palace], I mean that's so far out of my remit. One of the comments that really got me was another sex worker saying "She's just in it for the money." I was like, "Bitch, please! What the fuck are you in sex work for? The outfits!?" I mean it's become tough to differentiate between what is trolling and genuine criticism.'*

We also spoke about processing anger. 'I have a lot of empathy for the anger in our community, it's so justified, but that doesn't mean I wasn't hurt. I was holding space for it but I'm not made of stone.' Jacq was exhausted; it was only relatively recently that she acknowledged the whole online attack as a traumatic experience, and how empathy is often absent when righteousness is on the table. I got the impression that she had been trying to shoulder a tremendous weight, which was other people's suffering. 'I will say the silver lining was that it forced me to draw better boundaries. I'm working actively to use my privilege for good, which means passing the mic as often as possible.'[8]

A few months later a planned event came to my attention. A venue in Hoxton was organising a 'sex worker's careers advice' evening, and when I saw the event description online I was initially concerned. The event itself looked poorly thought out, like people latching onto a zeitgeist. I didn't think much more about it until days later when I got a message from a fellow activist spitting bile, furious at the event organisers. 'There's no point attacking them,' I said. 'You'll just alienate people who may be genuinely trying to be good allies.' I watched the situation unfold a bit more and soon realised what had happened. Sex workers on Twitter had been raging about the event all day, but hardly anyone had actually reached out to the individuals concerned. I recognised one of their names, Victoria Rose, from an online network we were both part of so I wrote her a private message to ask what was going on.

We started chatting and I quickly got a fuller picture. A backlash of fury had been working up all day online, and when organisers got the picture that the sex worker community weren't happy they immediately pulled the plug and cancelled the event. The next day I ended up on a call with the programme manager of the venue, and it was clear they didn't understand why there was so much anger. 'We only have the best intentions, like we really want to support the community.' It sounded like the venue weren't fully clued up on the laws that make sex workers vulnerable, they didn't know enough about the Parliamentary protests, the history of SEV licensing, or have a firm enough grasp of decriminalisation. They also didn't know that advertising an event offering sex workers careers advice could have violated Section 52 of the Sexual Offences Act 2003, which states that inciting prostitution is a serious offence carrying a sentence of up to six months in prison.

When I spoke to Victoria on the phone a while later, she explained more about herself and her intentions behind the event. 'I wanted to take part in the event to share my experience as a sex worker and to advise others on how to stay safe. But I started to get told by other sex workers that I shouldn't be giving advice because I didn't have the experience, although they didn't know what experience I did or didn't have. Sex workers who didn't know me were targeting me on Twitter; I feel like in any community where you aren't known, people are more likely to attack you instead of taking their time to reach out.' Victoria pointed out how when she approached individuals privately she was able to have more productive dialogue and receive feedback, but she had to do the work of reaching out to them. 'Rumours spread fast and it took me a couple of days to talk to everyone. I felt very unsupported, like I wasn't accepted as part of the community. Sex work can be such an isolating job so to be rejected and attacked by other sex workers was really difficult to deal with. It was like my own experiences were not valid because I hadn't worked in specific areas, like street work or brothel work, or done exactly the same job as them.'

Speaking to the organisers I could hear how genuine and well meaning they were. I could also hear that they were right at the beginning of their journey as activists and allies. There was years of catching up to do, and I knew it couldn't all be done in one day. The sense of urgency is always felt among activists, like, there isn't enough time for someone to get it wrong and learn from their mistakes. If only there was an update button somewhere, and you could just upload all the important campaigning knowledge in one go. In reality it was going to be months if not years of research, hours of unpaid labour, squeezing meetings into busy work schedules, snatched conversations with fellow organisers, and a lifetime of overcoming personal constraints that stand in the way of social justice. I knew they didn't need another constraint put in their way; they didn't need the collective rage of our community pointed at them. I wasn't going to add to the cancel culture by ostracising them further.

There is a reason I reached out to Jacq and Victoria; I went through something similar myself. During the first year of forming the East London Strippers Collective, as an activist I quickly found myself in situations that I wasn't really ready for. I was hungry and impatient to challenge the injustices I had been observing in strip clubs for years, but I didn't have a solid understanding of sex work laws, I was missing essential knowledge and wasn't completely prepared for the responsibility of being an advocate for sex workers. I was trusted to speak on an important platform at an event in the Houses of Parliament hosted by ECP. It was entirely unplanned, I hadn't had any warning or ample preparation, I was basically handed the mic and asked 'What do strippers think about decriminalisation?' I misread the situation completely and made an error of judgement, saying things that were basically whorephobic. What I thought at the time was a useful contribution turned out not to be, and I probably deserved some of the collective rage I received soon afterwards, although it took a long time before I properly understood why.

Several members of the sex worker activist community decided I was part of the problem, that my lack of awareness and blind spots meant I was basically an enemy and not to be trusted. That lack of trust is still felt to this day as I move through activist spaces, particularly digital spaces where faceless collaborators with up to three different names each try and organise together. I am hypervigilant to any possible hostile energy among groups I'm trying to collaborate with and I'm less able to relax into any real role with confidence in case I sound defensive or insensitive; I'm terrified that I will be misunderstood. I am permanently on edge around people who I don't know and don't know me, ready for criticism *that never comes, but maybe unspoken. Occasionally I feel validated, but more often I expect rejection from the people around me. Or was it my imagination? Does that person think I'm whorephobic? Am I being too self-absorbed? Am I taking up too much space? Do I sound like an attention seeker? Why is it always about me, why can't I switch off this chronic anxiety and actually be part of the group? Does that person know about that thing I said years ago? Who is actually a friend or even an ally in this room?*

Anxiety is exhausting. These fears undermine my cognitive functioning in these spaces. Solidarity relies on trust, but trust and trauma do not go hand in hand. Trauma leaves an imprint, shaping my experience accordingly. I watch how my behaviour unconsciously helps bring my worst fears to life, proving my worst core beliefs about myself; that I'm difficult, intimidating, out of step, socially impaired, disliked, self-obsessed. My mental health spirals towards a destructive self-image, and I spend more time piecing myself back together over and over again than I ever let on.

More recently, I started reading about trauma theory and how traumatic experiences are stored in the body and nervous system. Trauma that hasn't been processed and resolved, particularly during childhood development, comes back up to the surface via triggers. The triggered psyche cannot tell the difference between the past and the present, and essentially relives past trauma over and over again, until it is processed and integrated. It's like a piece of the past is turning up, asking to be healed. I was triggered that weekend after I spoke in Parliament. The shock of waking up to a tirade of abuse online before deleting content and blocking users brought to the surface a massive backlog of unprocessed trauma from my background; trauma which is nobody's business but mine.

Being attacked online left me with a creeping long-term psychological unease around activism. I spent the weekend in bed without sleeping, suffering a flare up of Crohn's disease (which included internal bleeding), unable to feel safe because the world of the internet was no longer outside of myself. It was in my bedroom, in my hand as I held my phone, inside my head. I don't go near Twitter now. When I trigger around activism, I re-experience the bullying and neglect, the confusion and anxiety I felt continuously as I was growing up; I can't recognise who is a friend and I don't feel safe. Suddenly everyone and everything becomes symbolic.

It's by no means the worst adversity a sex worker can experience – far from it. As a white, English stripper, with community and social support, I am in the least at-risk group of sex workers. Trans sex workers of colour, street workers, those on the edge of poverty with no access to power and resources are immeasurably more vulnerable than me; the fact I am even passed a mic in Parliament is an extreme level of privilege I'm acutely aware of. But trauma doesn't care about that.

I watch how the activist community trigger each other, how one person's trauma response awakens another person's trauma response and so on. I ruminate on how trauma is something that many sex workers have in spades, and I try to get wise to it, learning to separate other people's from my own. I work hard on processing my early trauma, and it turns out the Buddhist chanting I have been doing nearly every day since I started stripping is a remarkably powerful tool for resolving trauma. Only recently I learned that chanting is like a form of breathwork stimulating the auto-

nomic nervous system, which is responsible for all sorts of self-regulation,
from sleep to concentration levels. I'm able to come back into a state where
I can tell the difference between the past and the present; by telling myself
'that was then and this is now' I'm able to keep moving forward. Time
will tell if we can process our collective trauma, and resolve our common
triggers as a community. I believe we can.

THE POWER OF COLLECTIVES

It appears that the post #metoo and #blacklivesmatter world
is no longer the dominion of rich, white men. These global
movements are proof that ever-increasing populations are
calling time on systemic privilege and entitlement. Public
appetites cannot be ignored. Millennial generations don't
want to participate in economies that are known for their
relentless exploitation of labour; emerging consumer habits
reveal trends towards more ethical decisions about everything
from food, to fashion, to lifestyle choices. These global trends
are also reshaping the sex industry, which is notoriously good
at changing and adapting to market forces. And people are
still interested in sex. There is an ever-growing hunger to consume and appropriate sex workers' culture, with celebrities
emulating them and enjoying a more sex-positive image than
ever before. The box office takings for the film *Hustlers* proved

how much public appetite there is to see strippers on the big screen, yet this hasn't translated into increased earnings for strippers. In fact, strip clubs in the UK appear to be a dying business. The halcyon days are long gone; strippers have become sales personnel in a corporate hierarchy that sidelines them as much as it relies on them.

If strip clubs are to keep their doors open, then new business models are urgently required. Industry operators need to wake up to changing attitudes, and let go of financial practices they learned twenty years ago, or make way for something new. Ideally, sex workers themselves need to start taking control of their workplaces by creating their own. There is one clear strategy that confronts all four previously outlined obstacles, particularly the radical feminist agenda: *sex worker-led businesses*. In 2003 a strip club called the Lusty Lady became the first worker-led cooperative strip club when the dancers who worked there banded together and bought the business from its previous owners. Throughout the 1990s the club had become well known for its labour union movement among the dancers; in 1997 it became the first unionised sex business in the USA. The co-op ran for a decade before closing its doors in 2013. Businesses that are actually operated by workers themselves send out a powerful message; when sex workers operate their own workplaces, the most important message of all is one of autonomy.

There is a degree of discomfort within the sex working

community about entering into the power relationships that inevitably arise out of economic arrangements. Few people who feel so financially exploited are willing to profit from anyone else's labour; this is why labour movements are needed. If strip clubs, brothels and agencies are to exist without the exploitation of labour, then it is exactly these relationships that must be dramatically revolutionised. New business models that experiment with lateral power structures rely heavily on solidarity between sex workers and a community built on trust, which is why collectives matter. Over recent years flurries of collectives, businesses and grassroots efforts aiming to redesign the sex industry have materialised, from pop-up nights to life-drawing classes, theatre productions to union drives. The reimagining of strip clubs is already well under way.

In April 2014 ten women, all known to each other from working in the East London strip pub circuit, came together for a dinner party. They cooked and ate together, and sat round a large table taking it in turns to reminisce about what it was they still loved about their jobs, and what had drawn them to it in the first place. The collective power and energy in the room was palpable. The East London Strippers Collective grew out of a direct response to declining industry conditions. Since then the ELSC have experimented with different projects, from an art festival to running their own pop-up strip club. The most successful of these happenings is their sold-out weekly life-drawing class in Shoreditch. In March 2019 the ELSC were invited to participate in a late-night event at the Royal Academy of Arts, in Piccadilly's Burlington House, a huge accomplishment for sex workers who have long seen their labour consumed and discarded by the art world. In 2019 the Berlin Strippers Collective also followed suit and began running their own stripper life-drawing class. The Berlin collective was set up with the help of Chiqui Love, an original co-founding member of the ELSC; one of the all time queens of stripping, Chiqui is a Latinx legend who built her career as a stripper and Burlesque star in London before relocating to Berlin. With full assistance and support from the ELSC, Chiqui is sharing the formula for financial self-sufficiency with strippers elsewhere in Europe.

This reframing and repackaging of labour is being explored by many other sex workers. More strippers are finding a way of marketing their own labour to totally new audiences who wouldn't normally dream of stepping foot inside a strip club, nor could they afford it, but who are nevertheless still curious. Jacq the Stripper has inspired a new generation of sex working artists to begin capitalising on their own identities in the wider world. Exotic Cancer is an Australian artist and stripper who has grown a massive cult following, her merchandise now a badge of honour for thousands of sex workers worldwide. She has become known for her artistic renditions of the beauty and grimness she observes while working in strip clubs.

In this sense, she switches between multiple roles; as well as performing the role of object, being viewed in the strip club, she also takes up the role of viewer and subject specialist.

There has also been a number of UK pop-up performance events that centre the culture and labour of the sex industry, run by collectives that include sex workers. Juicebox events offer a safe and inclusive space for diverse audiences, welcoming queer women of colour who want to show their appreciation for strippers but don't feel protected in regular strip clubs. LICK events is a womxn-only space (cis female, female-identifying and non-binary) which runs an occasional pop-up strip night at a London SEV, For Your Eyes Only. Brazilian Wax is a 'party for off-duty sex workers' produced by ex-stripper and theatre maker Jo Nastari. Femmedaemonium productions are 'a female-led performance collective of sex workers and allies which exists as a platform for socially marginalised voices'. They create 'secret, role-play imbued theatre which is exploratory, safe and above all else, consensual'. Sexquisite are another collective of sex workers and allies, aiming to challenge stigma and raise awareness. Unionised strippers have also thrown parties to raise strike funds for fellow members of the UVW trade union.

In the summer of 2019 something very exciting happened. The first LGBTQ+ strip club in the UK opened its doors on 20 July, marking the possibility of a new era in sexual entertainment. Harpies, a weekly event celebrating queer strippers of all genders and persuasions by inviting an equally non-gender-conforming audience to come and party with them, has made a home at the East London Strip Club, Metropolis. Every Friday night, party-goers can come and throw money at an incredible line-up of gender-queer, non-binary performers. Harpies have made history, not only as champions for trans/queer visibility, but also as one of the first strip clubs to stop charging dancers to work. Harpies performers get paid a fee and keep all their earnings from private dances and tips. Profits earned from door cover charges and sales of alcohol are shared more fairly, and performers do not have to hand over a house fee or a percentage of their income. Harpies have provided an example of a workable business model that doesn't rely on the standard practice of charging dancers to work, throwing the gauntlet down for other industry operators.

Following in the footsteps of Carol Leigh who pioneered sex worker theatre as a genre, theatre productions have also been used to disrupt mainstream attitudes towards sex work for decades. The Sex Workers' Opera, a five-year-long community theatre project running from 2014 to 2019, was a multidisciplinary show featuring sex workers' stories from seventeen countries, performed and produced by a cast and crew of sex workers and allies, of whom at least 50 per cent membership of the team at any time were sex workers. Strippers also using their stories to make theatre, to much critical acclaim, include Jo Nastari's *Fuck You Pay Me* (2018), Chase Paradise's *Ho Life or No*

Life (2017), and Nicole Henriksen's *Makin It Rain* (2016). Once again we see power relationships shift dramatically when sex workers are on stage in control of their own narratives. Strippers are immediately changed from voiceless object to becoming the subject, speaking loud and clear to paying audiences. The potential for these productions to reach sizeable audiences and influence public attitudes about sex work are not insignificant. Unfortunately, the costs of producing theatre are almost prohibitively expensive. Without considerable funding, making theatre can often end up looking just as (if not more) financially exploitative for performers as sex work. While the potential to make an impact on public perceptions often makes up for the lack of income, for many it's a vastly unsustainable career path.

It could be said that these new endeavours aren't new at all, that strippers have long been turning an income from their identities in the wider world. Sex worker autobiographies are plentiful, and strippers have long been known for their entrepreneurialism.* Strippers who go on to establish Burlesque troupes, like Jo King and Gypsy Charms, or open pole fitness studios, like Felix Cane and Suzie Q, are also examples of the business

---

* A common enough 'exit-strategy' is to make the move into the beauty industry. Countless retired strippers and sex workers own or manage hair and beauty salons all over the world, or complete training to become beauty technicians. Fake nails, hair extensions and skin treatments are big business and it seems entirely logical to capitalise on the years of knowledge that come from learning beauty tips and tricks in an industry where looking good creates value.

acumen among members of the industry. Sasha Diamond and Tequila Rose are both UK-based strippers turned pole dance instructors specialising in stripper-style pole, sharing the skills they picked up from the strip club with their students.

PROCEED WITH CAUTION

There are also a small number of entrepreneurial strippers who have built personal brands as coaches to other strippers. Strip and Grow Rich, Survive the Club and Racks to Riches are all businesses started up by strippers that have carved out a niche selling advice and support to other new hopefuls entering the industry, or to any experienced dancers wanting to increase their earning potential. Their years of learned experience carries a value within the industry, and finding a customer base among their colleagues is a shrewd business move. While these stripper coaches support a narrative that the answer to a worker's success is their own skill and willingness to work hard, it must not be forgotten that these efforts are made within a *context* of labour conditions and lack of employment rights. Not only can strippers learn moneymaking tips from each other, they can also share invaluable knowledge and advice about their legal rights.

Survive The Club publishes a blog and advice column. One previous blog post contains advice to dancers on what to do if standards start slipping at their club:

If you really love your club, try and talk to the managers . . . Be humble . . . Be articulate and let them know that you understand the business and money is everyone's objective. Understand that more girls for them equals more money, but explain that when they saturate your market and lower their standards, it hurts your money. Desperate girls can really hurt your profits. Once your manager knows that you understand his or her point of view, they will be more likely to hear you out on yours. If you have always been professional and you are consistent and polite to your co-workers and have been a generous tipper throughout your career, this is when it pays off. Then ask your manager if you can work at a discounted house fee. There are clubs where I have never paid to work, just tip outs, and I have never had a manager deny me a negotiation.[10]

Being courteous and polite is always sound advice for maintaining good working relationships and improving a business environment. But universal conditions in wider labour markets that drive down standards on a local, national and international scale, not just in strip clubs, can't be ignored. We must also acknowledge the culture within unregulated industries of workers being fired en masse for questioning or raising complaints; all workers should have due legal process for raising workplace grievances or whistle-blowing, and should not have to rely on currying favour and preferential treatment with bosses.

The Neoliberal dream is a vision where marketplaces have no rules, where there is no state welfare and social responsibility is located entirely within enterprise; if individuals are free to nurture personal brands and pursue their own self-interest, then the market will take care of everyone's needs, right? Building collectivism out of twenty-first-century late capitalism is far from easy. It is not the intention of this book to criticise the choices made by individuals, and there is no doubt that all the examples of sex worker-founded businesses and projects mentioned above are creating value in society. It is a basic human right for every individual to earn a living, and it is every sex worker's right to use their experience (as it is to use their body) to make an income, however they see fit. Sex workers keeping themselves out of poverty always has to come first. The question is not whether any strippers should use their relative privilege to profit from their own work – that is, unquestionably, their right. The question is more about how strippers with relative privilege use that power to challenge and dismantle the systemic conditions that keep all sex workers in a socially vulnerable position.

For example, if a stripper opens a pole studio to feed her kids and provide long-term financial security for her family – that's an achievement not to be underestimated. But if she has students who come to her pole studio and start making whorephobic comments about stripping and sex work, or parroting radical feminist rhetoric about victimhood, she has a choice.

Does she keep quiet, not wanting to lose paying customers and risk hurting her brand? Or does she intervene by challenging them to see things from her point of view, confident that if they leave, her integrity will help the brand grow stronger? It's these micro-acts of solidarity that the sex working community needs more than ever.

One unfortunate example of a failure of solidarity centres on the club, Metropolis. From Tuesdays to Thursdays Metropolis operates as a regular cis-het strip club, with all the usual house fees and working conditions. However, over recent years, thanks to the legendary queer club nights that take over the club at weekends, Metropolis has earned cult status as a venue within the queer community. In 2018 Metropolis announced that East Creative, the team behind Sink The Pink (a queer club night which went on to become a megabrand, selling out major concert venues like The Troxy), had been contracted as creative directors of the club. The weekend nights at Metropolis provided a healthy revenue for the club owners, and their popularity has shored up the venue's financial security for years to come. From an outside perspective it would seem that the arrival of queer, non-gender-confirming people in a strip club marks the dawning of a glorious new age, challenging the gender stereotypes which female exploitation relies on.

But a 2015 article in *Time Out* magazine, in which the founders of Sink The Pink describe their first visit to Metropolis, sums up the problem perfectly:

There were about nine girls dancing and two men watching,' says Amy of her first visit. 'It was quite awful. There's a bleakness that hurts your soul when you realise: oh God, that industry still exists . . .' And yet, confronted with its lasers, decent sound system, stripper poles, mirrored walls and insanely seedy sand-covered lounge, STP had finally found their dream venue. Last month, the crew launched Savage, a new weekly Saturday-night takeover of Metropolis. In a classic 'only in east London' move, it was out with the dirty old men and in with the glitter-soaked [queens].[11]

It was a huge oversight that by getting rid of the 'dirty old men' they were also erasing another vulnerable group's ability to make a living.

Sales of alcohol at weekends easily keep the business afloat the rest of the week; presumably any income from the midweek stripping is pocket money for the cis-het male owners.[*] The rest of the week, dancers pay their fees and commissions just like any other club.

Morgan (not their real name) is a performer based in East London, well-known among the East London Queer community. They have performed regularly at weekend club nights at

---

[*] In January 2019 Metropolis was bought by Columbo Group, a major London hospitality and entertainment company owned by two men, Steve Ball and Riz Shaikh. Columbo Group have a thriving portfolio of venues, including the Blues Kitchen, Camden Assembly, XOYO and the Jazz Cafe.

Metropolis, including Savage Disco for a couple of years, and also for Harpies on several occasions. According to Morgan, dancers working during the week did not reap any direct benefits from the club's success. 'As far as I know there were never any efforts made on the part of East Creative or Savage to integrate the dancers of Metropolis with the weekend club nights.'[12] They were, however, offered bar shifts at weekends, presumably at minimum wage or London Living Wage, but not to perform. Bar work may have been a helpful option for some dancers, although perhaps not for everyone. But aside from the issue of employment, the segregation of workers from different groups seems to have maintained the status quo despite an obvious opportunity to genuinely challenge it. As Morgan articulates,

> It's an oversight to assume that there weren't any queer people working in that venue to begin with. Most people have a fixed impression of a stripper, they assume she is this straight, rich, lonely woman. It's such a generalisation, but for that to come from another member of the queer community is really sad. It might have been an interesting trajectory to have built a bridge between both worlds inviting dancers to strip at weekends for queer clubbers and making stronger alliances between different groups.'

Narratives in the public domain about the protection of queer venues are also focused on the prospect of reclaiming spaces that were previously off limits to queer people. But there was no public dialogue about the employment status or exploitation of strippers still going on at Metropolis while it was rapidly becoming a destination venue for the LGBTQ+ community; as usual they were left out of the conversation. Perhaps if East Creative had been able to use their relative power and status as leverage to advocate for the weeknight strippers, it might have been the act of solidarity that sex workers so desperately need. But it seems unlikely they had the power to do so. The LGBTQ+ community are also badly in need of visibility and solidarity. It shouldn't have to be the job of one marginalised community to uplift another – but nor should empowering one community come at a cost to anyone else.

CAPITALIST NIGHTMARE

If Sasha Rakoff and Charlotte Mead get their wish and strip clubs shut down tomorrow, thousands of women will be even more precarious. Some will turn to full-service sex work, others will go back to the private bookings. That may not be so bad for some, but looking at Sheffield as an example, online agencies can't be trusted with women's welfare any more than strip clubs. And, as Laura's story of the mystery shopper in Westminster tells us, neither can government officials. The drive for welfare in the sex industry must be led by sex workers themselves.

The challenges for strippers listed throughout this book mirror those faced elsewhere in the sex industry, but as explained, they do not include the added burden of criminalisation or risk to life carried by full-service workers. For the moment strippers working in licensed premises are some of the most privileged sex workers. As outlined at the beginning of this book, it was never intended to incite divisions between different sex workers, quite the opposite. One of the primary goals of unionising strippers in the UK is precisely because establishing workers' rights in strip clubs brings us one step closer to full decriminalisation of sex work and the recognition of labour rights for all sex workers.

There do already exist structures outside the UK where strippers and sex workers cooperate and work alongside each other. In New Zealand, under decriminalisation strip clubs and brothels co-exist without much difficulty. In Berlin, where sex work is *legalised*, Chiqui Love works in a strip club called Angels Cabaret, whose owner also operates a nearby brothel; she describes a functioning arrangement where she is able to uphold boundaries in a more clearly defined way. One might assume that an environment where anything goes may lead to coercion and lack of boundaries, but Love's description is quite the opposite; it turns out that allowing sex workers the freedom to define their own boundaries opens the door to greater levels of solidarity between one another, rather than competition. Despite working in a country where full-service work is legal, she is not expected to perform any labour she hasn't chosen. In this respect her power lies in the freedom to choose.

Like so many other veteran strippers, she talks about how the industry has changed dramatically. 'It used to be years ago that strippers were like these Goddesses and no one could dare to touch them. I used to feel offended if someone said to me that I was a prostitute or sex worker. But now I see things very differently. I started to see that we are all pretty much the same family, and started to have a bit more respect for each other and understand what women have to do, or people have to do to survive.' It hasn't escaped Chiqui's notice how much the economy has changed since the start of her career. 'Financially, I think money has had a lot to say; it has changed our perceptions of what we do for money.'[13]

There is no doubt that the economy has changed since Chiqui first auditioned in a strip club in the early 2000s. There are greater levels of financial disparity, higher levels of female poverty, saturation of informal labour markets, and political dismantling of employment protections in favour of profit. While the new precariat class may be vulnerable to wide-scale exploitation, there is also a new body politic forming in the margins. More and more demographics who are feeling the squeeze of present day economics are able to ally themselves with others who are in similar dire straits. Times are a lot harder for a lot more people; Niki Adams from ECP deftly summed this up: 'many more younger women are switched on to what it must be like to end up selling sex. They may imagine doing it themselves, or are more likely to know someone who has. This empathy is growing and it needs to build towards change for sex workers so that vulnerable women aren't left at the bottom of the pile.'[14]

Nobody understands hardship better than those living through it. As the labour movement grows within the sex industry, it becomes clearer by the day that sex workers' rights align and intersect with so many more movements, from immigration, gender violence, poverty, homelessness, addiction, LGBTQ+ rights, BIPOC rights, precarious and invisible work, unemployment . . . the list goes on. The call for political change that is needed to alleviate the financial and material insecurity that tightens around the necks of so many of the global population is deafening. Sex workers are adding their voices to the commotion. In a few succinct sentences, Chiqui Love flawlessly clarifies the plight of her community; her words could just as easily be applied to any other field of work. 'I feel like there has been an impact on my industry that has made us do a lot more to get, perhaps, even less money, so I think there has been a bit of a wakeup call for everyone . . . we realise that fellow sex workers are actually just like us, you know, and everybody is just trying to survive in a fucking capitalist nightmare.'

AFTERWORD

So much has happened since I began writing this book. Just a matter of days after delivering the first draft of the manuscript to my publishers in March 2020, the world changed almost beyond recognition. It's hard to overestimate the impact coronavirus has had on individuals, families, communities, businesses, economies and nations – to a large extent, the virus has shown up exactly how precarious people are, and what being precarious really means.

When I emailed the manuscript over in the first week of March it felt like auspicious timing: over the last few years the International Women's Day protests on 8 March have become an important day for sex worker-led activism, and there was a lot planned that Sunday. I'd been invited to perform at an afternoon stand-up comedy event at the Museum of Comedy, and decided to do a short routine from *Ask A Stripper,* the Edinburgh Fringe show I co-created with my work-wife, Gypsy

Charms. After the gig, my friends and I joined the sex worker-led march through central London, followed by a massive event produced by Femmedemonium at a soon-to-be-demolished old public bath-house turned hipster event space in Hackney Wick. The entire day felt like a festival of sex workers' rights and it was the perfect way to celebrate my hand in.

The street demonstration turned out to be one of the last mass-gatherings to happen before lockdown was declared. A massive crowd of sex workers, allies and organisers met at Soho Square before marching through central London. Hundreds of protesters had turned out for the rally, which stopped traffic in London's West End and caught the attention of thousands of onlookers who gawped at the colourful throng with curiosity. Sex workers are no strangers to using aesthetics to make an impact, and public demonstrations are no different – all the usual symbols of political dissent were accompanied by red umbrellas, high-heeled shoes, stockings and thongs, sound systems pumping out strip club classics, and tongue-in-cheek signs with phrases like MY DADDY'S YOUR DADDY.

As the march snaked through London's prestigious Covent Garden, past the Royal Opera House and several international embassies before arriving at its destination, the Royal Courts of Justice, the mood was electric. The choice of location for the final stop was not lost on us; turning the final corner onto the Strand we were greeted with a magnificent show of power. Outside the gates of the Royal Courts of Justice, lit up in giant LED letters hung on the railings by organisers, were two simple words – DECRIM NOW. The protest erupted into a spectacular climax with a choreographed dance performance by members of the trade union branch United Sex Workers. It was one of the most empowering moments I've ever felt as an activist, and a huge deal for members of a community so alienated by legal policy to see the fight for sex workers' rights being brought straight to the epicentre of the British legal justice system.

Change felt like a very real possibility, not least because the crowd were celebrating a very real and recent victory. It had been all of two weeks since Sonia Nowak took her strip club boss to court and won. Sonia, a friend and fellow activist, had fought a year-long legal case against her previous club and on 24 February an employment tribunal ruled in her favour, setting a legal precedent and opening the door for dancers all over the UK to begin demanding change. Her win was a massive step towards establishing our labour rights, and the jubilance felt that day was unforgettable. We'd had two clear weeks of employment rights in the sex industry – a whole fortnight in which we dared to believe enormous change was on the way.

Amid the collective euphoria, however, was a creeping unease. News reports had been getting more persistent throughout the month of March about a killer virus that was spreading rapidly across the planet. The coronavirus that orig- inated in China in late 2019 and spread throughout the rest of the world in 2020 has made an impact on almost every living soul on the planet; major global economies have been brought to their knees as citizens have experienced unprecedented levels of restrictions on their movement, in an effort to control the spread of the pandemic. The devastating effects of the virus cannot be underestimated, as lives and livelihoods have been decimated by the crisis. In November 2020, finance min- isters announced that the UK economy was expected to shrink by 11.3 per cent, the steepest downturn in 300 years. The Office for Budget Responsibility estimated that by June 2021 unemployment would have risen to 7.5 per cent, the highest since the 2008 financial crisis, while government bor- rowing would be the highest outside of wartime to cope with the economic impact.

It's hard to know where to begin when trying to put into words how a pandemic that has wreaked so much destruction, and left so many people grieving loved ones and living with long-term health outcomes, has impacted the sex working community. There has been a wide consensus that the virus and its consequences have disproportionately harmed lower income, working poor families and individuals – i.e. people who have had no choice but to continue placing their health at risk in order to survive. While there are so many narratives competing for headlines – government complacency and policy failures, virus transmission rates and death counts, the strain on just about every key public service, and the rise in domestic violence – stories of people using sex work to survive have been unsurprisingly few and far between. And predictably, the effects on sex workers have gone largely unreported.

When UK officials announced a lockdown on 23 March, every strip club in the country closed its doors for business overnight; but as virus rates went into decline over the summer, most regular businesses were given permission to reopen, so long as they followed necessary guidelines. SEVs, however, were not included within those government recommendations, meaning they appear to have been closed indefinitely. This is despite the fact that licensing conditions have required strippers to socially distance for years. Many SEVs following the 'three-foot rule' went to the effort of building infrastructure, such as podiums, to make sure dancers were always at least one metre away from customers, so they ought to be well ahead of the game in terms of reduced contact. Efforts were made by a tiny percentage of clubs to reopen by freezing their SEV licence and opening as a regular bar. A club in Bristol reopened for a few weeks with the strippers serving drinks instead of dancing, for which they weren't being paid but had the potential to earn tips or sell VIP time to sit and keep customers company (at a social distance). Another Soho club opened briefly during the day with a complicated set of protocols involving dancing behind tables, no full strip on stage, and strict rules about where dancers could and couldn't walk.

For the most part, dancers have been left with nowhere to work, and – more importantly – no financial safety net. The government furlough scheme provided financial assistance to employees by guaranteeing 80 per cent of their wages while businesses were closed during lockdown – but in the case of strip clubs, this doesn't include dancers. Appallingly, this has meant that managers, bar staff, security staff and any other in-house strip club employees have been receiving consistent income throughout the pandemic. Misclassification of our employment status means we fall through the cracks, relying either on self-employment grants (which are denied to newly self-employed people) or the paltry income from the national benefits system, which has never recovered from the austerity measures after the 2008 crash.

Online stripper forums have been buzzing with urgent pleas for advice and suggestions from women suddenly struggling to make ends meet. One viable alternative has been selling adult content online; the rise of Onlyfans.com has been one of the more documented consequences of the pandemic. Covid-19 has been reshaping adult entertainment, as shown by the numbers of people subscribing to online platforms. Once again we see a familiar business model – the platform takes 20 per cent commission from all creators' earnings, and since Onlyfans.com saw a 75 per cent increase of users *per month* from the beginning of lockdown, online sex work has quickly become one of the fastest growing market sectors. Celebrity endorsement has certainly boosted this growth; Bella Thorne, the latest Disney Channel child-star-turned-sex-symbol, has become one of the first major celebrities to create an Onlyfans account selling nudes to the public, arguably making her a sex worker. The sex working community don't see it that way, though, since non-sex workers appropriating our culture doesn't help us in the long run.

Unsurprisingly, many strippers who are not in a position to create adult content online, thus digitally identifying themselves as sex workers, have turned to full-service sex work (which can be advertised anonymously) to survive. In many ways, the pandemic has really shown up the meaning of survival: for anyone relying on the sex industry to escape poverty before the pandemic, things have got drastically worse. On 18 April 2020, just a few weeks into lockdown, the International Committee on the Rights of Sex Workers in Europe held a virtual seminar to discuss the impact of Covid-19 on sex workers. Juno Mac, speaking for SWARM, described some dire situations being faced by sex workers in their network: 'People are dealing with food shortages in really unprecedented ways, finding their local food banks empty. A lot of people are single parents, dealing with mental health difficulties that are being exacerbated by being in lockdown with their families, carrying the pressure of worrying about income for those families.'[1]

In the same seminar, Niki Adams, speaking for ECP, stated, 'we heard of a couple of women who were stopped and arrested as suspected vectors of disease . . . It seems like the police and authorities are using this crisis to reinforce that kind of stigma and prejudice.' Hearing these stories, I was reminded of the descriptions of the sex workers who were rounded up under the Contagious Diseases Act 1864 and found myself wondering how much has really changed over the last 156 years. A deadly disease has once again created divisions between those who can afford to prioritise their health and their communities, and those without enough choice or social status to do anything other than take risks, thus opening up lines of viral transmission. Government furlough schemes mean nothing to people whose jobs are not recognised as jobs, and there can be no doubt that there have been some desperate people in grave situations turning to survival sex work, regardless of the virus, throughout 2020.

A close friend of mine, writer and sex worker Tamara Macleod, shared with me some of the invisible impacts the virus had for escorts:

I was inundated with messages from men inquiring about my symptomatology and how I might be designing ways to 'keep them safe'. Ordinarily the sex worker is already objectified as a carrier of disease; having this amplified was too much for me, and I am grateful I could take the time off. Most workers are not so lucky. Without access to any financial support and with much of the economy shut down, I know people who have had to continue working throughout lockdowns.[2]

Adultwork.com is one of the biggest advertising platforms for sex workers, with a booking function to allow clients to book time with an escort. Once the booking has been completed, both the escort and client can leave feedback for each other on the site, which is then visible on their profiles. If a new client approaches an escort she can see whether the client has good feedback from other workers, helping both clients and escorts build up trust and increased levels of safety. People tend to behave well if they want repeat business. If a client has no feedback then a sex worker knows to take extra security precautions when meeting a new client, or may decline the booking. When the UK announced a national lockdown, Adultwork.com switched off its booking and feedback system. In practice, this meant sex workers were suddenly vulnerable to time-wasters, boundary-pushers and dodgy behaviour. A feedback system is a simple way to help workers screen clients, and without it there is no way of knowing if a new client has violent or abusive intentions.

It wasn't just that organising bookings became more fraught, so did peer networking and support. Twitter in particular fast became a space for virtue signalling; privileged workers taking time off were policing and shaming workers who were still seeing clients,' Tamara explained. 'With Adultwork shutting down its booking system and workers deterred from admitting they are still seeing clients during lockdown, there was effectively a blackout, the kind of thing we experience when we are forced offline. The work continues but moves underground to avoid policing, both institutional and internal.' Working in the sex industry without support is precisely what leaves sex workers vulnerable, and when peer support breaks down there is precious little to be found elsewhere.

Finding safe spaces to work has always been one of the biggest struggles for full-service sex workers, and is arguably the most significant factor in terms of sex worker safety overall. Hotels have historically been some of the safest places for sex workers to offer incalls, since the social infrastructure all around them largely reduces their vulnerability to predatory clients. The hotel industry more or less collapsed under Covid-19, with hotels no longer operating in ways that allowed sex workers to remain discreet. Escorts have turned to private rentals such as Airbnb; one of the few silver linings of the pandemic has been that since tourism has collapsed, luxury properties available on Airbnb have dropped prices so dramatically that pop-up brothels have become more opulent than ever. That is, of course, for the privileged sex workers who have access to such resources; at the other end of the scale, all sources indicate that street prostitution has noticeably risen.

ECP reported that hundreds of women were enquiring about starting sex work, since their jobs as teaching assistants, waitresses, cleaners and beauticians were no longer viable.

Underground strip clubs have continued underground throughout the pandemic, even during lockdowns – as have the exploitative conditions that can be found in underground spaces. In June 2020 a Scottish news story confirmed that illegal events and gatherings were still happening, with agencies offering private bookings to dancers around the UK, mirroring all the same problems identified in Sheffield in Chapter 6 (except this time with the added burden of criminal liability for breaking lockdown laws). The same summer, a colleague from the ELSC was approached online by someone looking to book dancers for a 'private party' who was offering a paltry fee for the dancers' time; in return, he wanted to keep 90 per cent of tips earned at the event. I wondered if he was also going to pay the £10,000 fine if the party got busted. We politely declined his offer. At points it seemed like the pandemic was bringing all the manipulators to the surface: our social media accounts were bombarded by scammers posing as sugar daddies, looking for vulnerable sex workers to trick into paying *them* money in return for pledges of future financial support. Their schemes sound laughable, until the uncomfortable reality sinks in that for untold numbers of precarious people the promise of 'being looked after' is a very real device for coercion.

While the nightmare unfolded, however, some incredible developments were also going on. Some sex workers have taken matters into their own hands, and grassroots organising has been paying off in dividends, not least when it comes to community fundraising. SWARM responded to the crisis by immediately mobilising to set up a mutual aid fund, stating in their call for donations on 13 March: 'Like other precariously employed workers, sex workers do not have a monthly salary we can rely on. We don't get sick pay. Many of us exist without savings of any kind. The most marginalised are the most at risk. We often have nowhere to turn if clients stop coming to see us, and can face poverty or homelessness. Our community is facing a crisis.' By 30 June, with match funding from Vivastreet (an online advertising platform used by escorts) they managed to raise a staggering £251,000, which was paid out in grants of £200 to 1,255 sex workers in the UK. Another sex worker-led organisation in Scotland, Umbrella Lane, also ran a mutual aid fund for sex workers in crisis, which distributed just over £10,000 cash directly into the pockets of Scottish sex workers.

In May, an announcement from the Scottish government that £62,000 of public funding would be made available to support sex workers was met with much media fanfare. It took no time at all for sex workers in Scotland to realise that the funding was actually being given to the Encompass Network, nine organisations that offer support to trafficking victims in the form of rescue services, counselling and exit strategies. Dr Anastacia Ryan, director of Umbrella Lane, the only sex worker-led initiative in Scotland, explained a crucial point: 'They gave the money to be distributed through the Encompass Network, which Umbrella Lane is not welcome to join since we do not agree to use a prostitution-as-violence-against-women definition in our work.'[3] To the disbelief of the sex working community, Umbrella Lane would not be eligible for any funding, since they don't sign up to the Encompass Network's ideology that sex work is gender violence. 'We approached the Scottish Government directly to ask for a contribution to our crisis fund,' said Ryan, 'and they refused.' In a very real sense, support was only made available to sex workers in Scotland who identify as victims rather than workers – yet another example of the victimhood industry calling the shots, rather than sex workers themselves.

Sex workers have been left high and dry, relying on what we do best: supporting ourselves, and each other. Mutual aid fundraisers and events have been frequent, with Soldiers of Pole, Lysistrata, Black Sex Workers Collective, ELSC and more all tapping into social media followings to raise funds for vulnerable sex workers. Soldiers of Pole used Instagram Live to curate a twelve-hour striptease show, with performers all over the world signing up to perform for thirty-minute slots, raising money by asking viewers to send dancers' tips directly to their mutual aid link.

One of the most exciting responses to the pandemic has been the formation of a new collective, Cybertease, the first worker-led online virtual strip club. A group of sex workers, all known to each other through trade union activism (including Victoria Rose), formed a crew and began organising their own events online, splitting all money raised from each event equally between themselves, and thus creating exactly the kind of business model that disrupts conventional industry practices. Cybertease events are fun and interactive, and – more importantly – diverse. Their website invites guest performers of 'all genders, all sexualities, all backgrounds and identities, all abilities, all ages', further disrupting the regular heteronormative stereotyping that typical strip clubs have stubbornly held on to for decades. The arrival of Cybertease marks the beginning of a new era for the sex industry: businesses where sex workers create their own working conditions, without being beholden to greedy bosses or problematic licensing regulations, must surely be the future of adult entertainment.

The summer of 2020 also arguably saw some of the biggest cultural moments for sex work, indicating that mainstream cultural influencers might be finally starting to get the message. Ex-stripper icon Cardi B released her international hit single, 'WAP' (acronym for Wet Ass Pussy), featuring Megan Thee Stallion, which contains some of the most sexually explicit lyrics ever recorded by two female rap artists. The choreography for their music video is straight out of a strip club. Mainstream channels lit up with dialogue about women taking back control by sexually objectifying men and reversing the one-way system that has always allowed male artists in RnB and hip-hop to express their sexuality in the exact same way. Another smash hit, Megan Thee Stallion's other single, 'Savage', remixed with lyrics by Beyoncé that mention Onlyfans, led to a 15 per cent surge in subscriptions to the online platform in the twenty-four hours following its release. Singer Kehlani released a music video for her single, 'Can I', which marked a departure from the relentless misappropriation of sex workers' culture by mainstream media. Instead, she acknowledged sex work in the best way possible by featuring sequences from actual webcam performers, while she placed herself in the position of viewer rather than trying to duplicate their style. A political statement at the end of the video draws attention to the global demand for the full decriminalisation of sex work; one of the few examples of celebrity endorsement for sex workers' actual political demands.

Another cultural icon made a stand for sex workers during lockdown, this time much closer to home. Performing artist FKA Twigs launched an online fundraiser to support sex workers on the platform Gofundme.com. Twigs made an initial donation of £10,000 and invited public contributions, raising a total of £26,700. When the fundraiser was launched, Twigs released a public statement on her Instagram account, which soon caught media attention.

I was nineteen when I learnt my first pole move, I learnt a back hook spin from a stripper when I was working as a hostess in a gentleman's club. For those of you who don't know, hostessing is when one person pays another person for their time, anything from a conversation over dinner to sex work, and the club gets a cut of the fee. My lived experience as a very young woman in these environments has not only informed the strong and formidable woman that I am today but also a lot of my work as a music and visual artist – sometimes even subconsciously.

I feel like now is the time for me to step forward, pay respect, and shine a light on the challenges facing sex workers, especially during these uncertain times. Sex workers I know and have met have discipline, craft, talent and work ethic – not only do they deserve better long-term, but their income has been wiped out by the lockdown and many are invisible to the financial aid available to others.

Unfortunately, there was already growing unrest within the sex working community about Twigs' use of sex worker culture. As a professional performing artist it hadn't taken Twigs very long to master the art of pole dancing, which she executed with breathtaking skill in her 2019 music video for 'Cellophane', completing the stripper look by wearing a pair of iconic Pleasers. It wasn't the only time she'd used imagery from the sex industry: in 2015 she turned herself into a blow-up sex doll for her EP, 'Melissa'. She also produced a video titled 'We Are the Womxn', released in 2020, which contained images of her dancing in a strip club. The story behind the video was one of female empowerment; as part of her recovery from cystic fibroids, Twigs had taken up pole dancing in 2016 to help her rebuild core muscles (she even approached the ELSC back then, ending up training on the pole with one of our members, Lauren Elise). Her journey towards healing led her to Queen Afua, a healer whose dance and movement ceremonies release generational trauma for participants. Twigs and Afua collaborated first with a full moon ritual followed by a ceremonial trip to the Blue Flame, a legendary Atlanta strip club, for a female-only event where women danced for each other. The video footage includes Twigs getting ready backstage with the Blue Flame strippers, who welcomed her into their world. Once I learned that Twigs had been a sex worker, I wasn't at all surprised; I privately speculated whether she'd used so much of the imagery in her creative practice as perhaps it was her way of processing some of those early experiences mentioned in her statement. But I also knew it wasn't my place to assume; her story, like her body, is her business, after all. Projecting my assumptions onto her would be every bit as harmful as any SWERFs projecting their assumptions about sex work onto me or anyone else.

Other sex workers were angry at what they perceived was

more celebrity misappropriation but didn't know that behind the scenes Twigs was working with sex workers directly on the fundraising campaign. I saw the familiar pattern of a well-meaning potential ally being publicly shredded on social media. As all the completely valid arguments about misappropriation fired up online, it became tricky to know what to think.

So when Twigs finally released a public statement that she had in fact worked in the sex industry herself, some sex workers initially had trouble trusting her. This also didn't surprise me. I already knew how fiercely defensive sex workers can be about protecting each other, and how much the movement is built on trust, and I thought endlessly about how sex workers struggle to accept potential allies since, for the most part, no one has our back. I realised that allyship takes time, and can't be done overnight. I also wondered how many other celebrities are out there, with the secret that they too at some point in their lives engaged in some form of sex work to get where they were going. I thought about how bold FKA Twigs was: while other celebrities were lending their support to more mainstream causes, she had chosen to offer hers to an utterly maligned and isolated group. I imagined how powerful a public social media hashtag campaign to support sex workers could be – something like #yesasexworker, for women (as well as men and non-binary folk) to take the plunge and finally risk their reputations and careers by publicly declaring their own histories in the name of anti-stigma and solidarity.

That seems a far reach from where things currently stand. In December 2020, Instagram and Facebook introduced tighter restrictions to their community guidelines resulting in even greater levels of censorship. At the same time, the after-effects of FOSTA/SESTA have grown, with the suggested SISEA (Stop Internet Sexual Exploitation Act) – a bill that seemingly aims to protect against exploitation by apparently banning all suggestion of sex on the internet. In the same week, on 9 December, Diane Johnson MP introduced a private members bill in Parliament to introduce the Nordic model in the UK. The vote was passed, and has been moved forward to the next stage of creating new legislation – a Parliamentary debate. Will this debate go the same way as the one led by Sarah Champion MP in 2018? Will anyone from ECP or SWARM be in the room when ministers decide our future? Will harm-reduction prevail over moral panic? I only hope that the groundswell of resistance is growing fast enough to prevent the law from being passed.

If the Nordic model is introduced in the UK, it will harm us. We need support from the public; we need the wider community to catch up with the politics around sex work, and evidence-based policies of harm-reduction. That means you, dear reader. This is your call to action. Can you help? There are countless sex worker-led organisations that could use your support, donations, voluntary power, resources, platforms, awareness, press coverage, funding application skills, labour of any kind.

Thank you for reading this book. The main objective of writing it has been to share enough insight into the sex workers' rights movement in the hope of inspiring readers to become allies. If any part of it has moved you to want to act then it has achieved what I set out to do. Please bear in mind some of the lessons learned so far about becoming an ally. Remember how fiercely protective and vulnerable to being misrepresented we are. Ask sex workers what support we need, contact organisations directly and ask them what resources would serve them best. Most of all, listen to sex workers' voices, forget everything you've heard about strippers, and see us as we would like to be seen.

ACKNOWLEDGEMENTS

This book could not have been written had I never encountered the fortitude and resilience of the hundreds of women I've met working in the sex industry. I wish to thank in particular the strippers and sex workers who have given me their time and support, as well as their stories while writing it: Jo King, Gypsy Charms, Keri Gold, 'Emily', Sasha Diamond, Edie Lamort, Niki Adams, 'Laura', Jordan Kensley, Kitty Velour, Jacq the Stripper, Victoria Rose, Chiqui Love, Tamara McLeod.

I'm also extremely grateful to all the supporters who helped crowdfund this project. Thank you for your patience while I have kept everyone waiting.

With special thanks to my editor, Sam Boyce.

NOTES

INTRODUCTION

1 Mac, J., Smith, M. *Revolting Prostitutes: The Fight for Sex Workers' Rights*, 2018, Verso, p. 55

2 https://www.citywide.ie/assets/files/pdf/decriminalisation_and_public_health_the.pdf

CHAPTER 1: ETHICAL STRIPPING

1 https://www.bizjournals.com/bizjournals/news/2014/11/13/cindy-gallop-makelovenotporn-bitcoin.html

2 Easton, D., Hardy, J. W. *The Ethical Slut: A Practical Guide to Polyamory, Open Relationships and Other Adventures*, 1997, 2009, Celestial Arts, p. 4 (2nd Edition)

3 https://www.who.int/hiv/topics/sex_work/about/en/

4 https://www.otago.ac.nz/christchurch/otago018607.pdf

5 http://spl.ids.ac.uk/sexworklaw

6 https://www.independent.co.uk/voices/sex-workers-decriminalisation-of-prostitution-new-zealand-new-law-works-research-proves-sex-workers-a7761426.html

7 Mac, J., Smith, M. *Revolting Prostitutes: The Fight for Sex Workers' Rights*, 2018, Verso, p. 56

8 https://www.vice.com/en_uk/article/qbemmm/protest-sex-workers-frankie-mullin-942

9 https://www.thesun.co.uk/news/2530991/stacey-tierney-british-woman-melbourne/

10 https://www.change.org/p/victoria-police-demand-answers-from-victoria-police-what-happened-to-dreams-dancer-stacey-tierney

11 https://www.news.com.au/lifestyle/real-life/true-stories/why-would-you-watch-somebody-die-mums-agony-at-daughter-left-to-die-alone-in-melbourne-strip-club/news-story/7f03735027d1b7be78d0f9e2093ead1a

12 https://overland.org.au/previous-issues/issue-236/feature-after-hours/

13 https://overland.org.au/previous-issues/issue-236/feature-after-hours/

14 https://www.theguardian.com/commentisfree/2017/jan/09/stacey-tierney-deserved-the-same-right-to-a-safe-workplace-as-any-of-us

CHAPTER 2: LICENCE TO STRIP

1 Paul Raymond Interview with Elaine Grand on *Good Afternoon*, Thames TV, first transmitted 27 November 1975. https://www.youtube.com/watch?v=XTp-99nvthE&t=1282s

2 Berkowitz, E. *Sex & Punishment: 4000 Years of Judging Desire*, 2013, Westbourne Press, p. 373

3 Berkowitz, E. *Sex & Punishment: 4000 Years of Judging Desire*, 2013, Westbourne Press, p. 162

4 *Mrs Henderson Presents*, 2005, Director Stephen Frears, Distributor Pathé Distribution

5 *The Look of Love*, 2013, Director Michael Winterbottom, Distributor Studio Canal UK

6 https://www.dailymail.co.uk/news/article-6304091/Iconic-Windmill-Theatre-strip-club-Londons-Soho-loses-battle-renew-licence.html

7 http://www.legislation.gov.uk/ukpga/1982/30/schedule/3/crossheading/requirement-for-licences-for-sex-establishments/1997-03-31/data.htm?wrap=true

8 https://www.mirror.co.uk/news/uk-news/peter-stringfellows-lap-dancers-went-12677464

9 https://objectnow.org/overview/

10 https://publications.parliament.uk/pa/cm200809/cmselect/cmcumeds/492/8112508.htm

11 https://publications.parliament.uk/pa/cm200809/cmselect/cmcu-meds/492/8112507.htm

CHAPTER 3: GATEKEEPERS OF DESIRE

1 Srinivasen, A., 'Does Anyone have a Right to Sex?', *London Review of Books*, March 2018

2 https://burlexe.com/burlexe/the-burlexe-burlesque-show/jo-king-from-london-academy-of-burlesque/

3 Interview with Jo King by email, April 2019

4 Interview with Gypsy Charms by phone, October 2019

5 Interview with Keri Gold by phone, October 2019

6 Cook, C., Davies, P. *Olympia Moments Ltd*, 2014, Back in Black Publishing, p. 13

7 Interview with 'Emily' by phone, October 2019

8 Interview with Sasha Diamond by phone, October 2019

9 Mac, J., Smith, M. *Revolting Prostitutes: The Fight For Sex Workers' Rights*, 2018, Verso p. 38

10 https://observer.com/2018/04/amazon-britain-harsh-working-conditions/

CHAPTER 4: IS STRIPPING SEX WORK?

1 https://www.eastlondonstripperscollective.com/our-manifesto

2 Leigh, C. 'Inventing Sex Work'. In Jill Nagle (ed.), *Whores and Other Feminists*, 1997, Routledge, p. 225

3 https://www.who.int/hiv/topics/vct/sw_toolkit/115solution.pdf

4 www.bbc.co.uk/bbcthree/article/d6ad2e6d-2c72-4a35-9281-daaeed-f029ee

5 https://www.theguardian.com/commentisfree/2013/nov/01/sex-workers-hands-off-my-whore-france-prostitutes

6 prostitutescollective.net/wp-content/uploads/2019/03/About-Us.pdf

7 https://www.legislation.gov.uk/ukpga/2009/26/section/27

8 https://www.thescottishsun.co.uk/news/3141573/immigration-raid-seventh-heaven-glasgow-police/

9 https://www.transequality.org/sites/default/files/Meaningful per cent20 Work-Full%20Report_FINAL_3.pdf

10 https://vimeo.com/17724591

11 https://www.bbc.co.uk/news/av/uk-11981314/local-vicar-joins-fight-to-keep-local-strip-clubs-open

12 Interview with Edie Lamort by phone, December 2019

13 https://publications.parliament.uk/pa/cm200809/cmselect/cmcumeds/492/8112508.htm

14 https://hansard.parliament.uk/commons/2018-07-04/debates/50911795-3525-4F4A-B047-EF87047B5176/CommercialSexualExploitation#contribution-E681A1BB-D054-4FEE-A8DE-D68D265C6012

15 Interview with Niki Adams in person, December 2019

16 Interview with Niki Adams in person, December 2019

17 http://www.legislation.gov.uk/ukpga/2003/42/section/55

18 https://jezebel.com/tearing-down-the-whorearchy-from-the-inside-1596459558

CHAPTER 5: WHAT'S WRONG WITH REGULATION?

1 https://www.thetimes.co.uk/article/the-television-vicar-who-supports-the-rights-of-strippers-80dvhlgngw5

2 https://democracy.towerhamlets.gov.uk/mgAi.aspx?ID=58736

3 Interview with Laura by phone and email, March 2019

4 https://committees.westminster.gov.uk/documents/s31289/Platinum%20Lace%20report%20redacted.pdf, p. 26

5 Laura is referred to throughout Jenkins' report by her stage name, but in order to protect her identity her stage name is not mentioned in this chapter.

6 https://committees.westminster.gov.uk/documents/s31289/Platinum%20Lace%20report%20redacted.pdf, p. 26

7 Interview with Laura by phone and email, March 2019

8 https://committees.westminster.gov.uk/documents/s31289/Platinum%20Lace%20report%20redacted.pdf, pp. 36–7

9 https://committees.westminster.gov.uk/documents/s31289/Platinum%20Lace%20report%20redacted.pdf, p. 36

10 Interview with Laura, March 2019

11 https://journals.sagepub.com/doi/10.1111/1467-954X.12278

12 https://www.get-licensed.co.uk/licence/sex-establishment-licence

13 https://www.gov.uk/premises-licence

CHAPTER 6: OBJECTIFICATION

1 https://www.nytimes.com/2005/09/18/books/chapters/female-chauvinist-pigs.html

2 notbuyingit.org.uk/about-us-2/

3 https://oneworldaction.wordpress.com/100-unseen-powerful-women/human-rights/sasha-rakoff-dr/

4 https://notbuyingit.org.uk/sites/default/files/SR%20Objection%20Not%20Buying%20It%20Rakoff.pdf

5 https://www.theguardian.com/uk-news/2018/apr/26/sheffield-strip-club-protesters-judicial-review-spearmint-rhino

6 www.thetimes.co.uk/article/clubs-accused-of-forcing-lap dancers-into-sex-acts-b5s2rfkcx

7 https://www.bbc.co.uk/news/uk-england-south-yorkshire-47806257

8 www.womensequality.org.uk/sev_uvw_allegations

9 https://www.jusnews.net/womens-equality-party-candidate-stands-by-campaign-to-revoke-strip-club-license/

10 https://www.bbc.co.uk/news/uk-england-south-yorkshire-53558430

11 Private conversation with Heather Watson, Facebook, April 2019

12 www.notbuyingit.org.uk/sites/default/files/Myth%20Buster%20Starter.pdf

13 www.gov.uk/government/publications/revenge-porn

14 https://notbuyingit.org.uk/background/

15 Killing Us Softly 4: Advertising's Image of Women. Director Sut Jhally, writer Jean Kilbourne. Northampton, MA: Media Education Foundation, 2010. DVD.

16 Hakim, C. *Honey Money: The Power of Erotic Capital,* 2011, Penguin Books Ltd

17 https://www.party-strip.co.uk/female_strippers.php?S=10&A=Yorkshire%20-%20South%20&T=Sheffield

CHAPTER 7: THE VICTIMHOOD INDUSTRY

1 Bayard, K., *Pimp State: Sex, Money and the Future of Equality,* 2016, Faber & Faber, p. 48.

2 https://www.versobooks.com/blogs/3162-in-full-sight-the-pimp-lobby-at-the-amnesty-agm

3 https://www.independent.co.uk/voices/prostitution-sex-trade-punters-pimps-womens-rights-exploited-hiv-condom-rule-a7913121.html

4 https://www.thetimes.co.uk/article/feminists-have-fallen-for-the-strip-club-myth-vt3fm2vkv

5 https://morningstaronline.co.uk/article/f/sex-work-organising-lot-hot-air

6 https://beta.charitycommission.gov.uk/charity-details?regid=275048&subid=0

7 https://www.theguardian.com/uk/2009/oct/20/trafficking-numbers-women-exaggerated

8 Eden, I. 2003. 'The Lilith Report on Lap Dancing and Striptease in the Borough of Camden'. https://childhub.org/sites/default/files/library/attachments/poppy_03_lap_dancing_0109.pdf, p. 15

9 Eden, I. 2003 . 'The Lilith Report on Lap Dancing and Striptease in the Borough of Camden'. https://childhub.org/sites/default/files/library/attachments/poppy_03_lap_dancing_0109.pdf, p. 10

10 https://www.youtube.com/watch?v=3sDiMS9hbUM&t=348s

11 https://www.theguardian.com/world/2008/mar/19/gender.uk

12 http://www.newquayvoice.co.uk/news/5/article/2950/

13 https://www.scribd.com/document/47185652/Green-Paper-Camden-Lilith-rape-stats, pp. 1–2

14 https://www.scribd.com/document/47185652/Green-Paper-Camden-Lilith-rape-stats, p. 7

15 Eden, I. 2003. 'The Lilith Report on Lap dancing and Striptease in the Borough of Camden'. https://childhub.org/sites/default/files/library/attachments/poppy_03_lap_dancing_0109.pdf, p. 11

16 Eden, I. 2003. ' The Lilith Report on Lap dancing and Striptease in the Borough of Camden'. https://childhub.org/sites/default/files/library/attachments/poppy_03_lap_dancing_0109.pdf, p. 13

17 http://www.womenssupportproject.co.uk/userfiles/file/uploads/profitable%20exploits-1.pdf, p. 17

18 https://www.scribd.com/document/47185652/Green-Paper-Camden-Lilith-rape-stats, p. 8

19 https://www.unodc.org/documents/treaties/UNTOC/Publications/TOC%20Convention/TOCebook-e.pdf

20 Roach, C. M. *Stripping, Sex, and Popular Culture*, 2007, Berg, p. 131

21 Roach, C. M. *Stripping, Sex, and Popular Culture*, 2007, Berg, p. 131

22 Mac, J, Smith, M. *Revolting Prostitutes: The Fight For Sex Workers' Rights*, 2018, Verso, p. 72

23 Mac, J, Smith, M. *Revolting Prostitutes: The Fight for Sex Workers' Rights*, 2018, Verso, p. 4

24 https://glc.yale.edu/sites/default/files/pdf/sexual_politics_of_new_abolitionism_.pdf

25 Agustín, L. M. *Sex at the Margins: Migration, Labour Markets and the Rescue Industry*, 2007, Zed Books Ltd, p. 7

26 Agustín, L. M. *Sex at the Margins: Migration, Labour Markets and the Rescue Industry*, 2007, Zed Books Ltd, p. 96

27 https://find-and-update.company-information.service.gov.uk/company/01322750/filing-history?page=1

28 https://pcc-cic.org.uk/sites/default/files/articles/attachments/poppy_evaluation.pdf

29 https://www.theguardian.com/uk/2009/oct/20/trafficking-numbers-women-exaggerated

30 http://andreanetwork.pbworks.com/f/trafficking.pdf

31 https://www.theguardian.com/lifeandstyle/2008/sep/10/women.social exclusion

32 https://childhub.org/sites/default/files/library/attachments/poppy_08_brothel_summary_0109.pdf

33 https://www.theguardian.com/uk/2009/oct/20/trafficking-numbers-women-exaggerated

34 https://web.archive.org/web/20170222194344/http://www.eavesforwomen.org.uk/news-events/news/closure-of-eaves-another-nail-in-the-coffin-for-the-women-s-sector/

35 http://wbg.org.uk/wp-content/uploads/2016/11/WBG_2016Budget_FINAL_Apr16-1.pdf

36 https://www.ohchr.org/Documents/Issues/EPoverty/UnitedKingdom/2018/NGOS/English_CollectiveofProstitutes.pdf

CHAPTER 8: HUSTLERS

1 https://twitter.com/jeanho/status/1173423744439635970?lang=en-gb

2 Interview with Jordan Kensley by phone, September 2019

3 https://www.thecut.com/2015/12/hustlers-the-real-story-behind-the-movie.html

4 www.vulture.com/2019/09/hustlers-the-real-story-behind-the-movie.html

5 https://www.autostraddle.com/im-not-a-stripper-but-i-play-one-on-tv-why-hustlers-wont-change-the-game-for-sex-workers/

6 https://www.thecut.com/2015/12/hustlers-the-real-story-behind-themovie.html

7 https://www.thecut.com/2015/12/hustlers-the-real-story-behind-themovie.html

8 https://www.meetup.com/Life-Drawing-With-ELSC/

9 https://www.youtube.com/watch?v=r1Mql1z-Afw

10 www.imdb.com/title/tt5503686/?ref_=tt_urv

11 https://www.vice.com/en/article/43knng/hustlers-movie-closed-new-york-show-palace-strip-club-to-film-and-dancers-lost-thousands

12 Interview with Kitty Velour in writing, October 2019

13 https://www.whoresonfilm.com/

14 https://nowtoronto.com/news/what-s-lena-dunham-got-against-sex-work/

15 https://www.change.org/p/instagram-uk-meet-with-rebecca-crow-katsandcrows-to-discuss-sex-worker-rights-on-instagram

16 https://www.youtube.com/watch?v=r1Mql1z-Afw

17 https://medium.com/pulpmag/the-film-hustlers-is-ugliness-wrapped-in-j-los-silky-chinchilla-2d9b861766d

CHAPTER 9: SEIZE THE MEANS OF TITILLATION

1 https://www.picuki.com/media/2212584733607247091

2 https://www.dailymail.co.uk/news/article-2251856/Stringfellows-lap-dancer-Nadine-Quashie-loses-unfair-dismissal-case--gets-compared-church-organist.html

3 https://www.supremecourt.uk/cases/docs/uksc-2017-0053-judgment.pdf

4 https://uklabourlawblog.com/2020/04/30/dancers-are-workers-nowak-v-chandler-bars-group-ltd-and-the-history-of-dancer-organising-in-london-by-katie-cruz/

5 https://www.gov.scot/publications/guidance-provisions-licensing-sexual-entertainment-venues-changes-licensing-theatres/

6 http://www.jacqthestripper.com/blog/2017/2/15/inquisitive-strippers

7 Interview with Jacqueline Frances by phone, September 2019

8 Interview with Jacqueline Frances by phone, March 2020

9 Interview with Victoria Rose by email, February 2020

10 https://www.survivetheclub.com/thehustle/2017/6/6/what-to-do-when-the-standards-drop-at-the-strip-club-you-work-at

11 https://www.timeout.com/london/clubs/Sink-The-Pinks-savage-new-party-in-a-London-strip-club

12 Interview with Morgan, 2021

13 Interview with Chiqui Love by phone, December 2019

14 Interview with Niki Adams in person, December 2019

AFTERWORD

1 https://www.youtube.com/watch?v=OikVw4FBqvo&t=302s

2 Interview with Tamara McLeod by email, December 2020

3 Interview with Dr Anastacia Ryan by email, April 2021

INDEX

Unbound is the world's first crowdfunding publisher, established in 2011.

We believe that wonderful things can happen when you clear a path for people who share a passion. That's why we've built a platform that brings together readers and authors to crowdfund books they believe in – and give fresh ideas that don't fit the traditional mould the chance they deserve.

This book is in your hands because readers made it possible. Everyone who pledged their support is listed below. Join them by visiting unbound.com and supporting a book today.

Sarah Ainslie

Carolina Are

Chris Attey

Camille Aubry

Sharon Bakar

Jeffrey Barth

Andrew Barton

Louise Beaumont

Sarah Bee

Meli Berney

Kieran Bevan

Jo Biddulph

Arian Bloodwood

Sara Bolognini

Roger Brackin

David Brown

Brian Browne

Emily Burgardt

Kimberly Burke

Alexandre Caillol

Kevin Cannell

Gypsy Charms

Craig Clark

Lexi Cross

Patrick Cullen

Sasha Diamond

Kari Dickson

Glenn Dietz

Ima Doll

Dtp

Jo Ellis

Meni Etim

Finbarr Farragher

Jamie Finch

Andy Fortytwo

Alix Fox

Jessica Furseth

Frank Gambino

Ruth Gammon

Kassandra Gardner

Malcolm Gibson

Fiona Gilbertson

Tania Glyde

Daryl Goodwin

Lj Gray

Emma Green

Mike Grenville

Colleen Sylvia Haasbroek

Peter Harrison

Laurie Hartley

Michelle Harwood

Moe Hashimi

Lucy Haskell

Thomas Hazell

Paula Hedley

Samuel Hedley

Charlotte Hockey

Emily Hodder

James Edward Hodkinson

Ellen Hornsby

Charlotte Hughes

Imogen Humphris

Fifi Hunt

Mike James

Aaron Jones

Lynnford Jones

Tamika Jones

Naila Kabeer

Mila Karwowska

Anna Kennedy

John Kenton

Dan Kieran

John Kinley

Grégory Kinsman-Chauvet

Mahari Kismahass

Marc Knapton

Krzysztof Krygier

Julie-ann Laidlaw

Anna Lange

Thomas Lawrence

Stuart Learmonth

Helen Lee

Anselme Lenga

Marianne Lester-George

Anastasia Lewis

Ginny Litscher

David Llewellyn

Hannah Logic

Kate Lynch

Frankie M

Baret Magarian

Vee Maksimova

Cory Mann

Simon Manning

Clive Mansfield

Pamela McCarthy

Rosie McLean

Ewen McNeill

Bairbre Meade

Alice Metcalfe

Jasmine Milne

John Mitchinson

Dafydd Monks

Gillian Monks

Matthew Moore

Madeline Moran

Neil Munro

Carlo Navato

Kirsten Neil

Tony Newbolt

Peter Newman

Hazel Nicholson

Gary Nicol

Kevin O'Connor

Trelby O'Connor

Gregory Olver

Stacey Orr

Tuppy Owens

Camilla Pallesen

Els Payne

Glory Pearl

Sassy Penny

Jared Philippo

Charles Philpot

Dave Pickering

Justin Pollard

Tina Price-Johnson

Trevor Prinn

Elizabeth Rao

Millie Robson

Jarvellis Rogers

James Rose

Kalina Rose

Tequila Rose

Lizzie Rubbisher

Darren Russell

John Sanders

Raoul Sansonetti

Maggie Saunders

Scott

Dante Semmens

Omar Shahryar

Nikki Shaill

Laurence Shapiro

Len Shenker

Spelling Mistakes Cost Lives

Lizzie Stanton

Emily Starling

David Stevens

Georgia Sykes

Daniel Tenner

The Women's Rugby Show

Tibs

Jollean Tomsin

Cheyne Towers

Wendy Tuxworth

Martin Underwood

Kim van der Hulst

Antonio van Vurren

Amber Vaske

Kitty Velour

E. K. Victor

Gilly Vincent

Nadja Voorham

Eleanor Walsh

Courtney Waters

Xanthe Whittaker

Louise Wilkinson

Sarah Williams

Christopher Witter

Simon Woods BABADip

Marcus Wright

Ottilie Wright

Alys Zaffre

Omar Zeid